ZANZIBAR TO TIMBUKTU

ANTHONY DANIELS

Zanzibar to Timbuktu

John Murray

© Anthony Daniels

First published 1988
by John Murray (Publishers) Ltd
50 Albemarle Street, London W1X 4BD

Typeset by Spartan Press
Printed and bound in Great Britain by
Butler & Tanner Ltd, Frome and London

British Library Cataloguing in Publication Data

Daniels, Anthony, *1949*–
Zanzibar to Timbuktu.
1. Africa South of the Sahara. Description
& travel – Personal observations
I. Title
916.7′04

ISBN 0–7195–4533–1

CONTENTS

A map of the journey will be found on p. ix

So geographers in Afric-maps
With savage pictures fill their
    gaps;
And o'er unhabitable downs
Place elephants for want of towns.
Jonathan Swift

Oh Africa, mysterious land!
Surrounded by a lot of sand . . .
Hilaire Belloc

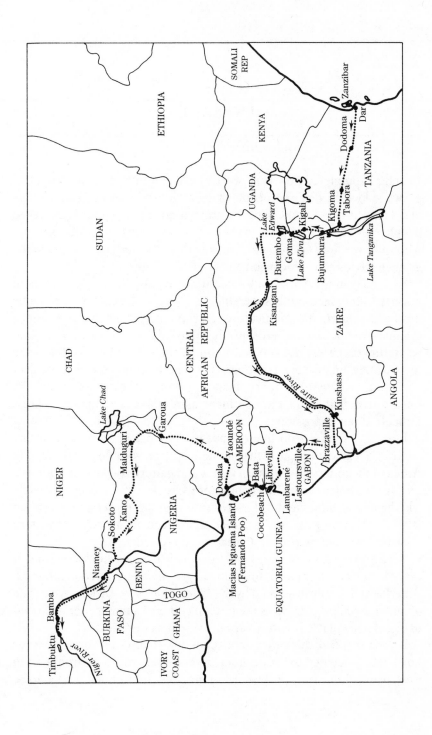

PREFACE

In 1986 I completed two years' work as a doctor in rural Tanzania. I had grown to love the ordinary people of the region, whose courtesy, courage and cheerfulness in the face of great hardship put more privileged people to shame. I then went on short visits to Ethiopia and Mozambique for *The Spectator*. Not surprisingly, perhaps, I came to the grim-mest possible conclusion about Africa's future.

Every day in my work I saw – could not avoid – the consequences of poverty, ignorance and superstition. I encountered the economic mismanagement, the omnivorous corruption, the unchecked demo-graphic growth, the soil erosion, the petty tyranny of bureaucrats and party functionaries, the inflated political rhetoric which leaders were increasingly unable to distinguish from reality, and the disregard of education as anything more than a means of extortion from the uneducated that beset the continent as a whole and made progress difficult, if not impossible.

Indeed, I found it no longer easy to say what progress *was*, in the context. I came to regard the sudden but irrevocable intrusion into Africa of ill-understood western values and patterns of consumption as a disaster leading with the inevitability of a Greek tragedy to some terrible Malthusian denouement. The favourite pastime of commentators on Africa – ascribing blame, whether to African incapacity or western rapacity – will not help at all. Perhaps nothing will.

Yet life is not fully encompassed by statistical tables, however exact, of ever-downward trends in the annual *per capita* production of food. America is not fully described by the crime figures, or Britain by the rate of unemployment. Africa, as the foreign editor of a newspaper once said to me, is a big place. It is very varied, even in its miseries.

It was to capture this variety, and if possible to discover some cause for hope, that I decided to return home by travelling overland from east to west, using public transport wherever possible. It was not intended to be a journey to reach where no human foot had reached before; still, to an averagely comfort-loving European, the prospect was daunting enough. Even the best hotels of Dar es Salaam are not without their drawbacks.

In the first chapter of his *Zanzibar; City, Island and Coast*, the great Victorian traveller and linguist of genius, Sir Richard Burton, wrote: 'Of the gladdest moments in human life . . . is the departure on a distant journey into unknown lands. Shaking off with one mighty effort the fetters of Habit, the leaden weight of Routine, the cloak of many Cares and the slavery of Home, man feels once more happy.' I am afraid this does not quite summarise my emotions on departure. I was subject to no Mighty Shakes, only to invisible quivers. I took with me pills and lotions against lice, fleas, worms, scabies, typhoid, typhus, dysentery (bacillary and amoebic), malaria (chloroquine sensitive and resistant), fungus and gout; and a copy of *Moby Dick*, the reading of which I surely could not find more boring than sitting doing nothing whatever in god-forsaken African villages waiting for a lift. I trembled inwardly also at the prospect of encountering the philosophy of *Mobutuism* in action. Sir Richard Burton faced greater hazards than these, of course; but then he was made of far sterner stuff.

ONE

Zanzibar

The first taxi I hailed in Zanzibar broke down after a hundred yards. It was dusk and the sky glowed carmine through the canopy of palms. The driver, aided by a passing bicyclist and two small boys, was confident of effecting the necessary repairs before nightfall. But the ancient British vehicle had given up the ghost, and my fare was subcontracted to a passing pickup truck of later model.

I was taken to the Bwawani Hotel, where it was assumed all respectable visitors stayed. The hotel was built on the orders and design of Sheikh Karume, great leader of the Zanzibari Revolution, who had a vision of a New Zanzibar, a modern, efficient, socialist, totally rational state.

Bwawani means In a Pond. Actually, Sheikh Karume had it built in a swamp. Mould had eaten holes in the deep pile carpets, and damp separated the wallpaper from the concrete walls. When the door to my room was opened there was an overpowering musty exhalation, as though it were an ancient underground family vault and not an hotel room at all. I half-expected to find Vincent Price inside.

The porter – charming, courteous and friendly, as are all Zanzibaris – smilingly demonstrated the use of the lavatory cistern to me. In the absence of the handle, all I had to do was to poke my forefinger down a small aperture and fish about for a time . . . He called for the insect-sprayer. (The attack rate of malaria in Zanzibar is ferocious.) He arrived, grinning broadly and carrying one of the old-fashioned hand sprays that I remembered my father using twenty-five years ago to rid the roses of aphids. To the smell of must was now added that of a choking insecticide.

In the morning I was able to study this gem of revolutionary architecture in greater detail. It was built of concrete in five storeys. At these latitudes, concrete seems to weep grey-black tears that stain the surface indelibly. The upper two storeys were closed – a notice in the lobby mentioned refurbishment, but it had obviously been posted for a long time – and one or two of the windows had been replaced by plywood. To the front was the swamp, to the back the gardens and then the seashore, complete with rusting hulks. Not far away was a mud flat, on which rested several dhows. In the gardens were a large upturned concrete saucer – serving both as rainwater gatherer and modern abstract sculpture – and a statue of Sheikh Karume, giving the dates of his accession to power and subsequent assassination. He was founder of the Afro-Shirazi Party (Shirazis are the Africans native to Zanzibar); and from the state of the statue, he may yet be the founder of the Zanzibari guano industry.

I moved from the Bwawani, which is some way out of the old town of Zanzibar, to the Africa House that is in the midst of it and used to be the old British Club. Two small cannon stand guard at the entrance; over the stairs are still some hunting trophies that, though high on the wall, have mysteriously tilted to an angle. On the first floor, completely open to the sea breeze, is a billiard table and marker, with raised benches for spectators, referee and waiting players. But there are no players waiting now, for there are no balls or cues, and the sound of Swahili and Zairean music relayed as loud as possible over the radio has replaced a hush broken only by the click of ivory on ivory.

Some of the rooms retain their labels over the lintels: Ladies' Powder Room, Gents' Wash Room, the Committee Room. This latter is the location of a remarkable library that was not long ago the subject of a long article in *The Times Literary Supplement*. I asked the reception-ist – an extremely polite and obliging man who was trying to improve his already excellent English by reading an abridged version of *King Solomon's Mines* – whether he knew of the article. He didn't, and I promised to send him a copy when I returned to England.

The books that remained were undisturbed, still carefully cata-logued. (I met a man who remembered a post-revolutionary bonfire of books in the street, however.) There were never more than a couple of hundred British on Zanzibar, and I suppose the library of their club offers an insight into their collective mind. Of course, the British passion for horses and for killing fish, fowl and fox was catered for: *Chasing and Racing, with a foreword by Lord Lansdowne*. There was an emphasis on the imperial and military: *Forty Years a Soldier; The Life of*

Buller. There was a strong streak of Germanophobia: *My Fight with Kaiserism*; *Bismarck, Some Secret Pages of His History* (in three volumes). And for the homesick there was *Sussex in Bygone Years*.

But the collective mind was not quite as unreflecting or philistine as this might suggest. There were scholarly works also, of history and economics; and the best literature of the time. Of great interest to me was *The Prevention of Malaria* by Ronald Ross. While I sat reading it one of the staff entered and asked me what I was reading with such concentration.

I in my turn asked him whether he had heard of Ronald Ross.

'No,' he replied.

'He was the man who discovered that malaria was spread by mosquitoes.'

He was astonished. Did it need to be discovered, then? He thought everyone knew malaria was spread by mosquitoes.

I walked out into Stone Town, as the old quarter of Zanzibar is called. Here the streets are narrow and the houses tall, in the Arab manner that produces such gratifying coolness in even the hottest of climates. Of course, none of the houses had been whitewashed in a quarter of a century and the cumulative shabbiness would alarm anyone unused to urban Africa. But things were much worse in the nineteenth century, according to the accounts of Victorian travellers, who found the town pervaded by the stink of carcasses rotting on the beach. It was the moral qualities of Zanzibar, however, that really inflamed their imaginations. Zanzibar, wrote Professor Henry Drummond in 1888, was: 'a cesspool of wickedness Oriental in its appearance, Mohammedan in its religion, Arabian in its morals . . . a fit capital for the Dark Continent.' Alas, I saw no wickedness all the time I was there.

Next door to the Africa House was the house of Tippu Tip, the half-caste slave and ivory trader who carved an evanescent empire for himself in the eastern part of present-day Zaire. Small children played with banana skins on the steps of the dark, cavernous entrance hall, through which I could dimly make out moorish arches. The children greeted me enthusiastically and shouted *Picha! Picha!* (Take a picture! Take a picture!) I had no camera with me, something beyond their experience of foreigners, and they appeared bewildered. As I approached to look indoors they scattered in fright, shrieking. But I told them not to be afraid, and they soon gathered again to resume their game.

The narrow streets and alleyways were not crowded and passers-by greeted me ceremoniously. The full form of greeting is quite lengthy, but hurry does not come naturally to such a people or in such a climate. The American Consul advised Stanley as he started out on his expedition to find Livingstone: 'Be patient, don't fret . . . or you won't live long here'.

I continued up Shangani Street, a broad thoroughfare as streets go in Zanzibar, which follows the contour of the shore. I passed the old British consulate where Stanley was told by the then consul, Sir John Kirk, that Livingstone's character was by no means purely angelic. Further on was the old Portuguese fort, opposite the Jubilee Gardens, Bandstand and Fountain (no flowers, no band, and definitely no water). Then came the single most imposing building in the old town: the Beit-el-Ajaib, the House of Wonder, once the Sultan's guest house but now occupied by offices of the *Chama Cha Mapinduzi*, the ubiquitous Party of the Revolution. Built in three storeys, the lower two each as tall as a house, painted white and with an enormous verandah supported by iron pillars, it must once have seemed a marvel of Victorian technology, as improbable as a man walking on the moon. The clock of the clock tower, decorated with filigree ironwork, had stopped.

Behind the Beit-el-Ajaib I found what seemed at first like a small bomb site. On closer inspection it proved to be a graveyard. Inside an enclosure of crumbling masonry, among a tangle of weeds, was an important-looking tomb with a long inscription in Arabic. An engraved stone translation, fading fast, was inserted into the crumbling masonry:

In Memory of His Highness Sayyid Said Bin Sultan, Imam of Oman and Sultan of Muscat and Zanzibar.

Sayyid Said was born . . . in AD 1791, and succeeded his father in 1804. He visited his East African dominions for the first time in 1828, transferred his capital from Muscat to Zanzibar in 1832 . . .

He died at sea on the 19th October 1856 . . . His body reached Zanzibar six days later and was interred here.

Sayyid Said was a great ruler and a faithful ally and firm friend of Great Britain. To him is due the credit of establishing the clove industry in Zanzibar and Pemba.

This memorial was erected by His Highness Sayyid Sir Khalifa Bin Harub . . .

Written and carved by order of His Highness, by Saleh Bin Ali, Interpreter, in 1925

Perhaps it is too soon after the revolution that overthrew Arab hegemony on the island to expect the Zanzibaris to care for their historical monuments from an age of oppression. Perhaps it is the very dilapidation of such places that lends them charm – if they were carefully tended and preserved they would seem curiously soulless and sterile. Or maybe the matter goes deeper than that. The neglect is not the result of a conscious decision to be revenged on a repudiated historical tradition, since everything seems neglected equally. Rather, it is still too intensely oral a society to attach much importance to tangible relics of the past.

I entered the warren of streets – paths, really – between the close-built houses. Before long I came across a small shop presided over by a tiny wizened Indian. I caught his eye and he beckoned me in. He dealt in bits and pieces: unused sepia postcards from the 1950s, copper coins, a few stamps. Stacked against one wall were a hundred or so books which he had somehow inherited from the defunct Zanzibar Book Club (no member to borrow more than three books at a time or to keep them longer than ten days). I asked for and received permission to browse, and was soon covered in bookish dust. The worms that bored so neatly, pedantically almost, through the pages, had done so undisturbed for many years.

'You will not find volumes such as these anywhere,' said the owner, pressing into my hand a very heavy green-covered book so dense that even the worms had made no impression upon it. 'I have a set of three, very valuable.'

The set of three comprised the report of the British Military Commission on the Russo-Japanese War. I assured him that I should certainly have bought them, fine volumes all, were it not for their weight, which might prove inconvenient as I travelled across Africa. However, I was short of reading matter and I bought, for about thirty cents, Sinclair Lewis's crude political fantasy *It Can't Happen Here*, the *It* of the title being a fascist takeover of the United States.

As if disbelieving his luck, or fearing that I might change my mind, the trader quickly said he must shut the shop now and go to mosque.

Shortly afterwards I met another Indian trader, the only man on the island I saw dressed in collar and tie. He too beckoned me into his shop, a much larger establishment, but also devoted to junk. Cheap carvings gathered dust and cracked crockery, the detritus of departing families, mouldered on shelves.

'I have real antiques,' he said forlornly, meaning, I supposed, things that dated back to the 50's, as remote now as any epoch in history. 'Is there anything you want?'

A friend of mine had wanted me to inquire the price of a Zanzibar chest.

He took me to a gloomy back room and pointed to a plain wooden box with brass fittings.

'You will not find such a chest in Zanzibar – at least five hundred years old.'

On the lid was a brass label:

MOHAMMED AMIN 1897

The deception was so transparent it wasn't really deception at all. He had long since given up hope of genuine trade. He was seventy-six now, rheumy-eyed, and we sat down to have a little chat. I asked him how things were before.

'Before what?'

'The Revolution.'

He laughed: a bitter laugh.

'It was paradise in Zanzibar,' he said.

His son, in his forties, and balding, joined us.

'For everyone?' I asked.

'Put it like this,' interposed the son. 'If you owned a house but the tenants controlled it, wouldn't you eventually want to control it yourself, even if you weren't able?'

'But they don't understand, they don't understand,' lamented the father. He had been captain of the Zanzibar cricket team that played teams from visiting warships in the 1930s. 'Now it is football, only football.'

The violence after the Revolution was terrible. They guessed that 20,000 had been killed. (The generally quoted figure is 5,000: but even that is the equivalent in Britain of 800,000.) For years they had suffered the shortages and insane paranoia of the new regime. Only recently had things improved. Food was available, there was little to fear. But of course, it would never be like the old days, when they had dealt in fine silver and objects of rare beauty.

'Now only junk,' said the man who a few minutes before had claimed possession of real antiques.

They asked me whether I wanted to change money at favourable rates: the old man would never leave Zanzibar now, but his son needed dollars to emigrate.

'You want to see my treasure?' asked the old man, searching under the old newspaper that covered the table at which he sat.

It must be a thin treasure, I thought, wondering what it could be.

At last he found it. He stroked it as he handed it to me.

It was a year-old article from the *New York Times* in which was inset a small photograph of him. He had acted as the reporter's main informant and for a day his life had once more attained significance, after more than twenty empty years. I left him to linger over his treasure.

I emerged into the old Slave Market, now the site of the University Mission to Central Africa Cathedral Church of Christ. It was here that Edward Steere, first Bishop of Zanzibar, chose to erect his cathedral, building the altar over the very place where there had been a whipping post for slaves. There were no architects in Zanzibar at the time, so the bishop designed the building himself, experimenting with a mixture of coral rock and cement which the local population thought would soon crumble to nothing, the more so as a sign of God's disfavour. The first service was held when there was as yet no roof; later, a tower and steeple were added, the Sultan requesting that they should not be higher than his palace, a request with which the bishop was happy to comply.

The yellowish-grey building is both Arabic and Victorian gothic in inspiration, a contradictory mixture of styles that somehow contrives to be entirely consonant with its surroundings. It is, in fact, a building of considerable *tact*, not a quality one normally associates with the endeavours of Victorian missionaries.

In the vestibule was a notice giving the times of daily communion. A footnote was appended:

N.B. English Survice on Request

I walked round the interior, now very neglected. The plasterwork was peeling, some of the stained glass was broken. There was a crucifix fashioned from the wood of the tree under which Livingstone's heart was buried. Livingstone made but one convert in all his life, and he backslid; and even now the congregations in the cathedral are pitifully small (the Catholics have fared better). Attached to the walls were brass plaques commemorating those who died in Zanzibar and elsewhere on the coast to bring light into what they considered darkness. At a slight angle, under a broken stained glass window, was a general dedication:

> To the Glory of God and in memory of Livingstone and other explorers, men good and brave who to advance knowledge, set free the slave and hasten Christ's Kingdom in Africa, loved not their lives, even unto death, this window is dedicated by their friends.

I walked out into the bright sunlight and then into the Cathedral Bookshop. Two titles were available: *Towards Party Supremacy* and *Reform or Revolution?*

Across from Stone Town are the famous Michanzani Flats, a workers' paradise built by the East Germans at a time when it was still the hope of the revolutionary government to do away with the old town altogether. The flats line two intersecting triumphal boulevards down which tanks might safely roll; the flats continue faceless and unbroken along the boulevards for more than a quarter of a mile. They were built on the assumption that what was good for East Berlin or Karl Marx Stadt was good for Zanzibar – the architectural manifestation of the latest ethnocentric doctrine Europe has sought to impose on Africa.

Explaining the failure of missionaries in Africa, Mary Kingsley wrote they had: 'a tendency to regard the African minds as so many jugs which have only to be emptied of the stuff which is in them and refilled with the particular doctrine they . . . are teaching.' Poor Africa! This tendency has not by any means been confined to Christians, and now Africans feel obliged to search for a doctrine that is truly their own. The problem is that even the idea of a doctrine, complete and self-consistent, is un-African.

Livingstone's House, or more properly the house which an Indian merchant lent him in the interval between his expeditions, is half a mile from Stone Town. A hundred-and-thirty years ago it must have been isolated, but now the new concrete town is catching up with it. On my way there Saif, a butcher in the market, bought me a mangosteen to taste, just out of friendliness. Travelling – but especially in Africa – one learns to suspect friendly gestures as leading inevitably to fraud or theft; and then, on the occasions that they don't, one feels guilt that sophistication has cut one off from simple human kindness.

Livingstone's House was large and airy, but no special effort had been made to preserve it. A notice outside explained that it was now used for government 'quaters', including the Friendship Tourist Bureau. They were indeed friendly in the bureau – six of them – but unable to help in any way. There were no tours, no books, and no boats. My problem, touristically speaking, was that I was not a Prearranged Group. But I could look around Livingstone's House if I liked.

In the corridor was a map of Africa. A bookworm had forged a path all the way across Portuguese East Africa, while others had started trading posts in Italian East Africa (including Ethiopia) and the Anglo-Egyptian Sudan.

Returning to Stone Town, I was approached by an African bent with age in Muslim dress.

'Excuse me, sir,' he said. 'Are you Irish?'

'No, English.'

'Do you know my master, Mr George McGregor? He was my master.'

'I'm afraid not.'

'He taught me the bassoon. We played in the bandstand. He was my bassoon master. Do you know him?'

'I'm sorry, I don't.'

I expected a flood of reminiscence, but instead he rushed onwards, an ancient bassoonist in flowing robes.

Across the bay at a distance of two miles is an islet called Prison Island. It shimmers tantalizingly in the noonday heat. It was first used as a centre of correction for recalcitrant slaves. (Too often when they shivered with vicarious horror at the East African slave trade the Victorians forgot that many of the slaves were destined for *European* plantations in Mauritius and Reunion, where a far harsher fate awaited them than in Arabia.) Then a prison was built which, however, was used as an isolation hospital and quarantine post.

I went across in a boat called *Start a Fire*. Its anchor was the cylinder block of an internal combustion engine. We landed at a tiny sandy inlet. Across the turquoise and azure water the town of Zanzibar looked much as it did in nineteenth-century prints. Frolicking naked in the clear water were some Italian tourists, providing the Zanzibari boatmen who had brought them with much salacious delight. They roared with laughter at one enormously fat lady who looked like a bronzed mother-in-law from a Donald McGill postcard.

The ground was strewn with the fragrant flowers of frangipani. The superintendent's house, not yet ruined beyond the powers of restoration, had still a magnificent wooden spiral staircase. On rusting iron hospital bedsteads a few Zanzibaris slept. In the garden wall a plaque commemorated a sailor of the Royal Navy who had died in Zanzibar in 1902. The ship's littérateur had improved slightly on Shakespeare:

> Fear no more the heat o' the sun,
> Nor the furious winter's rages,
> Thou thy worldly work has done,
> Home art gone, and ta'en thy wages.

Amongst the luxuriant undergrowth the roofless ruins of the hospital crumble before the assault of the vegetation, which finds sustenance even halfway up a plastered wall. The hospital's origins as a prison are clear enough in the rusting iron bars of the cells, but as a site for a sanitorium there can be few more beautiful. Even the latrines, built over the sea on overhanging ledges, offer a vision through their openings of the placid, coruscating aquamarine water below.

The only inmates now, though, are the giant tortoises which flee slowly through the undergrowth and give up every five yards, as though they suffered from angina. They flee more for the sake of solitude than to escape danger, for no enemy could be slower than they. They view the world with a baleful glare which is somehow more than reptilian. They want nothing but to be left alone, these saurian hermits.

At the far end of the islet is a building connected by iron pipes to an extraordinary rusting contraption that must once have been a boiler. Inside the building is a giant cylindrical autoclave, built of iron three inches thick and tall enough for a man to stand in. It is rusted – rusted solid. The door is immobile, congealed half-open on a wheel-and-rail system, so that it is impossible to make it even judder or vibrate. The whole has the air of being a Jules Verne invention for the exploration of some unlikely region of the globe – Zaire perhaps?

*   *   *

The passenger ship, the M.V. *Mapinduzi* (Revolution) that normally ran between Zanzibar and the mainland was ferrying workers to Pemba for the clove harvest: designed for 600, it was carrying 3000. There used to be more than one ship, but that was long ago.

Instead, I found a small wooden boat to take me that much resembled the *African Queen*, less Hepburn and Bogart. It was to depart from the Dhow Shed, as the harbour was called, but no-one was able to say when. The Zanzibaris, in common with most Africans, have little sense of the passage of time, or a very different one from ours: with one notable exception. Every weekday afternoon at two-thirty, with a punctuality by which one could set one's watch, the workers in Zanzibari government offices rush out to scramble for places in the Land Rovers that take them home. In all other matters it is useless to expect an awareness of time; and the European, who rushes even when he has nothing to do, must swallow his frustration and learn to smile. The nearest anyone would come to stating a departure time was, 'when there are enough people who want to go'.

The organization of the Dhow Shed was rudimentary, to say the least. Although Tanganyika and Zanzibar are united into one republic (a much-trumpeted achievement for the cause of African unity), there were still immigration and customs procedures to be gone through. Customs formalities consisted largely of shouting across a counter at a man with a piece of white chalk, so that he would mark one's baggage in preference to that of all the others who were shouting at him. The sale of tickets was conducted along the same lines, with the result that it took much time and energy. However, there was little doubt that being the only white was greatly to my advantage.

After an hour or two of collective panic, during which the boat had been loaded with baskets and sacks of durian, a large, prickly green fruit with white flesh, it was time to embark. Amazingly, a queue formed; but the captain decided it was in the wrong place and had it move further along the quay. Then he decided that the first place had been the right one after all, and had it moved back; by which time, needless to say, the queue had turned into a seething mêlée.

Our boat was reached by clambering over three other boats moored parallel to the quay. It was an obstacle race for short pregnant women with much luggage and a baby strapped to the back, but they completed the course with remarkable aplomb and good humour. Our boat, on which one might hesitate to take a dozen people up the Thames in midsummer, soon filled so that late arrivals were scarcely able to find room. In all, there were a hundred and fifty passengers, and when the boat began to list heavily they all shrieked with laughter and shouted *Twende! Twende!* (Let's go! Let's go!)

I found myself squeezed between a sack of durian and the exhaust pipe, much rusted and resoldered, that emerged from the engine below deck. It exhaled a thick black smoke. (To prevent the solder from melting one of the sailors threw water over the pipe from time to time). As for the durian, Sir James Scott wrote in 1882: ' . . . the flavour & odour of the fruit may be realised by eating a garlic custard over a London sewer.' I was next to an elderly Arab, who spent much time examining the contents of my bag and marvelling at the quality of my possessions and their cheapness, even when translated at the black market rate of exchange. As refreshment on board there was a bucket of water and a tin mug, and a large bag of biscuits, rock-hard, that it needed the perfect teeth of Africans to break. The passengers shared with me their oranges and baked cassava flavoured with salt and chilli which they had brought for the journey – very poor people share as a matter of course, unselfconsciously.

At last the boat left the quay and the verdant coast of Zanzibar slipped slowly by. I think I was the only person aboard to torture himself with thoughts of danger. For everyone else, whether we arrived or not was *shauri ya Mungu* – God's affair. I was impressed – as I had been many times before – by the way Africans made the best of an unenviable situation. Under the beating sun, with an unpleasant pitch and roll, too cramped to move, amid fumes of diesel and durian, they yet remained cheerful and well-mannered. They chatted amicably or slept peacefully, mothers breast-fed and comforted their babies, no-one complained. I have often wondered whether this cheerfulness in the face of adversity is the outcome of conscious philosophy or of ignorance that anything could be different. Stanley wrote of the Zanzibaris:

> . . . they may be seen carrying huge loads on their heads, as happy as possible, not because they are kindly treated or that their work is light, but because it is their nature to be gay and lighthearted, because they have conceived neither joys nor hopes which may not be gratified at

will, nor cherished any ambition beyond their reach, and therefore have not been baffled in their hopes, nor known disappointment.

One of the passengers, a young man, asked me whether we had boats such as this in my country. The question implied ignorance, no doubt; but also a subliminal idea that perhaps life could be less harsh than this.

The journey took six hours, and we were never out of sight of one coast or the other. Still, a single large wave might have done for us, and I was relieved enough to see the harbour of Dar es Salaam. Disembarkation was as much of a struggle as embarkation: we had to transfer to yet smaller boats and then climb with stiff limbs over the oily decks of several moored vessels. But still everyone laughed, even when the customs officers made them open their pathetic packages. To remain polite at such moments is politeness indeed.

The first bus I saw on my return to the mainland listed every bit as heavily as the boat. Painted on its rear was a motto:

IN GOD WE TRUST – 100%

TWO

Tanzania

I stayed with friends in Dar es Salaam. They lived in Msasani, the affluent suburb of the city, where diplomats and aid workers go home at night to forget they are in Africa. This was not the best training for what I assumed would be the long and arduous journey ahead. I had only to drop my dirty clothes upon the floor for them to reappear two hours later cleaned and pressed as new. Every night I ate copiously and drank French or German wine. It was a dangerously seductive and luxurious prelude.

Msasani is built on a peninsula which gives fine, sweeping views of the Indian Ocean. The houses there are large, as are their gardens. I drove along the ocean road with someone who remembered Msasani as it was: better kept and grander still. He pointed to the house, now an ambassador's residence, where he had lived as a boy forty years ago. One of his neighbours – from time to time – had been the Aga Khan.

A few houses in Msasani were now inhabited by Africans. Most of them were easily recognizable by the neglect, the goats in the garden, and the replacement of flowers by cassava and maize. Rubbish was burnt by the side of the road. One could not blame the Africans, of course, for any man with a good job was immediately descended upon by his extended family, and even the best paid were not far enough away from subsistence to lavish effort or resources on the creation of mere beauty. Perhaps, too, it was only justice that in a city where a few months before food had varied from the scarce to the unobtainable, and where in the rains the telephones don't work and the roads are so potholed that it is advisable to have a four-wheel drive vehicle, something of the squalid world beyond should obtrude on the otherwise gracious realm of the expatriate. But then I thought, is no-one to enjoy anything beautiful or even pleasant, until there is perfect justice in the world?

The *security situation*, as everyone called it, had become serious. Dar es Salaam – Haven of Peace – was a haven of peace no longer. Before going for a walk along the beach it was wise to divest oneself of one's watch and valuables. Even so, there was no guarantee of safety: the young son of my friends had found himself forcibly divested of his clothes as well. The news of every fresh incident swept like contagion through the expatriate community. Not only were all doors locked and windows barred, but steel gates constructed across corridors within the house. Daylight afforded protection no longer. Even a memsahibs' coffee morning had recently been disrupted by a gang intent on rape as well as theft.

The British felt doubly under threat, thanks to Mrs Thatcher's handling of the South African question. And recently a man thought to have been an Arab had asked street traders outside the British Airways office to keep an eye on his briefcase while he left it there for a few minutes. No-one leaves their belongings for an instant in Dar, and a suspicious taxi driver asked him what was in the case. The man fled, taking his presumed bomb with him. Such incidents did nothing to calm already jangled nerves; but neither did they prevent the diplomats of some countries from taking advantage of the duty-free emporium in Dar, run on concession by the Palestinian Liberation Organization.

The house in which I stayed was protected by a new security system, imported from Kenya (which is more advanced than Tanzania). Around the corner, twenty-four hours a day, waited a pickup truck with a group of men equipped with steel helmets and bullet-proof vests, riot shields and clubs. At an electronic alarm signal from any of the households that subscribed to the system, they rushed to the scene, sirens wailing and lights flashing, to assail any undeparted thieves, with no questions asked as to resulting injuries or even deaths.

I wondered how long it would be before Dar gangs stumbled on the solution devised by their Nairobi counterparts. There, the guards are diverted by several simultaneous false alarms, while accomplices attack the real target (often with machine guns and battering rams). House-holders who resist are murdered. The thieves especially prize video cassette recorders.

Yet I felt this violence to be uncharacteristic of the Tanzanians. I knew them as a gentle and forgiving people, not easily roused to anger or resentment. They have no special predilection for violence, and I should not have expected them to take to armed robbery with any great alacrity.

But I was accustomed also to apparent contradictions in their character. I had been at once impressed on my arrival in the country by the courtesy of their social relations, which often put our comparative brusqueness to shame. But I soon learnt that whatever the outward forms, no real trust existed between them. A friend of twenty years would unhesitatingly take off with his companion's property, never to be seen again, if he thought he had a chance of not being caught. When a Tanzanian explained this to me, amused at my naivety in thinking otherwise, I protested that without such trust life must be very sordid indeed.

'Why not, sir?' he replied. 'This is Tanzania, this is Tanzania.'

There are several ways in which the expatriates of Dar escape temporarily from Africa. Perhaps the most bizarre is an American icecream parlour called *Sno-Creme*. Inside, it is a small Disneyland, with cardboard cut-out figures dangling from the ceiling and polystyrene castles on ledges on the walls. At the far end is a telephone in the shape of Mickey Mouse. Sno-Creme was celebrating twenty-five years of continuous service in Dar. It was one of the first fruits of independence and survived the years of Tanzanian socialist excess. To mark the historic anniversary, all the sundaes were of South Sea Island inspiration: Tahiti Treat, Aloha Sunrise, Pago Pago Boat (a Frutti Fantasy), and Pukapuka Delight. Hawaiian music twanged over the loudspeakers and the African staff wore garlands of frangipani and hibiscus blooms in their hair.

I ate my sundae, composed of reconstituted icecream powder, artificial syrups, aerosol cream, tinned strawberries, and a few slices of real banana and pawpaw (Tanzania's contribution). It cost the equivalent of the minimum weekly wage. Slightly nauseated by this chemical assault on my digestive tract, I staggered to the exit. On the wall by the door was a framed encomium from the *Los Angeles Times*: 'The secret of Sno-Creme's success is its innocence'.

Outside Sno-Creme sat one of two beggars who operate there in shifts. One of them has an artificial leg which he disconnects and props conspicuously against the wall. The other is a leper with a pushed-in nose and spatulate, fingerless hands which he upturns in supplication to departing customers. It is a psychologically acute place for them to beg: one could not reasonably claim to be either poor or in a terrible hurry as one emerged.

I gave the leper a small note which he manoeuvred with surprising dexterity into his shirt pocket. Another seventeen customers such as I, and he would be able to buy himself a Frutti Fantasy.

A further haunt of the expatriates, rather up-market, is the Yacht Club. Its rules are so complex that the Common Law of England is simple by comparison; its politics so secretive that the Politburo seems positively publicity-seeking. There is a waiting list for membership. During the school holidays the visiting adolescent children of aid workers are anxious to be seen on the quarterdeck, to prove their passage to adulthood. There are a few African members, half of whom do not pay their bar bills, but they are influential people with access to scarce goods the club needs, so nothing is said.

One eats well there: at least, better than elsewhere in Dar. It is very pleasant under the stars, a few lights twinkling across the bay, the rhythmic plash of wavelets on the shore below, a sea breeze cooling but not chilling. The expatriate feels that life in Dar is, after all, bearable.

At another table sat a prominent member of the club, of uncertain nationality and occupation. He was pointed out to me as being someone of whom the Africans were afraid.

'Why?' I asked.

'Because he's killed two of them.'

The second of his victims was his night-watchman who, failing to open the gate fast enough, caused him a certain irritation: so he squashed him to death against the wall with his car.

'But how could he get away with it?' I asked.

'Simple: he paid the family some money and that was the end of it. They might even have thought they got a bargain.'

Whatever the demerits of the old colonialists, they knew how to build for the climate. They relied on breezes, shutters and broad verandahs to keep buildings cool, and in the process built elegantly and on a human scale. There is nothing quite so uncomfortable as a modern concrete tower in Dar es Salaam when things go wrong – as, of course, they do. For some reason, sewage then starts flowing upwards.

I visited a friend in another part of Msasani. Conversation faltered and we watched an American movie on the video. The cook emerged from the kitchen and watched spellbound as carloads of gangsters emptied bullets into one another, with much loss of ketchup.

'Europe?' he asked.

'America,' we said.

He shook his head.

'*Africa ni takataka*,' he said: Africa is rubbish.

Much of my time in Dar was taken up with my application for a visa to Zaire. Apart from a valid passport, current vaccination certificates for cholera and yellow fever, photocopies of one's traveller's cheques, a letter of recommendation from one's embassy, an air ticket out, three passport photographs and a form to be filled out in triplicate without use of carbon paper, all one needs for a visa to Zaire is patience. A loss of temper would probably be fatal to one's chances.

In all, I went to the embassy ten times. It was not an impressive place. It had been a respectable house once, but it had not been repainted and the windows were cracked and dirty. The eaves were disintegrating. The garden was mainly of gravel and dust, into which the garden boy poured a jet of water from a hosepipe. He aimed it at a single spot, creating a pond of mud. He kept his aim for minutes at a time. What was he doing? What, if anything, was going through his mind? I gave up the question as insoluble. Meanwhile, the ambassador's Mercedes was polished and repolished until it gleamed.

I was interviewed by the consul. He seemed to find the whole idea of my going to Zaire faintly ridiculous. But he assured me my visa would be issued next day; but next day the embassy was closed. I was told to come back tomorrow, at two o'clock. I pointed to the notice stating that the embassy closed at one. Nevertheless, I should come at two. The embassy was closed.

When at last my passport was handed to me, on my tenth visit at the precise time stated the day before, there was not a flicker of recognition of my previous nine visits.

I felt as though I had achieved something so worthwhile, admirable even, that it almost made the journey itself superfluous.

Outside the embassy was a Frenchman, an aid worker in Mali, who had so far been to the embassy three times without even obtaining the application form.

Zaire's national motto was inscribed on the wall: Peace, Justice, Work.

Visiting a friend in the Asian quarter (Asia in this context being synonymous with the Indian subcontinent), I was impressed by the modesty with which even rich merchants live. They are, of course, reluctant to display their wealth in a country still officially devoted to the ideals of socialism, and in which they are a conspicuous and much-criticized minority.

It is alleged they are hated because they send money away to foreign bank accounts. Do not all Africans who are able do the same? It is alleged they are hated because they treat Africans badly. I can only say I have never seen it: on the contrary, I have never seen an African in need turned away emptyhanded from an Indian shop. It is alleged they are hated because they are exploiters and profiteers. But they sell at whatever price they can get, often in places where no-one else is prepared to trade. Without them, all commerce would cease. The hatred, if it exists, is that of poor people for those who seem to profit from them. It is the antisemitism of East Africa.

I knew an Asian trader in a small town who, during a crackdown on so-called 'economic saboteurs', was arrested for possessing twelve cups and saucers. He went to prison – in his late fifties – for six months, while the soldiers who arrested him sold his goods and drank the proceeds. In prison he contracted tuberculosis and beriberi. He was released when there was nothing left to buy in the town and people complained. Later, he was cleared of all crimes (but not compensated).

'Are you not bitter?' I asked him.

'No,' he said. 'I like this country. The ordinary people are good.'

At one of Dar's few bookshops, whose stock was so small it could be taken in at a glance, I met an assistant called Ali, who was studying a textbook of civil law behind the counter. His excellent English was self-taught: he had gone to school at a time when the teaching of English was deprecated (and it was hoped that Swahili would become a world language by spreading through Africa). He hoped one day to go to university and qualify as a lawyer. He did not consider his present income – $9 a month at black market rates of exchange – sufficient on which to marry and raise a family.

He asked me what I thought of Tanzania, how it compared with other African countries, and so forth. He was young enough to think the violent overthrow of the government was necessary and would lead to felicity. I cautioned him against the comforting illusion that Tanzania's problems could be quickly overcome: and if Tanzania's government was not the best possible, it was very far from being the worst possible.

The next day was the Muslim festival of Id el Haj, and Ali invited me to lunch at his uncle's house. He met me in a battered blue Peugeot 404 that had to be coaxed into action and seemed, on Dar's cracked and pitted road surfaces, to have square wheels. Ali's uncle, who had actually raised Ali, lived in what Ali called a 'suburb'. It turned out to be one of those pullulating districts on the edge of the city that are not really urban, but only African villages expanded a thousand times. The houses were perhaps a little closer together than in a village, but the wandering chickens and pigs, the mango trees and patches of maize, provided links with everyone's recent rural past. The resulting conglomeration might not have been tidy or hygienic – in the rainy season one always hears of cholera epidemics in Dar – but it was more human than the attempts at modern rehousing schemes in other parts of the city, where the drains block, the water and electricity supplies fail, noise reverberates, anonymity strikes and everything is grey.

A reddish pall of dust hovered over the whole district, trapping the heat. There was no wind and the Party flag, a drab green ground with crossed hammer and handhoe in yellow in one corner, drooped from bamboo flagpoles at every Party building – that is to say, every hundred yards. The main thoroughfares churned with traffic and petty commerce, and were lined with mud-hut bars named after South African cities.

The house of Ali's uncle, though also of mud, was larger than most. Ali's uncle was a small businessman who owned a decrepit bus and several other enterprises. He was also a *Ten Cell Leader*, that is to say the Party representative and supervisor for ten households. This system of political control is perfectly adapted to maximize corruption and petty tyranny. For example, if a pupil wishes to continue his studies he must not only pass the examinations but gain a certificate of political suitability from his ten cell leader. In practice, political suitability boils down to a willingness and ability to pay a bribe. Ali's uncle, however, despised the system and had joined the Party for business reasons only: it made obtaining licences easier. He exacted no bribes and sometimes even paid the forced contributions to Party funds for all his ten households, rather than ask them for money he knew they could not afford.

Ali's uncle wanted to be rich and had no time for dreams of equality. Already he was prosperous – he had a refrigerator – but he still had no running water. He wanted to live in Msasani one day.

Our conversation was constantly interrupted by visitors who entered without knocking, for which Ali's uncle apologized, but said it was the African way to extend hospitality to whoever came: there was no such thing as privacy, and no-one felt the need of it. Some friends, all Muslims, arrived with a bottle of Zanzibari whisky – called Gold Label – which smelled of paint remover. I declined a tot, on the grounds that I was too good a Muslim.

Ali was so in awe of his uncle that he spoke not a word throughout my visit: to have done so would have been an impertinence. He returned to life only as he drove me back to Msasani. He told me how he had once gone to Somalia because he had heard people were well paid there. They weren't, but still he dreamt of promised lands, like Burundi and Sudan. He asked me if I knew anything about wage rates there.

A policeman suddenly stepped out in front of the car, which was now travelling crabwise over a pebbly road, and stopped us. We only just avoided a collision (which probably would have done more harm to the car than to the policeman). He demanded to see Ali's documents. Ali said he had left them at home: it was all too obvious he had none. Only my presence, he said later, had saved him from having to pay a hefty bribe.

Ali refused my invitation to a cup of tea. He was too shy, he said. His instinct was probably right: the living room would have echoed with silences, pregnant with yet more silences, as subjects of conversation fled further from our minds the harder we sought them. Goodwill alone is not a sufficient basis for friendship.

It was time to leave Dar. On the afternoon of my departure, my friends discovered there was a flight direct from Tanzania to Mali.

'Are you sure you wouldn't rather fly?' they asked.

I wasn't sure; but I didn't.

I had been warned against the Tanganyika Central Railway by no less an authority than a member of the Tanzanian Parliament. He used it regularly to attend parliamentary sittings in Dodoma and was eloquent about its manifold shortcomings, particularly the overcrowding, the absence of doors and windows, the passengers in the toilets and the thieves on the carriage roofs who descended at night through the absent windows to relieve the passengers of their belongings.

'You must go by aeroplane,' he said in a tone that brooked no contradiction. 'You will be safe in Dodoma in no time.'

On the other hand, an expatriate friend of mine who had been brought up in Tanganyika and gone to school in Mwanza, on Lake Victoria, remembered the train as it was: how one ate with silver cutlery off porcelain as the train cleaved herds of gazelle in two.

'And the Africans?' I asked. 'How did they travel?'

They travelled, of course, as they have always travelled, and always will travel.

I had been warned also that the train *never* left on time, that is to say at 6.10 p.m. On this occasion, however, it could not have been more punctual had Mussolini been in power. We chugged gently out of the decrepit station at exactly 6.10 p.m.

The railway from Dar es Salaam to Lake Tanganyika was built by the Germans. It took them nine years, from 1905 to 1914. The sleepers of the single track still bear the date of their German manufacture, progressively later as one travels along the line. There are piles of unused German sleepers intermittently along the whole length of the railway, abandoned from a project to build a second track.

The rolling stock was not as bad as the member of parliament had led me to expect. Admittedly, the seat in my first class compartment seemed to have been deeply excavated by a foam-rubber devouring rodent, the lights did not work and the window would not remain shut without a specially-fashioned wooden prop lent out for the night by the guard. More importantly, however, the door locked and there was only one other passenger in this compartment designed for two. He was a secondary school pupil aged twenty-two (it was not uncommon to find such aged schoolboys in Africa) who spoke not a word of English. He was the son of the police chief of Moshi and was travelling first class on a warrant issued by his father. In fact, I was the only first class passenger who had actually *paid* for his ticket: all the others were friends or relatives of someone empowered to give them a warrant.

In the evening light, which lent a majesty even to tin roofs, we passed through Dar's semi-industrial district. It is semi-industrial because, while there are plenty of factories, practically nothing is produced there. We passed, for example, the small pharmaceutical factory whose owner I had once met. His factory had then been making nothing for several months, thanks to a lack of raw materials, but such was the tenderness of Tanzania's social conscience that he was not allowed to fire a single worker; with the result that he was running down his financial reserves paying twenty men to sit idle in his factory until he went bankrupt.

Having put the last of Dar behind us, we came to a halt in a landscape of lush green valleys where banana trees grew wild and fireflies drifted tantalizingly, emitting flashes of an astonishingly pure light. And, as if the effort of leaving so punctually had been too exhausting, that is where we stayed till morning.

It took fifteen hours to reach Morogoro, less than three hours away by road (potholed and crevassed as it is). No-one was able to explain the delay, nor did they think it required explanation. Delay was part of life, like death and the weather.

As soon as the schoolboy woke he asked me for money, claiming to be penniless.

After Morogoro, the countryside grew decidedly drier. Tanzania's fertile land lies around the rim of the country; the central plain is arid semi-desert. The rivers had dried out and were no more than scars in the landscape. The red earth and the baobabs reminded me of Australia. Baobabs have an unreal quality, like pantomime trees that one half-expects to walk away with an actor inside them. As for the people who lived there, I found it difficult to conceive how they could survive. Their villages were of long, low, mean-looking huts of crumbling mud, with thatch roofs. We stopped at each of them, however small; and each specialized in selling a single commodity to the passengers – baskets, hard-boiled eggs with calcium deficient shells, roasted manioc, peanuts, bananas. There was no sign of cultivation and I wondered where they obtained their produce. It was certain they made little money by it: most were in rags and some were in sacking. No child that was old enough to hold something was too young to participate in this petty commerce. Toddlers of less than three walked up and down the train, carrying a single banana for sale.

One village, more prosperous than the rest, specialized in providing lunch. Beside the train sat women with enamel bowls of rice and stew. I bought some chicken, the toughest I had ever eaten, and some goat kebabs. The train continued its slow progress through the desert with the passengers eructating in greasy satisfaction.

We arrived at Dodoma at 5 p.m. It had taken twenty-three hours to travel a distance covered in six hours by Land Rover, itself no racing conveyance.

Dodoma was something of an oasis in the bone-dry landscape. The light was mellow and golden after the harsh glare of the day, the temperature was dropping after the suffocating heat of the afternoon. It was a great relief to see some green again.

Across from the station was the Dodoma Railway Hotel, a colonial relic. All rooms were taken, however: the National Executive Committee of the Party of the Revolution was meeting in Dodoma. I was relegated to the Mapambazuko Guest House, simple but surprisingly clean. One washed in the courtyard from a tank of well-water.

Having been long confined in the train I was anxious to stretch my legs. I was warned, however, to return by dark: there were many robbers in Dodoma after dark.

Around the guesthouse was a residential quarter of modest prosperity, neater and tidier than is usual in Tanzania. From a nearby field came the laughter and exclamations of an evening game of handball. Dominating the area, however, was a recently-built Catholic basilica, from which issued the sound of hymns sung in Swahili. A service was in progress, conducted by an African priest. The alabaster statuary was Italian and mass-produced. The figures in the decorative mosaics were black, except for Christ and St Paul, who were white.

I walked on from the basilica and came across a small, neglected cemetery, some of whose graves were hidden by undergrowth. It was Dodoma's cemetery for whites; and one could trace the decline of colonial society in the headstones. Until independence they were carved with precision, of slabs of marble or granite. The undergrowth once cleared away, they were as fresh as the day they were erected. But after independence there was no-one in Dodoma who could carve straight: the letters became rough-hewn, irregular and all at angles, hacked out of concrete. Later still, there were only tin crosses with cards attached.

There was a grave sacred to the memory of a young District Commissioner, one of the last of the breed, who died aged 28 in a hunting accident three years before independence. What a stir his now forgotten death must then have created in the little white community! I moved on before the banal reflections of a mediocre mind on the transitoriness of life engulfed me completely.

But further on was another graveyard. This one had military ranks of perfectly regular white crosses. They were the graves of South African troops, commanded by Smuts, who died during the campaign in the First World War to wrest Tanganyika from the Germans.

Next morning, the town was strangely, eerily quiet. All shops and offices were closed, though it was a weekday. I met a pale, plump New Zealand missionary teacher who explained the silence. Everyone was away at a rally to be addressed by the President. The subject of his address? The need for an Honest Day's Work.

Dodoma was chosen ten years ago as the nation's new capital. By way of explanation, one high official said: Tanzania is a country of villages, therefore we must live in a village. Nevertheless, it seems an eccentric choice. Admittedly it is geographically central, but its water supply is precarious and its climate may be expected to sap the already not superabundant energies of Tanzanian bureaucrats. In a word, the choice is madness. Dodoma, while no village, is no Brasilia either. In ten years, not a single stretch of road has been paved. Indeed, from my archaeological observations, I should say that those paved roads which existed before the fateful decision was taken have since been allowed to disintegrate altogether. Certain offices have been constructed, though: notably the new Party Headquarters, financed by oft-repeated voluntary contributions of Tanzanian workers – voluntary, that is, in the Engelsian sense of the word, freedom being the recognition of necessity.

But for all that, Dodoma is far from unpleasant. It is quiet and provincial. If every passing vehicle stirs up clouds of dust, at least there is not much traffic. And that afternoon there was no traffic. Policemen, some with two-way radios, stood at intervals along the road that led to the old Party Headquarters, an ugly rectangular building with louvred windows behind which hung the usual filthy curtains, their ends stuffed between louvres to create the maximum impression of shabbiness. Among the policemen I recognized the one who had stopped Ali and me in Dar, but he did not recognize me. He carried a swagger stick, and I thought he rather enjoyed pointing with it to the places where people should stand and wait.

In the dust by the side of the road, opposite the old Party Headquarters, sat a blind cripple, his eyes empty, skin-covered sockets. His teeth were brown, his face wrinkled. He was a musician, and he played a three-stringed instrument fashioned from a gourd. He sang in a high-pitched and tremulous voice, a heartfelt song of praise to Mwalimu Nyerere and his achievements.

Just then, emerging ahead of a billowing cloud of dust, came a large, new yellow Mercedes, making for the Party Headquarters. In the back sat Mwalimu Nyerere. The singer coughed in the swirl of dust and by the time it settled he had, at the insistence of the policeman, crawled away.

In the evening I went to the Dodoma Railway Hotel for dinner. I sat on the verandah, watching members of the *Ndugu* class return from their labours of the afternoon. *Ndugu* is the form of address favoured by Nyerere. It is to Tanzania what *Comrade* is to communist countries. It means brother in Swahili and has connotations of solidarity and equality, which Nyerere maintains were omnipresent in village life until Europeans first brought sin into the African world. No-one is ever called Ndugu, however, except in the newspaper. The common form of address for a man is *Bwana*, which can mean anything from Sir to mate and hey, you. But in the *Daily News*, Kim Il-Sung, Colonel Mengistu and the visiting Bulgarian Minister of Culture are all Ndugu, while Reagan is *Mr* and Botha is *Racist*.

The Tanzanian Ndugu are recognizable by their pennant-bearing vehicles, their safari suits, and above all by their girth. Most Tanzanians are thin, but the Ndugu are fat. They hold their stomachs before them in a peculiar way, like pregnant women. The most important of them waddle. Their girth is evidence of their success and authority.

Dinner was not yet ready and I drank *Safari* beer, served in bottles without labels. (Beer, often unavailable, never runs out when the Ndugu are in town.) As an anthropologist once observed in connection with Cameroonian beer, it is possible to go from a state of sobriety to one of hangover without passing through drunkenness. So it is with Safari beer. Before I had finished the second bottle, my temples throbbed as though men with pneumatic drills were working on the inside of my skull.

Dinner was announced by a waiter who banged the back of a plate with a spoon. There was a rush – the Ndugu were hungry – as though gold had been discovered. At one end of the dining room was a wall of corrugated iron, painted white. The crockery and cutlery were astonishingly greasy, a dactylographer's dream (or nightmare).

Unhappily, one of the things the British taught the Tanzanians was how to cook. First came a greyish soup, of ingredient or ingredients unknown. Then came the inevitable roast chicken, heated for hours without imparting any brownness to the skin, but nevertheless drying it out, served with roast potatoes with leather jackets, and carrots boiled to a mush, swimming in a generous helping of the water in which they were boiled. The *pièce de résistance*, however, was the pudding: a dried out sponge roll with a layer of evaporated jam residue, it was coated in a layer of tepid custard, complete with skin and lumps. No boarding house in Weston-super-Mare could have done better. This was the vision of luxury and sophistication bequeathed to the Ndugu by the British, and they treated the waiters with more than colonial scorn.

Replete – more than replete – I returned to the verandah to await my prearranged taxi. While I stared into the marvellously starry sky, a yellow Mercedes drew up. Mwalimu Nyerere had come for a chat with some of the Ndugu.

How natural he was! How without affectation! Just another man, in fact. Of course, he has made something of a career of modesty in a continent famous for its ostentation and corruption. But if he is so modest, I wondered, how can he go round the world – in a special jet – telling it how it ought to be organized? And if he is such an egalitarian, how is it that when his daughter is mildly indisposed she goes to an expensive London clinic rather than to her local dispensary? I stared once more into the starry sky. The universe has many mysteries.

I was lucky, I was told, to get a place on the train from Dodoma to Kigoma: a ticket and a reservation were not everything. I went second class, though I had paid for first, until Tabora.

There were ten others in the compartment, lesser officials who were entitled to second class travel warrants only. They spent long hours as we crawled through the ever more arid country, on which the sun seemed to beat down in pulses, discussing the time at which we would reach Tabora. This pointless conversation was carried on like a guerrilla campaign, with sudden bursts of ferocious activity. At such times it was almost as though they believed that by winning the argument they would actually influence the time the train *did* arrive in Tabora – the power of words in Africa being without limitation.

The man who sat opposite me had a milky opacity in his right eye. To judge from his clothes he had to struggle to keep himself respectable. At one of the stations in the near desert he leant out of the compartment window for a breath of scorching air. As the train moved off, someone jumped up from the track below and ripped his watch from his wrist. It all happened in an instant and was, from the purely technical point of view, performed with admirable skill. By the time he had realized what had happened, the train had gathered speed.

At first he was shocked and disbelieving, and looked round the compartment as though expecting to find his watch somewhere there. Then, with the full realization of its loss, he went into a state of mourning. Such a watch cost three months' salary, perhaps more. For the remainder of the journey he stared disconsolately at the floor. Perhaps he was revising his tariff of bribes.

We reached Tabora late at night. From there I shared a compartment with a young civil servant returning to post after a conference. He asked me what 'department' I worked for, a revealing way of asking my occupation. He was charming, with as yet no sense of his own importance. Waiting for our departure from Tabora, we discussed Tanzania's problems.

I have yet to meet a Tanzanian government minister or official who does not know what is the matter: the government and party bureaucrats try to control everything, but are both corrupt and incompetent. They depend for their income on the shortages and delays they themselves create. The worse the shortages the richer – relatively speaking – they become.

The civil servant admitted he was corrupt. If he were not, his children would starve. This was no more than the literal truth. In the name of equality, salaries have been pitched so low, and taxes so high (the highest rate being 105 per cent), that not a single person in Tanzania can live within the law. Only a clever fool like Nyerere could not have foreseen this.

Our compartment lacked the wooden prop to keep the window shut and the civil servant was much exercised by the prospect of a thief entering while we were asleep, the stretch of rail between Tabora and Kigoma being particularly notorious. Indeed, while we were discussing the matter a young boy descended from the roof and tried to enter the next compartment. I asked whether we had better warn the occupants.

'No.'

As for my suggestion that we entrust our luggage to passengers in a secure compartment, it was laughable. Tanzanians, he said, were socialists insofar as they regarded everybody else's property as their own. It was folly to trust anyone with anything.

'Would you trust me?' I asked.

'That is different,' he replied.

When we woke next morning we were pleasantly surprised to discover nothing had been pilfered in the night. The thief who had tried to climb in at the closed window had not assayed the open one.

My spirits rose: the countryside was green again, for we were approaching Lake Tanganyika. The civil servant praised the quality of the region's bananas (though it was in all other respects backward). To prove his point about the bananas he bought a bunch and gave me one to try. I found it hard to enthuse beyond saying it was 'nice'. Even the best of bananas is a prosaic fruit. I tried, with greater enthusiasm, the wild honey gathered from trees, sold in *Konyagi* – distilled maize spirit – bottles. I caught a first glimpse of the lake, a deep sapphire blue. Sir Richard Burton considered it – erroneously – the source of the Nile. On the map it is long and thin, but still one cannot see to the other shore. One readily understands how it was that these vast but unknown inland seas came to haunt the minds of Victorian explorers.

We chugged slowly into Kigoma. The old German station was a fine three-storeyed building, now a dirty pastel yellow, its windows sheltered from the direct glare of the sun by eaves of iron. In 1965, according to a fading plaque, it won the award for the best kept station in Tanganyika. The award had obviously gone to its head, for it had never been cleaned since and was now indescribably filthy. It was as much a market as a station, as much a sewer as a market. The crowd was enormous and noisy; no-one spoke but at a shout. The hubbub seemed expectant, but whatever it was that was expected had not arrived the next day, when the noise was just the same. Women walked with impossible loads on their heads, lepers shook their stumps at possible alms-givers (of whom, of course, I was foremost), old women sat by their piles of dried fish, while children relieved themselves where they stood and the odours mixed unpleasingly.

Perched on the shore beyond the station was the old German steamer that still plied the waters of the lake. It was being given a refit by the Danes. I recalled the words of an American diplomat in Africa.

'We have a saying,' he told me. 'When the Scandinavians finally grow disillusioned in Africa, disaster is at hand.'

The only clean hotel in Kigoma was full – there was a Party meeting. I went instead to the Four Flowers Hotel. My room was down a dark corridor. The bed I cannot bring myself to describe. The walls were covered in little smears of dried blood, where generations of well-fed mosquitoes had been squashed by angry guests. No-one had wiped them for months, possibly years. But then, commodity prices had fallen and Tanzania had no foreign exchange.

The famous town of Ujiji is a couple of miles from Kigoma. It was there that, as every schoolboy knows, Stanley met Livingstone and set England laughing with the most famous words ever uttered in Africa: 'Dr Livingstone, I presume'.

I found the mango tree under which the two men might have met; at least, it was the mango tree near which the Royal Geographical Society set up a commemorative plaque in the 1920s. It was in a walled garden next to a bungalow which is intended one day for a Livingstone museum. Living temporarily in the bungalow were three Britons who had spent the last two years following Stanley's footsteps from Bagamoyo to Ujiji. They had taken four times longer than Stanley – but of course, they could not use his ruthless methods. Asked how they had enjoyed the journey, they replied wryly that it had been an experience. They had learnt many things about Africa and Africans, and now viewed with contempt the assumption of western liberals that, with a little education and training, Africans could be turned into fully rational beings, like themselves. They longed for home. One of the things they had learnt during the trip was how to distinguish – symptomatically – amoebic from bacillary dysentery.

The town of Kigoma was riven by a dispute between witches and exorcists. At present, the witches had the upper hand. The witches had been denounced as such by neighbours and then forcibly subjected to exorcism, performed (for money) by the exorcists. Afterwards, the witches complained to the police that they had been assaulted. The exorcists were now languishing in gaol, awaiting trial. However, the tables might well soon be turned. The highest official for miles around, the Regional Commissioner, was about to return from the National Executive Committee meeting in Dodoma. It was thought that he would favour the exorcists. At any rate, he had once used them to purge his residence – a cake-like edifice high above the lake, once intended as Kaiser Wilhelm's African palace – of evil spirits.

I should like to have stayed for the denouement of the dispute, but the last boat to Bujumbura for two weeks was leaving, and I was informed by those in a position to know that Kigoma was no place to stay for two weeks.

THREE

Burundi and Rwanda

I left Tanzania, for all its faults, with some regret. As patients, the Tanzanians were the best I had known: stoical and trusting to an astonishing degree. As people, they smiled and laughed when, from an observer's point of view, they seemed to have little to smile or laugh about. They were also kindly: when I injured my leg and walked with it in plaster in Dar es Salaam, complete strangers came up to me and said *Pole sana, bwana* (very sorry, sir). But it came as no surprise when the immigration officer affected to find some irregularity in my passport, an irregularity that could only be smoothed away by a payment of 400 shillings for which a receipt was not forthcoming, and which disappeared – as I pretended not to notice – into his combination-locked, leather-covered executive attaché case.

Other would-be passengers had difficulties with immigration formalities, largely self-induced. The boat had docked from the Zambian shore of the lake, bringing with it several *wazungu* or white men. Five of them were New Zealanders, one an Irishman. They had already been refused entry into Tanzania at another border post because their passports had South African entry stamps; but across the Tanzanian stamp saying 'Entry Refused' they had simply scrawled the word 'Cancelled'. That done, without asking permission of anyone, they had walked into the town and were surprised and outraged at their return to find themselves in trouble.

They could not have made plainer their contempt for African officialdom, their feeling that, as white men, they were entitled in Africa to do whatever they chose. The immigration officer was both furious that his dignity had been thus insulted, and delighted to have the opportunity to display his power. There was also the fact that all infringements of the law, real or supposed, had a tendency to increase his income.

'I am trying to help you,' he told the now-chastened travellers. 'But it is very difficult. Perhaps you will not leave by this boat. I must telephone my superior in Bukoba.'

Their hearts sank. Everyone knows that it is quicker to go to Bukoba than to telephone it. The question was, whether they were to be detained as illegal immigrants (they had spent four hours in the country), or as spies?

The Irishman was approaching middle age. By profession he was a carpenter, who worked on film sets and earned enough in three months to spend the rest of the year travelling through the obscurer parts of the world. His mother, who wanted him to settle down and marry a nice Irish girl, did not understand his *wanderlust*; his brother, who did not understand it either, lived in Kilburn, drank in I.R.A. pubs, and watched television. He never asked his brother about his travels, and within a quarter of an hour of their reunion, had sat him in front of the television and told him not to speak. None of his friends or acquaintances was in the remotest interested where he had been, either; they merely inducted him at once into their parochial concerns. He had been travelling now for fifteen years, and had long since learned not to bore people with his observations of exotic places.

'But why *do* you travel?' I asked.

'I can't explain,' he replied. 'It's just everything else is futile . . . I just have to, or I'd go mad.'

He was at the end of his trip and on his way to Bujumbura, to catch a cheap Aeroflot flight to England, via Moscow. He wanted to be back in time to work on the sets of Steven Spielberg's next film. He said the most memorable country of his present journey had been Zaire. He had visited the pygmies of the forest and found them, to his surprise, heavily guarded by Zairean troops. This was not to protect them, but to prevent them from leaving their ancestral lands; for when they did so, they ate a better diet and their children grew. It could do a lot of harm to a potential tourist attraction.

'After all,' said the Irish carpenter, 'no-one's going to come thousands of miles to see a big pygmy.'

The miscreants were allowed on to the boat just as it was sounding its hooter for positively the last time before departure. The boat was nearly empty, in contrast to the journey across the lake from Zambia, when every inch of the decks had been taken and the New Zealanders, on the grounds that whites knew about such things, had been asked to assist at medical emergencies such as a miscarriage and a delivery. Very few people, it seemed, wanted to go to Bujumbura.

Among those who did were an American Peace Corps volunteer returning to his Burundian village, which he was teaching the art and science of sewage disposal, and Ricki, an ageing Australian flower child who thought that John Lennon was the most significant figure in the last forty years of world history. He spent nine months of every twelve travelling the world, returning to Australia to live on a beach outside Sydney and work as a statistician for a marketing company until he had accumulated enough money to go travelling again.

The boat left almost on time, just as the evening light began to fade. The lights of Kigoma were switched on – reluctantly and dimly, as though an air raid were half-expected. One is always aware in African towns of the precariousness of the electricity supply: the varying voltages, with the lights flickering as at a gaslit séance, remind one constantly of all the things that can go wrong, of oil supplies exhausted, of ancient generators giving up the ghost, of drunken maintenance men, of diggers of ditches transecting the cables, of floods and short circuits, of shanty towns that bleed the current and diminish it. Electricity is still a miracle in Africa.

Fortunately, the lake was glassy calm. Four hundred and fifty miles long and thirty wide, it is subject to sudden storms as violent as those at sea. But we were able to carry on our desultory shipboard conversations – strange how undescriptive long-term travellers are – and eat our dinner of rice and meat in perfect comfort. My purchase of a bottle of Dodoma white wine, as sharp as vinegar, was regarded (at least, until they had tasted it) as an act of almost reckless munificence, they being the kind of traveller to whom no sum, however small, is too insignificant to quibble over. And after dinner, mellow and full of wisdom, we gathered on the upper deck and watched the indistinct black line of the shore glide by. From time to time, like a beacon, we saw a small fire burning, where a peasant was clearing land.

Suddenly the Peace Corps volunteer exclaimed:

'Not an electric light in sight!'

An undeniable truth; but was one supposed to approve the fact because it meant the corrupting influence of industrial civilization had not yet invaded Arcadia, or lament it because it meant the people of the shore were so poor and backward? Perhaps both, simultaneously.

The Peace Corps volunteer was still touched by youthful idealism, though actually he was no more a youth than I. The question of Africa was one of knowledge and ignorance, he said, above all one of education. His main task was to educate.

I expressed the view that, in Africa, education was power, and power was extortion.

'In the short term,' he said.

'And in the long term?' I asked.

He looked at the shore. He loved Burundi; it, not the United States, was home to him now. He admired the way the people in his village lived lives of unremitting toil, yet were kind, generous and on the whole cheerful.

'But of course,' he said, 'the only future for these people is mass starvation.'

We glided on in silence, but for the plash of the black water against the bows. He was returning to bring safe sewage to the damned.

We reached Bujumbura very early in the morning, and the boat dropped anchor. I woke while it was still dark and the principal feature of the landscape was the red light at the top of the radio mast. Gradually, as the dawn spread across the sky, the ridges of hills that rose immediately beyond Bujumbura unfolded. Perched on the first and lowest hill was the University of Bujumbura, once one of the best institutions of higher learning in Africa, and by all accounts still with a good academic standard. All the more unfortunate, then, that it scarcely admitted students from the majority tribe in the country, the Hutu, who were nearly nine tenths of the population.

Soon visible were the minarets of the new mosque, the largesse of Colonel Gadaffi. As yet, less than a hundredth part of the population was Muslim: but at one time, the Colonel hoped to change all that. However, his influence in the country had waned ever since he had made a personal visit there. Not only had the goons he brought with him terrorised the entire city, but he insisted on treating the President of Burundi, Jean-Baptiste Bagaza, as a very junior partner in the enterprise of World Revolution. He then made a speech so intemperately anti-Zairean over the radio that the Burundians thought it politic to cut him off in mid-sentence. Moreover, with the falling price of oil the Libyans could ill-afford the prodigious aid they once hinted at; so no-one was converting to Islam.

Once released on to *terra firma*, I went to a hotel – built for the Franco-African summit of the previous year – and then into the city. Actually, it is still a small town, with very much a small-town atmosphere. Few buildings attain to more than three storeys, and from the main street, the Avenue Prince Louis Rwagasore (a nationalist politician assassinated at the time of independence), the hilly terrain that covers most of Burundi makes its presence felt. Across the Avenue the French and American Cultural Centres stare it out, vying for influence. No doubt the French consider it a fight to the death between Racine and Mickey Mouse, between *pâté de foie gras* and cheeseburgers; while the Americans consider it a struggle between democracy and *hauteur*, between what people really want and what they have been made to feel they *ought* to want.

Bujumbura is neither appallingly scruffy nor architecturally distinguished. There are a number of beggars but none gives an impression of desperation, and all say '*Merci, patron*' when given something.

Oddly enough, my first priority was to find a bookshop. A diet of nineteenth-century whales taken in large gulps had proved indigestible, like a diet of game only. But the city's principal bookshop was the site of a curious scene. Around the doors was gathered a large crowd, clamouring to get in, as at a run on a bank. The shop was closing for lunch – rather early, it must be said – but the crowd, mainly of schoolchildren, was desperate for Larousse or Euclid, and would have broken down the doors had it not been for the timely intervention of a Belgian nun. Later in the day I returned. Among the manuals of correct French, works of religious devotion and historical puzzles (including *What Would You Have Done If You Had Been de Gaulle?*), I found Turgenev, my favourite of favourites. He was dogeared and yellowed with age, but his price was unaffected by inflation. I felt I would need his lucidity, his poise and his humour in the days ahead.

Bujumbura is a quiet, even somnolent, town. At noon, it is quite literally so: the streets empty, the shops shut, the traffic disappears, and everyone goes to sleep. At three o'clock it comes slowly back to life, but not for very long. Being near the Equator dusk falls at the same time every evening and the streets empty once more. It is not a town that throbs with life at night: there is no exuberance, no flamboyance. It has something of the atmosphere of Wales on Sunday.

It is not easy to recognize in all this tranquillity the location, a few years ago, of one of the worst massacres in recent history.

The problem was, and is, in the ethnic composition of the population. There are two main groups: the third, the pygmoid Twa, are of no account, being less than one per cent in numbers and individually despised. Between eight and nine tenths of the population are the Hutu, a Bantu group that moved into the region a millennium ago. The remainder are the Hamitic Tutsi, who are thought to have migrated to Rwanda and Burundi five hundred years ago.

No-one knows exactly how, but the Tutsi, a pastoral people of immense height (often reaching six foot six or even seven feet tall) but asthenic build, established a feudal supremacy over the shorter, stockier Hutu. This supremacy, which at least in Burundi was moderated by a system of mutual obligations and was evident without being unduly onerous, has lasted to the present day. In 1972, with all the rhetoric of equality and human rights on their side, a group of Hutu raised a rebellion and started to murder Tutsi indiscriminately. Vengeance was swift. To preserve their dominance, and with the greatest possible ferocity, the Tutsi put down the rebellion. In the ensuing slaughter, at least a hundred thousand (and some say three hundred thousand) Hutu were killed, and half a million more made homeless. The slaughter was not entirely indiscriminate: it was aimed particularly at Hutu with even the slightest education, who were assumed to pose a threat to the *status quo*. Hutu children were shot in their classrooms, and by the time the slaughter was over, there were no educated Hutu left in Burundi.

I have always admired the way diplomats in embassies gather information about obscure and undeveloped countries like Burundi (and Burundi *is* obscure: there is not a single book about it in the library of the Royal Institute of International Affairs in London) while remaining seated in large and well-appointed offices and dressed as for their capitals of origin. How is it they are so well-informed? Sometimes they remind me of spiders at the centre of beautifully constructed webs; at others of professors of telepathy.

I went to the embassy of a large and influential western power to see if they could tell me anything useful about the country. The diplomat with whom I had an appointment was, I imagined, fairly junior; but still he had an office as big as the Ritz, with deep-pile carpet, a vast, elongated leather sofa, and air-conditioning so powerful it made sense of wearing jackets.

The diplomat turned out to be two diplomats, a kind of serious Laurel and Hardy act. One of them was thin and soft-spoken, the other fat and jovial (except that he did not smile with his eyes). When the latter offered me a cigarette, I suddenly had the uncomfortable feeling it was *they* who were asking the questions, not I. They were the classic interrogation team, I an unwitting secret agent.

'What can we do for you?' one of them asked.

Surely they knew already, otherwise why would they have agreed to see me?

Rather unusually for me, for I pride myself on my memory, I had made a list of questions I wanted to ask. First I explained I was a writer of sorts.

'Of course,' said the fat one, spreading himself across the sofa, 'we don't get many writers through here. It's just not important enough. And those we do get always want to write sensational stories.'

He paused before his partner resumed, and I felt it was incumbent upon me to tut-tut a little, and shake my head sadly.

'What this country needs is some responsible reporting. It's had a very bad press, in my opinion unfairly. They always write about ethnic conflict, Libyan influence, the church-state conflict, AIDS and over-population. You don't want to write about any of that, do you?'

'Oh no,' I said, looking down at my list. It read:

Hutu vs Tutsi
Libya?
Church vs State
Overpopulation
AIDS

'Good. It would be nice if for once there was something positive written about Burundi.'

'You see,' said the other, chiming in, 'this government is doing some very sensible things. For example, it's opening up the market and the economy in general, it's got several reafforestation and irrigation projects going, it's trying to introduce birth control.'

I said I should love to write about reafforestation and irrigation; but unfortunately, readers insisted on Massacres.

And so, in spite of everything, we talked a little of Burundi's ethnic divisions. The government of Jean-Baptiste Bagaza, they said, was genuinely attempting reconciliation. Bagaza himself, the previous president's cousin, was not implicated in the massacre because he was away at the time at Belgium's military academy. Indeed, he was only five feet six inches tall and hardly looked a Tutsi. There was intermarriage, the two groups spoke the same language, individuals had friends from across the ethnic chasm.

'And how many Hutu students are there at the university?' I asked.

My question was about as welcome as a fart at a tea party. My informant coughed: his colleague took over. I felt I was being sold something.

'I can't give you the exact figures . . . but there *are* some . . . perhaps ten per cent . . .'

'And there are several Hutu cabinet ministers,' said the other, by this time recovered.

I was sceptical, but I kept silent. In 1965, *Africa: A Handbook* had stated: 'Burundi faces a communal dilemma similar to that of Rwanda, but in a form far less acute.' That was the year in which Hutu soldiers in the Burundian army mutinied, forty of them were executed, and all Hutu deputies to parliament were killed. A year before the great massacre, the *African Contemporary Record*, under the editorship of Colin Legum, wrote: 'Micombero (the then president) seemed to have made some headway . . . there was evidence that Micombero was dedicated to a reconciliation of tribal differences; thus his Government still contained a number of Hutu ministers . . .'

We moved on to Burundi's economic prospects. I was surprised to hear that they, too, were good.

'We're very upbeat about the Burundian economy,' they said, almost in unison.

They admitted it was true the population was growing fast and the land was practically exhausted, but there might be oil under Lake Tanganyika and minerals in the hills. The price of coffee (Burundi's biggest export by far) was holding up, and there was always the hope of more aid from Europe. Which brought us back to reafforestation and irrigation.

My time was up. Simultaneously, they began to examine their watches. I had just time enough to slip in a question about AIDS.

The government, it seemed, was ignoring it, in the hope it would go away. International researchers had been allowed to study the problem in Burundi, on condition they did not publish their findings. Africans found the suggestion that the virus (like man) first evolved in Africa offensive: just one more attempt, in fact, to make them feel inferior. I asked as I left whether they considered the virus a grave threat to Burundi.

They were very upbeat about the virus.

'It could wipe Burundi out in twenty years.'

After the diplomats I found M. Leclerc, an elderly Belgian businessman, something of a relief. He was not trying to convince me of anything and I, at any rate, found the penumbra of gloom that moved around with him more congenial than the can-do optimism of the diplomats.

He lived in the north-eastern suburbs of the city, in what had once been (and still largely was) the Belgian residential quarter. The houses were secluded, the gardens green but splashed with tropical crimson, the quiet streets tree-lined. As I approached M. Leclerc's house I recalled, for some reason, what a Tanzanian had once said to me: Your dogs live better than we Africans.

M. Leclerc was a very large man, tall and rather overweight. He moved slowly, but even that was too much for him and made him breathless, his lips and cheeks turning blue and purple respectively. As he lumbered over to join me on the verandah he said:

'I'm tired.'

'I'm sorry,' I said, 'if I've come at an inconvenient . . .'

'Of life.' And then he added, hastily: 'In Burundi.'

He explained that he hadn't been home on leave for three years. In the old days that would have been nothing at all, but these days . . . however, he would be as right as rain on his return from Belgium.

He offered me a cigarette and then lit up.

'I hope you don't mind me mentioning this, monsieur,' I said. 'But I am a doctor and it's . . . well, my duty to inform you that in your condition you should not smoke.'

'I know, I know,' he said sadly. 'I've tried to give up. I even succeeded once. But then last year I was taking an important client to the airport. I had taken my car back from the garage after a service that morning. As we drove to the airport the car blew up. We were lucky not to be killed.'

'A bomb?' I asked.

'The service. That is what it is like here these days. Nothing is done properly. Do you know, there is not a decent garage in the whole of Bujumbura?'

M. Leclerc had lived a long time in Africa, over forty years. In that time there had been a lot of 'development', but he didn't know where it was all leading. It had taken the native – he used the word unselfconsciously, apparently unaware of the politicization of semantics – out of his proper element, and put him into one he did not understand, with consequent loss of contentment and dignity. He had several native friends high up in the administration, and they all admitted in private that they did not really know what they were doing, that they were leading the country to disaster, and that the Belgians had left too soon.

I asked him whether he had an opinion on the tribal conflict in Burundi.

'On the surface it seems calm,' he said, 'but we are all waiting for it to happen again.'

He did not speak of the Hutu and the Tutsi: rather, he spoke of the short ones and the tall ones. It was odd that a man who used the now-explosive term 'native' without qualms should adopt such euphemisms when talking of the ethnic divide. Perhaps it was a form of magical avoidance behaviour: by not naming the tribes, he would somehow help to reduce the friction between them. At any rate, I discovered he was not alone in this; almost everyone I spoke to used the same euphemisms, as though it were bad form to do otherwise.

M. Leclerc preferred the short ones to the long ones. The long ones were always polite and smiling, but you never knew what they were thinking. They were perfidious: whereas the short ones were as an open book. But none of the natives was as nice as they used to be.

As for the Europeans who came out nowadays as aid workers, they were not a patch on the old colonials. They came out first for their tax-free salaries, second to play tennis, third (especially if they were Scandinavians) to find black girls, and only fourth to work. Often they were incompetent. Only the Germans were any good, and even their social behaviour left much to be desired. Nobody was concerned any longer for collective racial dignity.

Burundi was facing disaster. When M. Leclerc went to the independence day celebrations he was always chilled to see the numbers of young children marching past in seemingly endless ranks. What was their future? What employment would there be for them? It was as good as mass suicide.

M. Leclerc walked me the short distance to the garden gate. As I left, he put a cigarette to his blue lips and lit up.

I met Ricki, the ageing Australian hippy, round town. We arranged to meet for a drink in the evening.

In fifteen years of travel Ricki had been everywhere: almost.

'I can't go to Singapore or Malawi 'coz of my long hair,' he said.

It was a fine, balmy evening. The stars were out, a breeze rustled the leaves, the beer was strong. It was time, as they say in Chekhov, to talk philosophy.

I asked Ricki why he travelled – travelled so much. What was he seeking?

'It's hard to explain,' he said.

I encouraged him to try.

'Well,' he said, 'I'm interested in this time and space thing. I'm trying to work it out.'

I asked him whether perhaps he wouldn't be better off learning physics at a university.

'Oh no. I don't want to do all that crap.'

He explained that as a mathematician who had also had a lot of mystical experiences through smoking dope, he was in a very good position to produce a completely satisfying theory of space and time, that united objective and subjective aspects of the matter. I still didn't quite see what this had to do with exploring the byways of Zaire, but before I could enquire further he asked what I was doing in Africa.

'I'm writing a book.'

'Yeah, I'd like to write a book – something really *great*.'

'Such as?'

'*A Hitchhiker's Guide to the Galaxy*.'

We met again for breakfast. He inquired minutely into the menu, to find the most calories for the lowest price. After breakfast, we went to change money on the black market.

It wasn't difficult to find someone in the market-cum-open-air-bus-station to change our money. The difficulty was that Ricki wanted 173 Burundian francs to the dollar instead of the 170 on offer.

'It's a matter of principle,' said Ricki.

As we trod warily through the rubbish and the open sewers of the market in search of the elusive three francs (which we never found), I reflected that I could never travel with anybody else. The strain of conforming to other peoples' ideas was just too great. And perhaps that was why we all travelled in the first place.

That same morning I caught a bus to Kyanza, towards the Rwandan border. Surprisingly, it took only one passenger per seat, though the seats *were* very close together. We did not leave at once, however: first there were repairs to be done to a vital piece of equipment, without which the bus could not travel, namely the cassette stereo system. It had to be restored to a condition in which it could blare out Zairean music at a volume to drown all thought, all conversation and even all engine noise. No-one seemed to care about the distortion that inevitably occurred at such a volume: volume was all.

And so we set out along the excellent made road to the north. It doesn't take long to leave Bujumbura behind, or very long either to realize what a population density of five hundred per square mile means in a country where practically everyone lives by farming, and everyone farms with hand-hoes. Oddly enough, the people do not live in villages but in scattered huts dotted about the hillsides. Their lives are hard enough without having to clamber up and down steep slopes while commuting to and from their fields. (This is a consideration that neat-minded theorists like Nyerere might be expected to overlook.) Clumps of banana trees grow by every hut, banana beer being one of the few material pleasures available to these hard-working people. Their fields are tiny, with some evidence of efforts at soil conservation, but it is a losing battle and one can almost *see* the topsoil cascading off the slopes to leave bare, eroded and reddish gulleys.

The hills of Burundi are not gently undulating, like the Cotswolds, but steep and in some places almost sheer. It made me breathless just to think about climbing one. Yet everywhere one sees people conscientiously working the fields, even old people (admittedly, probably old before their time). Every available inch of land seems already to have been used and a question runs through one's mind (in the brief intervals of silence) like one of those unwanted banal melodies: what will happen when the population is twice what it is now? Resettlement schemes to underpopulated parts of Africa have already been tried, and they failed: the Burundians do not take kindly to other climates and terrains, and they pined for their ancestral lands. The possibilities for increasing output through improved technique seem distinctly limited too. But no matter: the Zairean music, with its insistent, monotonous rhythm and its repetitiously cheerful cadences blunts the mind and empties it of thought.

One looks in vain for a piece of open land. Of Burundi, Hemingway would not have written 'miles and miles of bloody Africa'. There are few animals larger than rodents left, though a sad little Burundian tourist brochure mentions antelope, buffalo and a curious beast, the cynocephalus. It is a thoroughly domesticated land.

We reached Kyanza, a small, straggly town that seemed all corrugated aluminium roofs, after about two hours. Just after the town, the road that led to the Rwandan border branched to the left, and it was here that I was deposited. There was very little traffic and so I started to walk. At six thousand feet the air was cool and fresh. On my right was a large brick mission that looked deserted but not abandoned. It is said that Burundi is the most fervently Christian country in Africa. The first missionaries into the country, in 1880, were killed at once. Sixty years later Father Howell, in *Leaves From a White Father's Diary* (whose cover depicted Father Howell in white habit and solar topi writing at a portable desk in the bush while behind him native porters carried crates on their heads and a hammock slung on a pole), was able to write of the Burundians that they were 'a whole people . . . marching to God . . . Along the road we passed groups of natives who were on their way to the mission. Tomorrow some twenty thousand will have assembled to honour the Blessed Lady. Happy, happy country!' But now the state is in conflict with the church, to wrest control of education from it. Of course, the results will probably not be favourable, but what are results compared with principles?

A little further on, a prospect of Eden opened up. The road, following the crest of a hill, became an avenue between noble eucalyptus trees, whose scent filled the air. Below was a lush and verdant valley; on the upper reaches of the slopes were the deep green bushes of tea, manicured like a Japanese garden, and coffee bushes with crimson berries. There were people working far below in the fields and the sound of their laughter and conversation drifted indistinctly upwards. Burundi is one of the many 'one of the poorest countries in the world'; no article about or reference to the country would be complete without a mention of this fact; yet here life seemed far from unpleasant, at least for someone who was merely passing through.

An old lady walking in my direction signalled to me that I should carry my bag upon my head, rather than over my shoulder. Her instructions were in a language I could not understand, though I recognized a few words from Swahili. It took her a long time to realize I could not understand: perhaps she had never met anyone before who did not know her tongue, and was unfamiliar with the story of the Tower of Babel. She started to signal all the more urgently that I should put my bag upon my head. How was I to explain to her that her advice, while no doubt correct in itself, was as useful to me as mine had been to the mothers of malnourished children in Tanzania to give them beans and eggs and fish as well as maize porridge? That we in urban Europe had lost the elegant and economical art – if we ever had it – of carrying things upon our heads? After a time she gave up on me as a congenital idiot.

I found a lift to the border, which had been variously described to me as being twenty or two kilometres away, in a pickup truck. There were two others in the truck on their way to Rwanda, a pretty and a not so pretty young woman. The border was in a valley through which ran a small river. It was here that I had my first intimation of an all but ineluctable law of travel in Africa: whatever time you arrive at a border, it is lunchtime.

Still, it didn't really matter. The weather was clement, the sound of the water over the riverbed of stones conducive to inner peace. I settled down to read Turgenev.

I soon attracted the attention of two small boys. Where had they come from? Unusually, there wasn't a habitation in sight. They were friendly, but insistent they wanted my Turgenev. I asked them what they would do with it.

'Read it,' they said.

The idea of eight-year-old rural Burundians reading Turgenev amused me. I gave them groundnuts instead as being of more practical value to them, and they devoured them hungrily.

After lunch – only two hours, quite moderate, as I was to discover – the formalities were soon done. The two women and I waited for lifts on the Rwandan side of the border, there being no regular transport. At length a Mercedes appeared on the Burundian side of the border and a plump man in a well-cut mohair suit with a heavy gold bracelet around his wrist got out, followed by a minion carrying his attaché case. He was not the kind of man to bother with formalities when he crossed borders; he was more used to being saluted. That is what happened this time; and on the other side of the border another Mercedes was waiting to take him onwards. He paused only to select the pretty woman to take with him.

The less pretty woman soon found a lift with a fuel tanker. With the help of the immigration officer I found a teacher in a battered Renault who was going as far as Butare. He was a man who was afraid for the future of his country: it was more densely populated still than Burundi, and the average number of surviving children per family was nine. He himself had two children, and thought that four or five would be enough.

I was debating whether to spend the night in Butare, a pleasant, well-wooded hill town, the seat of Rwanda's university, where students mill idly in the streets after classes, but the teacher took me to the bus station and found a bus, already overcrowded, that was about to depart for the capital, Kigali. He refused a proffered payment and wished me *bon voyage*.

My arrival in the bus aroused momentary curiosity but it soon subsided and the important topics of the day took over. The driver, deafened by music, was an accelerator enthusiast, pressing it to the floor for the entire journey, regardless of circumstance. The result was an exhilarating, if hair-raising, ride through the Rwandan countryside at sunset. And the Rwandan countryside was, if anything, more intensely cultivated than the Burundian. The hillsides were less steep, but the fields were even smaller. The land was as yet still fertile and people worked it until after dusk.

We reached Kigali in the dark. The city was too haphazardly and dimly lit for me to be able to tell much about it, but it looked a not untypical African urban sprawl, with low buildings and tin roofs and naked light-bulbs exuding a yellowing gloom they call light. The streets were dark and shadowy, and to a newcomer, however safe they might be in fact, they seemed full of menace and urged the stranger to secrete himself somewhere safely indoors.

The bus took me to a hotel. As I was checking in I was approached from behind by a short Rwandan with bulging eyes, wearing a worn brown velvet jacket, blue corduroy trousers and platform shoes without socks.

'Good evening,' he said in English.

'Good evening,' I replied.

'I am doing research.'

'Into what?' I asked as I wrote down the date of issue of my passport.

'Enemies,' he said.

I admit I found his answer disconcerting. Could it be that the superefficient Rwandan secret service was on my trail already, alerted to the fact I was not just a casual traveller but might write something prejudicial to the interests of the state? On the other hand he looked too seedy even for a secret policeman. I decided to go on to the offensive.

'Enemies? Enemies of what? Enemies of whom?'

'Just enemies,' he said.

'Nonsense,' I said. 'Absurd. You can't have just enemies. This isn't a novel by Kafka. Enemies of what?'

'There are many enemies,' he said oracularly.

'Well, I'm going to my room,' I said, feeling slightly uneasy, though the man was clearly mad.

'I'll wait,' he said.

I fled. The guilty fleeth where no man pursueth.

Actually, Rwanda is not a sinister country (though a million or more of its citizens live outside its borders). The face of the president, General Juvenal Habariyama, is not as obtrusive as in some countries, and is in any case rather benign, if a little like the face of a boxer who has gone too many rounds in his career. He is by all accounts a hard-working and honest man who does not live in great state, and while it is not wise to criticize him in person, it is safe enough to criticize his government.

As for Kigali, the streets that had worn a menacing aspect by night seemed sunny and inoffensive in the morning. Kigali has seen phenomenal growth since independence in 1962, when its population was only 4000 and it had precisely 400 yards of paved road. Now it is a real African capital, with a main street full of embassies (with the Libyan directly opposite the American, displaying photographs on its notice board of bodies mangled in the recent air raids), and offices of aid agencies that have proliferated almost as fast as the city itself. No doubt there is something artificial and almost comical about this growth, the result of political rather than of economic development, and there is something laughable too about the grandeur of the bank buildings, which surely cannot have much money within; but yet it is all a cause of considerable pride to the Rwandans and who can blame them for feeling it?

They have settled the ethnic question in Rwanda once and for all. In Rwanda the Tutsi domination was more onerous than in Burundi, there having been a Tutsi monarch whose rule was absolute until the 1920s. Justice was harsh and rigorous, if appropriate to conditions: a murderer was buried alive with his victim, an unmarried girl who became pregnant was dropped into a papyrus swamp with a boulder tied to her leg. Early European observers were divided in their opinions of the Tutsi. Some thought them noble and aristocratic, a naturally superior race; while others, including Sir Alfred Sharpe, Governor of Nyasaland, were less flattering: ' . . . they do practically no work, except to relieve the Wahutu of the fruits of their labour . . . At one time, the Watusi must have been a strong and warlike race; but nowadays they are effeminate and incurably lazy; if a M'Tusi, for instance, has to travel for a short distance, he is carried by a Wahutu . . .'

Just before independence there was a civil war in Rwanda. The Belgians took the part of the Hutu, (the pygmies sided with the Tutsi), and a complete social revolution took place, at a cost – estimates vary wildly – of between 6000 and 108,000 lives. But the matter was settled and the Tutsi are now an all-but-spent force. Was I mistaken to discern on their faces in the streets of Kigali an expression of regret, sadness and defeat?

I wandered the market of Kigali, away from the groves of diplomacy. No doubt it would have seemed much worse to me had I arrived from Switzerland rather than from Tanzania. As it was, I thought it only moderately squalid. Absurdly, the black clusters of flies around the meat raised a theological question in my mind: would a perfectly benevolent God have created flies, at least in such numbers? A child with phocomelia (the deformity that thalidomide produced) waved his stumps at me, and seemed to take pleasure in the involuntary revulsion he inspired. I took a professional interest in that part of the market devoted to native medicines: a withered old lady, her advanced age a good advertisement for her wares, laughed at my curiosity. A young man in the process of choosing his medicine started to talk to me in a strange mixture of French and Swahili.

There was something wrong with his liver, he said, and European-type doctors had been unable to cure it. He looked a picture of health to me, athletic and cheerful, but he insisted he was nigh unto death. From a large glass jug the old lady poured a vile, heaving brown decoction into an empty bottle of Laurent Perrier champagne, which the patient had brought for the purpose.

'I will be better in two days,' he said confidently.

'If there's nothing wrong with your liver now,' I said, 'there soon will be after you drink that stuff.'

We shook hands and went our ways.

I took a small bus from Kigali to Kisenye, on the shores of Lake Kivu. It was so cramped that my leg began to ache from an old injury. We passed through hill country of great beauty, worked with diligence by the local population. The land was fertile and well-watered. 'Rwanda . . . is an excellent land for European colonization. Because of its temperate climate, its abundant waters, its extended pastures, its thick western forests, its abundant and hardworking population, this region, where malaria has not spread its ravages . . . remains an area with a great agricultural future, a huge field open to European initiative . . .' Thus the Bulletin of the Royal Geographical Society of Antwerp in 1919. Another idea, on account of its healthful climate, was to build sanatoria for tuberculous Europeans throughout the country. None of this came to pass, and with the exception of the road itself, the landscape had totally escaped European influence. There were not even tin roofs.

Kisenye, on the other hand, was a Belgian resort which looked as though it had been built with retired colonial officials in mind. It was strangely suburban and reminded me rather of Dolgellau. There being nothing so dispiriting as a resort in poor weather, I decided to continue to Goma, a town adjacent to Kisenye but on the Zairean side of the border. At the Rwandan post I met a British engineer coming in the other direction who, by coincidence, worked for the company that had employed me in Tanzania. We knew certain people in common. While we chatted, the border officials treated the passport of his girlfriend, who was Western Samoan, with great circumspection, as though it might explode. The engineer warned me to beware of the Zairean Anti-Fraud Squad waiting for me on the Zairean side. It was a newly-established unit charged with combating smuggling, but it should have been called the Pro-Fraud Squad. They had exacted a payment from him in exchange for the non-removal of the wheels of his Land Rover.

I walked towards Zaire with some trepidation.

FOUR

Zaire

T he first rule of travel is that one should never look too prosperous. Thieves and officials will then leave one, relatively speaking, alone. It is a dictate I have no difficulty in obeying.

Evidently not worth the robbing, I got past the Anti-Fraud Squad without hindrance. Only the Health Inspector made difficulties, and that because he was drunk: he saw double and insisted on inspecting my companion's vaccination certificates. How do you explain to a man that you are only one person when he has the evidence of his own eyes that you are two? The discovery I was a doctor cut the Gordian knot, however: he waved us on, and even saluted me, or us.

The road into the town was short and grandiose, a dual carriageway whose central reservation showed some signs of deliberate cultivation. This was not at all what one had been led to expect of Zaire. After a few hundred yards the road gave onto a roundabout at the very heart of Goma. The official buildings of the town looked at each other across the roundabout, on which was a plaster monument bearing the national emblem, a yellow torch with a red flame, and a peeling, painted slogan:

ZAIRE
One Country
One People
One Party
One Chief

I was tempted to add: And One Bank Account.

I found a hotel, a Belgian-run establishment of moderate comfort (hot water being ten per cent extra). I deposited my bag and went into the town.

From the roundabout led a wide street whose colonnaded single-storey small stores are to be seen in a thousand frontier towns in hot climates. It was all but deserted, this being Saturday afternoon, and except for the French language and the dilapidation, it could have been an Australian outback town.

Further on, however, Goma became more exotic, more truly African. The road opened on to a vista of two forested volcanoes, Nyamwagisi and Nyiragongo, ten and thirteen thousand feet high. They were not like the artistic and elegant cone of Fujiyama, but truncated, bad-tempered creatures which, illogically, put me in mind of Tenniel's drawing of the Duchess in *Through the Looking Glass*. They were menacing, they made me nervous whenever I looked at them; the nearer of the two, though six miles away, seemed to lower over the town and had last erupted only nine years before. It took no great effort of imagination to see its wide crater spewing red-hot ashes and molten lava, like geological rhetoric. If primitive people hereabouts performed propitiation ceremonies – no wonder! Yet the people of Goma went about their Saturday business with apparent unconcern.

The residential quarter of Goma had a squalor – but also a vivacity – not to be seen in Burundi or Rwanda, though the latter were, statistically, poorer countries. The black volcanic earth had been churned into slime, fertilized by the ordure of infants and the litter of households. It was paradise for pigs. The huts of black wood, polythene and cardboard were small and mean and smoky. But the whole quarter babbled with gossip and rang with laughter. Hygiene is not happiness. Most amazing of all, the young men, out to impress the young women, wore brilliantly flashy clothes, always of colours on which a fleck of mud would have stood out like blood in snow. Somehow, though mud was all around, they managed to preserve themselves from it and retain intact their dazzling cleanliness.

Appearance was evidently of importance to the people of Goma. Every few yards there would be a tiny hut of black wood, scarcely more than a box, marked *Haute Couture* or *Coiffeur de Paris*. Was this sad? Funny? Noble? It was all of these, and for the same reason: the contrast between aspiration and reality. But at least it expressed a spontaneous aspiration, one chosen by people themselves and not *for* them by some puffed-up autodidact who believed only he knew what *the People* wanted.

Many of the wooden hovels had slogans painted above their doors: *Mobutu Educateur; Mobutu Unificateur; Mobutu Artisan du Zaire; Mobutu Sauveur.* Was this for appearances too? Did anyone believe it? My question was unlikely ever to be answered, for I could hardly knock on doors and ask, 'Excuse me, but do you really believe Mobutu is your saviour?'

As the sky cleared, the mountains of northern Rwanda became visible. It was in these jungle-covered mountains that the celebrated American observer of gorillas, Diane Fossey, had not long ago been murdered. On her own admission, she had much preferred gorillas to men. Rumours about the murder were quite the rage in the town. A German tourist told me, after I had promised the story would not go a step beyond the southern hemisphere, that she was murdered by some villagers from whom she had kidnapped a child as a hostage for a baby gorilla the villagers had captured for sale to a foreign zoo.

I asked one of her hated humans whether there was any public transport in the direction of Kisangani. He told me there was a bus at six o'clock every Monday morning as far as Butembo, after which it was a question of hitching a ride.

We walked along the road together. To add to the amenities of the Goma slums, an airport runway had been built adjacent to them. Suddenly, with a tremendous roar, an aircraft would rise, phoenix-like, from the squalor. And when an aircraft landed it always looked certain to crash full into the pullulating alleyways of mud. At first it was disconcerting: there were a surprising number of take-offs and land-ings. But soon it meant nothing more than a brief pause in the conversation.

My new-found friend asked me to his house for lunch next day. He would be honoured, he said, by my presence. I returned to the hotel with an almost physical glow of goodwill towards Africans. Where in Europe do you go for a casual stroll and receive from a complete stranger in the street an invitation to lunch?

I had dinner in the restaurant of the hotel. It was surprisingly good. The restaurant was supervised by the manager's wife. She lived, of course, in a self-gratifying state of permanent exasperation: the natives can't lay tables, the natives can't arrange flowers, the natives can't add up bills, and if you turn your back on them for a minute, they'll do something stupid.

One sympathized. It is difficult to make Africans appreciate (except as customers, when they appreciate it at once) the vital importance of serving from the left and clearing from the right. The trouble is that *they* eat with their fingers from a communal bowl. When my mountain strawberries and *chantilly* were served from the right by a pygmy (in a maroon tunic) reaching *up* to the table, the head waiter – a giant with the soul of a school prefect – took him ferociously to task. He out-madamed madame.

I went to bed but woke in the middle of the night. I had a fever: malaria. The engineer at the Rwandan border told me that he had met a pickup truck with the body of a Japanese tourist who had died of cerebral malaria on his way to Kisangani.

'Was he taking his pills?' I asked.

'It was difficult to tell,' the engineer replied. 'He'd been dead three days. He smelt terrible.'

I took a curative dose of pills. For the rest of the night I dreamt I was already dead: only my sense of smell had been preserved.

Strangely enough, I woke up refreshed: completely cured. I decided to go to church, not out of religious feeling, but out of curiosity. I found an evangelical chapel very close to the runway. It was made of creosoted planks in various stages of disintegration.

I entered gingerly. It was very crowded, mainly with mothers with astonishing numbers of infants. Someone pushed a little boy off a bench to make room for me. The trouble with going to church services out of curiosity is that congregations naturally take you to be religious, and even expect you to make some contribution to the proceedings. Behind the altar, a table with a white cloth, were three preachers: an old man and two acolytes. There was also a man in the corner behind a lectern, reading snatches of the Bible.

The service came briefly to a halt on my arrival.

'Do you understand Swahili?' asked the old preacher.

'*Kidogo*,' I replied – a little.

'And French?'

'*Un peu.*'

With that, the service recommenced. Scores of heads turned back towards the altar.

The three preachers were like a sales team, continually taking up where the others left off, often in mid-sentence and changing from Swahili to French and back again. Their Swahili was gallicized: I noticed, for example, they used the French numerals instead of the Swahili ones, and sometimes their sentences were half-Swahili and half-French, with words almost alternating between the two. I wondered whether I was at the birth of a new language, or at least a new patois.

The preachers were enthusiastic about Heaven and Hell, Salvation and Damnation, but there was no disguising they were labouring under certain disabilities. For one thing, the high proportion of infants in the congregation made maternal concentration on the service very difficult: the infants crawled, excreted, demanded to be fed, vomited and gurgled through even the direst predictions of hell-fire. For another, the church seemed to be about ten feet below the flight path of every incoming and outgoing aircraft. Periodically the walls would shake as though Armageddon had already arrived. It wasn't long before I'd had enough. I muttered something about having a lunch appointment as, with lowered head, I escaped from the church, my departure as mysterious to the congregation as my arrival.

I met my Zairean friend as arranged. His name was Bamy. He had brought along a friend of his, a young man who had just qualified as an agronomist from an agricultural college. He was the unhappiest-looking man I had seen on my journey so far: a deep unhappiness, a profound, unliftable depression suffused his face. His eyes darted like those of an animal cruelly used: not once, but all its life.

'Where do you work?' I asked him.

'There is no work,' he replied.

'But surely . . . as an agronomist . . .' My voice faded.

Was not Zaire a country where researchers loved to find horrifying percentages of malnourished children; was it not a country which, despite its vast extent and agricultural potential, imported half its food?

'There is no office for me.'

'Do agronomists work in offices, then?' I asked.

'Yes.'

'What about a farm?' I was determined not to be crushed by his utter pessimism. 'There is plenty of land.'

'Plenty of land,' he echoed. 'But no capital.'

'Are there no banks? Is there not credit?'

'Not for people like me. I come from a poor family. I have no connections.'

There was a finality about the impossibility of a farm, of credit, that rendered all further questions not merely superfluous but stupid. I imagined him for the rest of his life seething with anger in a hut he knew to be squalid, too educated ever to use the hand hoe or cultivate anything on a small scale, his only chance of escape a revolution in which he would be the local Saint Just.

We walked together towards Bamy's house, past a technical college which had never been an architectural masterpiece but which was now an occupied ruin. How, why, had every window been smashed? How was it possible for a building to reach this state, even with the most ardent neglect?

'What do you think of Zaire?' asked the lugubrious agronomist.

'I have been here only one day,' I parried.

'What do they say of Mobutu in your country?'

'They say he is corrupt. They say he is one of the richest men in the world.'

Bamy looked round nervously, and then emitted a sound halfway between a cough and a laugh. I warmed to my subject.

'It is said he has a personal fortune of four thousand million dollars.'

Though they knew he was rich, they had never heard a figure put on his wealth. To them, a flight to Kisangani indicated wealth. They were silent for a moment as they pondered what four thousand million meant. They could not grasp it any more than I could.

'And we have no roads, no schools, no hospitals,' said Bamy's friend, storing away the figure in his mind for the better nourishment of his bitterness.

Bamy, on the other hand, seemed to find Mobutu's fortune rather comical.

We reached his home. The house was of wood. Inside it was dark, even in the middle of day. The door led into the cramped living room, the only other room being the bedroom. There was a deal table and four chairs, as simple as it was possible to fashion them. The only ornament was a cheap china pekinese. Bamy's wife, who welcomed me shyly, had to cook outside in the mud and flint yard, where stray children and goats relieved themselves and where mud-soaked tatters of rubbish accumulated in corners. She had difficulty with her charcoal stove, for the wind was up and the sky covered with menacing black clouds. A girl of eight, their daughter, helped her by fetching water and charcoal.

I asked Bamy whether he had any sons. Yes, one: he was away in Kinshasa, at school. To educate him cost practically all his income, but what other course was open to him if his son were ever to escape this poverty?

I asked the agronomist whether he was married.

'How can I marry and have children when I have no money?'

He was not so much thinking of the sustenance of his family, as of the purchase of a wife. Bamy's wife had cost two cows, commuted to money. And there was an inflation in bride-price as in everything else. He would be lucky to get a wife for two cows nowadays, and he hadn't the money to pay for even one.

Was there no possibility, I asked, of marriage without bride-price?

Perhaps there was in Kinshasa, but how was he to get there? Or what was he to do there? No, he would have to remain unmarried.

Not to have children is, for Africans, the greatest possible misfortune: so great as almost to constitute a crime. It signifies not only physical, but spiritual extinction. Without children life has no meaning and no purpose. All across Africa my positive desire *not* to have children seemed as alien as Martian philosophy.

I noticed while we were discussing marriage that the agronomist had a slight nervous tic of the left corner of his mouth and eye. This surprised me. I had met a few patients in Tanzania who stuttered, and they too had surprised me. Our mental picture of Africans as children of nature with simple and purely sensual joys and pleasures – a stereotype deeply embedded in European consciousness – does not allow for tics and stuttering and depression which, while undesirable in themselves, are held to point to a complex and sensitive inner life.

Lunch was served. As the daughter brought a miscellaneous collection of cutlery to the table I said helpfully that I was by now quite used to eating with my hands. Bamy was not exactly offended by this demonstration of my cultural broadmindedness, but he was not rapturously pleased by it, either.

'In this house,' he said, 'we eat with knives and forks.'

Before starting on the meal, Bamy called on his daughter to say grace. They all gave a heartfelt amen when she finished: for them it was not a form of words, but genuine gratitude. One does not take food for granted in Zaire.

There was a chicken and a goat stew, and *ugali*, maize porridge (in this case mixed with millet). I was, probably absurdly, torn between two competing impulses: on the one hand to eat sufficient to prove that I appreciated their food, on the other not to deprive them of what must have been luxuries they could ill-afford. Bamy's friend, though depressed, had an excellent appetite.

After lunch we sat and talked. The subject of corruption arose again. Bamy, who was a clerk of some description, said one had to be corrupt to live; the question was whether or not one was greedy. His agronomist friend only muttered: the chance to be corrupt would be a fine thing.

As our conversation flagged, two friends arrived. They ate the remains of the meal – with their hands, I noticed. Afterwards they talked; perhaps because my presence inhibited them, once the latest neighbourhood gossip had been exhausted, they fell silent. If there had been television, we should have watched it. The suburban Sunday had reached even Goma.

The rain fell in torrents, grey gusting sheets of water. Walking back to the hotel was out of the question: Bamy insisted on a taxi. His wife and daughter could take it on their way to afternoon chapel. The little girl jumped up and down with excitement, for she had never been in a taxi before, or so she said. Could she ride in the front? Bamy found a taxi and dismissed as nothing the soaking he had received in the search. The taxi was not a well vehicle: its engine had been replaced by a nest of machine guns, its exhaust by a rapid-firing howitzer. When we arrived, Bamy insisted – absolutely and categorically – on paying for the taxi himself. We exchanged addresses and vowed an eternal correspondence.

I was told, as a tease perhaps, that the bus to Butembo left at six in the morning. Africans think of whites as very late risers – the poor see more dawns than the rich. At any rate, I was the first by far to arrive at the bus stop, and my thought processes were too numb for me to read by the dim light of Goma's bookshop window, which displayed several copies of *Are Accidents Preventable?* (The answer, in African opinion, being over-whelmingly No, hence the need of a book proving the contrary.)

Slowly at first, and then quickly, the passengers arrived. We all had numbered tickets, but when the bus came it was discovered there were by a long way more numbers than seats. There was a scrum for places, compounded by the mountains of luggage to be stacked both on and in the bus. I ended up next to a baby with constantly soaked nappies and a mother whose broad, childbearing hips exiled me to the very margin of an already incommodious seat.

We started out after day had broken. Our passage was smooth for the first two miles or so, and I began to think it was not true what they said about Zairean roads. But after the airport terminal, with an almost absurd abruptness the road degenerated into a track. It was as clear a case of what has been called the Third World Airport Road Syndrome as one could wish to meet. Important people travel by air: what need, then, of roads? The route I was travelling to Kisangani was along two sides of a right-angled triangle, though the maps showed a road direct by the much shorter hypoteneuse. I was assured, however, that if I chose *that* road, I should never be seen again.

African frontiers have often been criticized as the arbitrary im-positions of Europeans who took desk rulers and drew lines across maps in accordance with the needs of the European power-politics of the day. At least as far as agricultural methods are concerned, the border between Rwanda and Zaire is, or has become, a genuine one. On the Rwandan side land is neatly parcelled without waste, with a population almost fanatically devoted to working it. But on the Zairean side, the banana groves are haphazard and untidy, a testament to an awareness that there is an infinitude of land beyond: Zaire is forty times the size of Rwanda and Burundi combined, with only three times their population.

The soil is black and volcanic; one has the casual impression that anything would grow there. But, apart from bananas with their broad shaggy leaves, nothing is cultivated. The local market is not large enough, and the road system has deteriorated so far that transport to distant markets is out of the question. The mere sight of all this unrealized potential, especially in the presence of such need, is apt to make the economically rational man tense with useless frustration; but the passengers on the bus, except for an Israeli couple who wanted to climb Mount Ruwenzori, noticed nothing, and went on chatting happily, laughing as the bus was catapulted into the air by another hidden ridge in the road surface.

Past the volcanoes and the town of Rutshuru we entered the Virunga National Park (formerly the *Parc Albert*). On the edge of the escarpment we had a magnificent view of a vast, grassy plain, golden-brown to the far horizon:

> Plains immense
> Lie stretch'd below, interminable meads,
> And vast savannas, where the wandering eye,
> Unfixt, is in a verdant ocean lost.
> Another Flora there, of golden hues,
> And richer sweets, beyond our garden's pride,
> Plays o'er the fields, and showers with sudden hand.
> Exuberant spring: for oft these valleys shift
> Their green-embroidered robe to fiery brown,
> And swift to green again, as scorching suns,
> Or streaming dews, and torrent rains, prevail.

Thompson never saw Africa, but it has never been described better.

At a bend in the escarpment road a truck had run into the ditch on the mountain side, leaving little room for us to pass on the escarpment side (there was a drop of several hundred feet). The driver, who evidently did not believe accidents were preventable, was all for having a go at passing the stricken truck, until the screams of the passengers gave him pause for thought. The passengers, only too willing to escape the bus, pushed the truck out of the way, as ants tackle a dead beetle. It was true, as the bus driver had protested, there had been room to pass, but only with the last inch of crumbling, stony escarpment to spare.

On the plains we saw zebra, impala, a sole buffalo, and some bush pig, comically ugly and with their tails erect. With the exception of baboons, they were the only large mammals I was to see on my journey across Africa. I was surprised that the other passengers scanned the horizon for game and were truly excited when they saw it. I had imagined they would be blasé. Possibly they were no more familiar with these animals than was I.

Past the park we entered a region of green mountain forest. From time to time there was a coffee plantation, usually only half-maintained, as though no-one quite believed in the possibility of profit. The bushes were not pruned, nor the spaces between them weeded. The signboards with the names of the plantations were always at an angle, as though fitted by drunken carpenters. My impression was of once prosperous country estates, now in the possession of reprobate sons interested only in an income to drink. Worse still were the dairy farms. There were valleys with grassland as green as any in England or Ireland, whose meadows had once been hedged or fenced; but the logs used as fencing posts had sprouted branches and leaves, and were trees once more, while the gates lay flat upon the ground keeping nothing in or out. The lush grass was tangled and overgrown. At the centre of the farms were large brick farmhouses in Flemish style, abandoned, mere ruined shells, as much objects for archaeologists as Angkor Wat or Pompeii.

My old instincts as a right thinking liberal tried to reassert themselves as I cast around my mind for reasons and excuses for this neglect and decay. The former owners of the farmhouses would have lived, no doubt, at a grotesquely higher standard of living than the Africans around them; but Zaire had not exactly adopted strict economic equality as a goal since independence, and at least those farmers had *produced* something. It might have been for the luxury end of the market, and beyond the means of most Zaireans to buy it; but those with means were not at present practising self-denial, merely importing what had once been produced in the country. In short, any attempt to rationalize the annihilation of those farms was the special pleading of a liberal conscience, forever accusing its possessor of a crime beyond expiation.

We passed into the forest once more and there, on a sharp bend, we stopped to buy tree tomatoes, cape gooseberries and mountain strawberries from some frightened-looking forest dwellers. The fruit was our only food till evening. Every thirty miles or so there was a village, perched on the tops of successive hills, with a surrounding area cleared of forest. Most of the clearing was for firewood: only the land immediately adjacent to the village was cultivated, and looked insufficient for the upkeep of the population. Every village had its first-aid post – a mud hut like all the others but with a red cross painted on it – and its school, where the African passion for many children was made visible in the massed ranks of toddlers in the muddy yards, marching in formation and saluting the flag. And everywhere, too, the spread of evangelical Christianity was evident, their churches and missions vastly outnumbering those of the Catholics. But the Word of God had not spread half so wide or half so far as roofs of tin. Corrugated iron had been anathematized by Mary Kingsley in the nineteenth century and the

modern French Africanist guru, René Dumont, as being hot in the
heat, cold in the cold, noisy in the rain and expensive in foreign
exchange. This is in contrast to native African roofing, which is
economical, aesthetically pleasing, suitable to the climate, labour in-
tensive, biodegradable, etc. Yet tin carries all before it: how perverse a
creature is Man!

It was eleven hours to Butembo, more than enough of teetering on the
edge of a hard seat, trying to establish a bridgehead against the massed
buttocks of multiparous African womanhood. It had been raining for
some time when we arrived: not a genteel, lightly refreshing rain, but an
intemperate downpour, making the air as impenetrable to vision as a
pea-souper, and turning the ground into a clinging, spattering red mud.
We slithered crabwise into Butembo.

The weather cleared a little and at a distance to our right we saw the
Ruwenzori mountains, the object of the Israelis' trip. The weather had
disheartened them, for once the rains started in earnest the mountains
were inaccessible. Nor was Butembo at that moment a town calculated
to raise anyone's spirits: an extended, meandering collection of low
buildings with one remarkable feature, a feature confined to modern
African towns: a total absence of beautification or ornamentation, a
functionalism so complete as to exclude colour or zig-zag lines or any of
the small artifices to be found in even the poorest of villages. A town like
Butembo, with its muddy roads that suck and squelch at the feet like the
tentacles of an octopus, crushes the aesthetic sensibilities of a man more
thoroughly and comprehensively than any other place or experience of
which I have knowledge.

The hotel, though, was not as bad as we had feared. The rooms were
not dirty; there was a hot water tap (though no hot water), and lightbulbs
(though no electricity). An account of Butembo written in 1937 read
oddly: was it the same town? 'At Butembo I stayed in a hotel which is run
by a Belgian Marquis and a Russian Countess. The hotel is built like a
village, and each guest has a small thatched hut of his own, set among
gardens of chrysanthemums, rose and cannas . . . This is popular tourist
country, with fine roads and scenery . . .'

I had dinner with the Israelis by flickering candlelight. One was a
medical student, the other a student of archaeology. Zaire was one of the
few African countries to which, as Israelis, they could travel, though
their prospects were improving, thanks to the fall in the price of oil. Zaire

in any case welcomed them: the Israelis had trained the Presidential Guard, Mobutu's most reliable support.

The waiter brought a warm beer that reminded me of England where, however, warm beer denotes a preference rather than a power failure. The meal, too, was not altogether alien in style: meat and potatoes. But meat in Africa is not butchered; it is hacked in chunks from a carcass and resembles, when served at table, the hurried attempts of a mass murderer to reduce the evidence of his crimes to manageable proportions, while the police are banging at his door.

The next morning was fine and confirmed it was not only the weather that made Butembo dismal. A small communal bus stopped to pick me up; it was going as far as the village of Oicha, thirty-five miles up the road. It was overcrowded, of course, and I sat as best I could on a sack of lumps. There was another white on board, a lean young man in a linen jacket and a panama hat, whose execrable French meant that he could only be English. Nevertheless, we spoke in French, and that but little. We had not been introduced. He was going as an assistant missionary to a village evangelical mission, and I supposed he thought too cordial a contact with me, merely because I was a fellow white, would destroy his standing with his new flock. Or perhaps he was just shy.

Past Beni, an old colonial administrative centre crumbling with neglect (though still inhabited), we were flagged down and an old man, skeletally cachectic, was brought forth and carried, log-wise, from his hut. I wondered where in the bus they would put him, since there was no room: the roof, perhaps? But overcrowding has its uses. They cleared a tiny space for him, and though he was far too weak to keep himself sitting up, there was simply no room for him to collapse.

Even raising his eyelids was a great effort, something for which he needed to summon up all his remaining strength. He was probably suffering from one of those longstanding debilitating diseases – tuberculosis, for example – that is especially liable in Africa to provoke suspicions of witchcraft. Now they were taking him *in extremis* to seek white man's medicine, or that version of it available hereabouts; which, failing to produce a cure, would confirm their original suspicions, and absolve them of the charge of negligence in not having sought white man's medicine earlier.

The village of Oicha straddled the road for two miles or more. I waited by a fork in the road: I was told there was a pickup that would 'soon' be leaving for Komanda, where the road north joins the road west to Kisangani. I stood under the shade of a tree, towards which other passengers drifted in desultory fashion. The word 'soon' has few connotations of urgency in Africa: it is used more for its soothing effect than as a temporal prediction. As I stood, a little girl emerged from a nearby hut and diffidently brought me a stool on which to sit, and then retired hurriedly, without saying a word, back into the hut. These little gestures of generosity and consideration have a disproportionate effect on the mood of the traveller – especially when he is just about to give way to misanthropic musings.

These musings returned with renewed vigour during the loading of the truck. The number of passengers turned out to be twenty (and three in the cabin). The passengers were not allowed on board until the back had been laden with hundred-kilo sacks of rice and manioc. On the best of roads it would have been inadvisable; on Zairean roads it was madness. How many times in Tanzania had I seen fearful accidents caused by overloading (or evil spirits, as victims, drivers and onlookers alike believed). I saw seven people suffocated to death when they fell off an army truck and illegally-transported sacks of maize fell on top of them; I saw an open truck driven by a drunk catapult twenty-three people to their deaths. But I was much too impatient to wait for another vehicle. In any case, it was unlikely I should ever have found one less overloaded, since most transport owners in Africa will happily wait a century for a single extra passenger, let alone a dozen or a score.

The forest started in good earnest after Oicha. From my position on the truck it was difficult to see anything but the green canopy overhead, scored by the blue and white of the sky above the road. After a struggle to raise myself, I made out the rest of the forest: the thick undergrowth, the trunks of noble trees that soared sixty feet into the air without a branch and then spread out like a green umbrella, the lianas that draped the trees as in green mourning. It was silent, except for us: engine noise and the sound of chatter, raised occasionally to a squabble about who was taking more than his fair share of room on the truck. I was the favourite target of such complaints, and for the first time I felt myself to be the object not just of amused curiosity, but of slight hostility. They talked about me for half hours at a time, made no attempt to disguise it, and called me *mzungu* – white man. Though I wasn't in any way threatened, I began faintly to understand the distress that being regarded only as an example of an alien race causes.

We stopped at a few tiny hamlets, whose clearings had been slashed precariously from the wall of the forest, to pick up further sacks of manioc, until the truck was so laden that its axles and chassis began to make noises of protest. We stopped also to buy a smoked dik-dik from some pygmy hunters who carried bows and arrows but had been civilized into wearing grey flannel schoolboy shorts. The price they asked was too high and we drove on, after which the passengers reflected unfavourably on the intelligence and greed of pygmies. From time to time we passed a freshly-killed monkey for sale, slung between two posts and looking as though it were being punished in some mediaeval way. I was assured that monkey was the very best eating.

The truck did break down twice, but was cobbled together again until the next time. Towards the end of the journey some of the passengers descended, often at isolated collections of three or four huts, not even a hamlet. Children would rush towards the truck in an ecstasy of pleasure, shouting 'Papa! Papa!' or 'Mama! Mama!', while the bent old figure of a surviving grandparent hobbled from a hut to greet the returning prodigal. The joy was unconfined. The unloading of goods created further excitement, and the fashionable clothes – especially of the men – were admired as wonders of the world.

We reached Komanda at four in the afternoon. Because it was at an important junction, I had expected it to be rather more of a town than the villages through which we had passed. But I soon discovered there was nowhere to stay, and my fate was a matter of the most profound indifference to my former companions on the truck, who had rushed to a hut where something fermented was sold. Heavy clouds were gathering again, the sky was illuminated in the distance by pink flashes of sheet lightning. My immediate future caused me some anxiety.

I had been told I might have to wait several days in Komanda to find a vehicle to Kisangani. But whether the information was intentionally misleading or I was just fortunate, I found a lift within half an hour. I saw a large and new Mercedes truck a hundred yards from where I had been set down, which looked as though it was just completing its loading. I asked the driver where he was going.

'Kisangani,' he replied.

I asked whether I could go with him.

He looked doubtful. The cabin was already full, he said, and I should therefore have to ride on top of the load. White men are generally regarded in Africa as physically weak and feeble creatures (though they are acknowledged to be clever), and the towering load on the truck was, in the opinion of the driver, beyond my strength to climb. Never the most agile of men, and with a knee injury, I too had my doubts, but I was prepared to try: the possibility of a loss of face being less daunting than that of a week in Komanda. And in the event I found it very easy. The other condition insisted upon, of course, was payment, no doubt doubled in my honour. I agreed without demur.

We were soon on our way. My companion on the top of the truck was a short young Zairean, whose body was as grotesquely muscular as that of Mr Universe: except that his musculature had hypertrophied spontaneously in the course of his work rather than as a result of pumping iron. He was the loader of the truck and the man who secured the tarpaulin over it with tightly-tied ropes. He clambered over the truck with the dexterity of a monkey. He was not, however, the most pleasant of companions. He was uncouth, drinking beer in huge gulps and then belching, spitting and blowing his nose over the side of the truck, snoring when he slept, jeering at everyone we passed, and chewing bread with his mouth wide open. He spoke no Swahili or French but, like many Englishmen, took ignorance of his language to be a sign of profound mental incapacity combined with deafness, to be overcome by repeated shouting.

The view from the top of the truck was lordly, though somewhat muted in aesthetic effect (in my case) by the fear of sliding off the damp tarpaulin. I felt almost equal to the trees, or at least to the creatures that inhabited the forest canopy. As for the villages below, their lives were laid out for me as they never could have been at ground level. As everyone knows, the day fades fast in the tropics, and I saw the women light fires for the preparation of the evening meal while the men took their ease on little stools outside their huts, their minds to all appearances as emptied as those of Zen masters. I caught the smell of roasting meat – forest game, no doubt – drifting upwards, and my appetite sharpened. With the casual envy of one who does not examine too closely the object that he covets, I even found myself envying these villagers a little. They knew where they would be in two weeks' time; their lives had a rhythm, and they possessed the deep security that comes of needing or desiring little. If monotony was a problem, at least they were prey to no torturing ambition. And their children passed their childhood in a world of wonder and magic, rather than in the prosaic suburbs of the west.

I had forgotten entirely my anxiety that I should not stay a week in Komanda.

When night fell, the dark forest was silhouetted indistinctly against the sky, slightly menacing. Who knew what dangerous beasts lurked behind the black wall of trees, waiting to pounce on a broken-down vehicle? Far ahead the sky was still lit up by the silent flashes of an electrical storm. The yellow beam of the truck's lights faded to nothing only a few yards ahead and, shaken by the ruts in the road, resembled the tentative searchings of a blind man's stick.

My companion wrapped himself up in a corner of tarpaulin and slept soundly. I kept a lookout for the storm, but it appeared to recede in exact proportion as we advanced. At midnight we reached a town called Mambasa, founded by Arab slave and ivory traders from Mombasa. By night, at any rate, it seemed no different from a thousand other small African towns, its main street a wide estuary of mud between petty traders' stores and innumerable bars. The shapes of the other trucks parked up for the night loomed in the blackness; many of the stores, and all of the bars, were still open, lit by guttering oil lamps whose light cast eerie shadows out of open doors and windows. From one of the bars came the sound of disco music and laughter, and when my companion woke and heard it he at once began to dance. By unmistakable gestures, he told me he was on the lookout for a girl.

But first he had to eat. In the courtyard behind one of the stores we washed our hands in a bucket and ate with our fingers from communal bowls of *ugali* and meat. My hunger overcame my culture-bound aversion to this way of eating, of scooping out the hot, glutinous porridge with its clear imprints of other peoples' fingers, and dipping it into a bowl of greasy stew. There is no surer way of offending people than by showing a distaste for their food, and so I ate as heartily as I was able.

Afterwards I climbed back on to the top of the truck, which was to serve as my bed. My companion went off into the dark in search of amorous adventure; I hope he did not find AIDS instead.

The disco continued well into the morning and then, the sky having cleared, it grew very cold, so my sleep was fitful at best. But the fact I survived at all and uttered no complaint seemed to create a favourable impression on the two drivers, who were noticeably friendlier in the morning.

We left Mambasa at half-past-five. The sun was up but it was still cold, and soon the road narrowed as it passed through long overarching thickets of bamboo. Bamboo is a graceful, elegant plant, well-suited to the exquisite, contemplative art of China and Japan; but on the top of a Zairean truck, it has the unfortunate habit of caning you across the cheeks, like some sadistic Victorian schoolmaster.

Then came the first of the army roadblocks. The officer was sitting on a deckchair under a flimsy straw shelter, leafing through a 'novel' in pictures. A faint movement of his arm indicated to his one subordinate that he should go and collect the bribe. There was a short discussion and some notes passed hands. After lifting the barrier, the subordinate trotted back to the officer, who had not looked up from his book. It was, in a manner of speaking, a very genteel shakedown, the officer being uninvolved in the vulgar business of handling cash.

There were several more roadblocks along the way, similarly without acrimony or menace. The worst days in Zaire (from the point of view of roadblocks) were over. Of late, the soldiers sometimes received their wages, and there was therefore less desperation about their exactions: except, perhaps, in the middle and the end of the month, when their salaries and mid-month advances ran out.

Some villagers had learnt from the example of the soldiers. With true entrepreneurial flair, they cut their firewood only where it was sure to block the road. With skill and determination, they made the road impassable and unclearable without their assistance. Nothing, except money, would induce them to clear a passage. Pleading and cajoling was so much wasted breath. The villagers claimed they could cut their firewood nowhere else, a somewhat implausible claim; they had, they said, to live. Like Louis XIV, our driver did not see the necessity. There was evidently hostility between the town and country dwellers. It was the latter who always emerged victorious from these small struggles, victories of which I was secretly glad. But I daresay the town, as usual, would have the last laugh, inasmuch as it could raise the prices of its trade goods.

The road descended gradually into the river basin. The heat became unpleasant and damp, like entering a greenhouse. We stopped for a chat with every passing vehicle, and stopped also in most of the villages where, it seemed, the truck's crew had 'wives' and children of uncertain paternity (many vehicles passing). Everything was relaxed, affectionate and natural about these relations, a reproach perhaps to our neuroses about such matters; but, a true child of my culture, I found the loss of time involved in these halts intensely frustrating.

We stopped in the middle of the day in a town called Bafwabalinga, which had as yet received no rain, and was therefore as dusty as Mambasa had been muddy. The heat was well-nigh unbearable, as insistent as a migraine headache. Most people were asleep, propped against their crumbling walls. For lunch there was only dry bread and warm orange drink, industrially sweet. We stayed two hours in this Zairean hell, where harp-ribbed dogs dug themselves into the dust to escape the heat; and although every step was to me a herculean labour, boredom and professional curiosity drove me into the unattended People's Pharmacy, where the shelves were cluttered with the same mélange of physicians' samples and outdated drugs that I had seen so many times elsewhere in Africa, collected and sent by charitable groups in Europe under the illusion they were performing a service, rather than poisoning the recipients with useless medicaments and impoverishing them into the bargain.

When finally we left Bafwabalinga we had three more passengers, a young woman who seemed well-acquainted with the crew, her daughter of three and her small baby. Rather ungallantly, the two in the cabin suggested that I, who had proved my mettle, join them there, while the woman and child climbed to the top of the load. I said nothing to disturb this arrangement. The view from the cabin was less good, but it was more comfortable, and as we accelerated once again through the overhanging thickets of bamboo I thought with a certain smug satisfaction of the blows I, at any rate, was not receiving.

The road deteriorated further: the Michelin map of Central Africa marked it as impassable in the rains. In the distance dark and menacing clouds were gathering fast. My anxiety rose: what if the rains should break while we were still two hundred miles from Kisangani? Would we have to wait until the next dry season? The two men in the cabin were unconcerned. They continued to stop at every village and hamlet for a chat, even as the clouds gathered, and to greet every passing vehicle. I supposed this is what they meant when they said that human values are still most important in Africa, though to me it seemed like irresponsibility. But they said we should reach Madula, only fifty kilometres from Kisangani, tonight; we should spend the night there, and arrive in Kisangani at eight the next morning. They were understandably much more concerned, once they knew I was a doctor, that I should treat their gonorrhoea, which both of them had had for several months. There were no proper medicines in Zaire, they said. I was able to oblige them from my small stock.

At five in the afternoon, with the blackest of clouds all but overhead, they decided to stop for another meal. It appeared to me the height of fecklessness: I did not trust to their knowledge of local conditions. It was not yet quite time for dinner, and so they went on a social tour of the village. I waited by the truck and read, an activity that caused some wonderment among the children who soon surrounded me. They were distracted, however, by a goat that wandered blindly out into the road from behind our truck, into the path of an oncoming vehicle. The goat was flung several yards into the air, its head half off, blood spattering the ground like a cartoon by Scarfe. A crowd gathered round the corpse in festive mood. There was much laughter at the foolishness of the goat. It was not every day in this village that a major event occurred, something that could be talked about for days on end. A man emerged from one of the neighbouring huts with a large machete. He had a determinedly matter-of-fact look upon his face, as though he wanted to set himself apart from the general excitement. He walked straight through the assembled crowd – let me through, I'm a butcher – and in one stroke of the machete, to the admiration of the crowd, severed the sinews that still connected the head with the body. In no time at all he had skinned the carcass and hacked the flesh into chunks. A child arrived to lead the entrails away, another the skin, and soon there was nothing to commemorate the passing of the goat other than a bloody smudge in the dust: and maybe a surfeit of stew in one of the huts.

The black clouds were now directly overhead and began to discharge heavy, pear-shaped drops. It was, however, time to eat. The driver led me to an untidy yard between two huts. The cook was a tall, fat, slatternly woman with her hand firmly round a bottle of Primus beer, which she finished in a couple of swigs before reaching for another. I guessed these were not her first bottles of the day, and she gave the impression she wouldn't have minded a fight. She was dressed in a flimsy piece of coloured print, very dirty, with a medallion portrait of Mobutu as a younger man across her ample bosom. It looked as though she had worn it ever since Mobutu *was* a younger man, for he was beginning to fade; and there was a tear right through the motto that underscored the portrait, *Toujours servir*, Always to serve.

The meal this time was of chicken stew and *ugali*, the chicken being well-flavoured but practically fleshless. I was not required to pay, for the driver had already done so and refused to be reimbursed. The rain had now started in good earnest, and the woman with two children joined us in the cab for the rest of the journey. Her daughter was eating a dry bread roll, and directed all her crumbs at my legs. I was in shorts, and the day having been hot and humid, my legs were damp with sweat. A hair shirt is like satin compared with crumbs in the cab of a truck going through the Zairean jungle.

Then I noticed that both children, who rubbed close up to me, had severe scabies, secondarily infected from their scratching. Close contact is, of course, the way this disease spreads, and I edged my way to the corner of the cabin. The daughter, however, thought this was a game, and followed me. My Hippocratic conscience led me to tell the mother that her children had *upele* (Swahili for scabies) and that I had *dawa* (medicine) for it. She was unimpressed. As far as she was concerned, all children had sores, and if they scratched a bit, it was only natural.

The rain was torrential and the road surface as slippery as a politician's answers. For scores of yards at a time we skidded and slithered independently of the driver's will, and it came as no surprise when, at the top of a slight rise, we saw a truck immoveably stuck at right angles to the direction of the road. It was clear there would be no further progress towards Kisangani tonight; and with my temperamental pessimism I thought maybe not for another three months.

By now, to add to the rain, an electrical storm of incredible violence had broken: more violent by far than any I had yet seen, though I lived two years in a region of Tanzania where, during the season of storms, several people were killed every year by lightning. The road through the forest and the forest itself were lit up for seconds on end, as repeated, brilliant and prolonged bolts of lightning struck not only downwards but across the sky, as though they would encircle the globe. The lightning continued when the rain had all but stopped, and it was then suggested that we in the cabin walk on to the next village which fortuitously was only a mile away, to leave the uncouth loader, who had been thoroughly soaked in the storm, to guard the truck. And so, with terrifying electrical discharges crackling in the air around us, and with fear in *my* heart, at least (a fear which, of course, I could not allow to be seen), we set out for the village. The deep ruts in the road and the glutinous mud doubled the length of the walk, as far as effort was concerned; but the little girl of three followed behind her mother without complaint, not even a whimper, already having learnt to accept whatever hardship befell her.

There was no disputing, in the abstract, the beauty of the lightning, but I was pleased enough when it showed us the village not far ahead: two lines of dried mud buildings separated by a wide thoroughfare of wet mud. There were rooms in the village for travellers: in fact, I discovered next morning that provision of such rooms was the main business of the village. They were of the simplest possible construction, but clean. There was a barrel of rainwater outside with which to wash, and a shelter where guests could cook. No doubt my small room afforded little protection against the lightning – I had known of several people killed inside their huts in Tanzania – but such is the primitive instinct to seek shelter in a storm that I felt considerably reassured nonetheless.

The two drivers were eager to search for women. They had not yet taken their medicine for gonorrhoea: they seemed to require courage to do so. But I doubted somehow whether they could spread their disease any further than it had spread already, so I said nothing. The rain fell again, as torrentially as ever. The sound of it on the roof – hated with puritanical hatred by René Dumont – I found quite soothing, insofar as it was rhythmical and a reminder of the luxury of being indoors: but yet it was disturbing when I thought about the state of the road, and imagined this hut might be my home for several months to come, with only Moby Dick for company.

I needn't have worried. The rain had stopped by the morning, and as these were the first rains of the season the muddiness was comparatively superficial. Somehow the truck obstructing the road had been moved and the drivers, elated by their nocturnal conquests, were certain we should reach Kisangani by lunchtime. This turned out to be over-optimistic, for not many miles further on another truck had slithered sideways to block the road. A solitary goat perched on top of the load; it had been thrown a bundle of leafy branches which it munched continuously while observing the humans below trying to free the truck by digging away the mud. What was merely an irritation and frustration to me was to the workers an almost festive occasion. Though the work was arduous – it is not easy to free twenty tons with spades – they laughed and sang and made light of it, and greeted each failure of the truck to budge with roars of merriment.

I noticed that the baby carried by my fellow-passenger was severely malnourished. Moreover, it had a fever, its brow running with sweat and its breathing rapid and shallow. I pointed this out to the mother, who was trying to fill its mouth with dry bread. But she was not unduly disturbed, and greeted my offer of help with indifference. All children, she said, had fever from time to time.

The rest of the journey was easily accomplished. A hundred miles from Kisangani the road improved, and fifteen miles from it the road was surfaced. The villages approaching the city were noticeably more prosperous, growing for a market rather than for survival. The frequency of roadblocks also increased, there being more money hereabouts, presumably, to extort. At the last of these roadblocks, in an area which was neither urban nor fully rural, a soldier stepped confidently into the road and held up his hand for us to stop. But instead of slowing, the driver accelerated. The extortions of the soldiers had not been onerous and would not have dented the profits of the journey: but it is, after all, small injustices rather than large ones that stir revolt. An accelerating Mercedes fifteen-ton truck fully laden is not to be lightly obstructed, and the soldier, who a moment before had been so confident, had to dive for safety to the side of the road.

'They'll shoot us,' I said.

'They've sold all their bullets,' replied the driver, accelerating further.

We knocked over a market stall, and chickens went squawking for cover, leaving feathers behind. It was just like in the movies. We whooped for joy: we heard the loader banging the side in appreciation.

'Bravo! Bravo!' I cried.

And that is how we came to arrive in the centre of Kisangani at seventy miles an hour, having averaged eight miles an hour for two days since leaving Komanda.

FIVE

Down the Zaire

K isangani – Stanleyville that was – stands at the highest navigable point of the Congo, or Zaire, river. It was once compared, in respect of its thriving trade, with Antwerp, but I doubt if anyone would venture such a comparison today. The Belgian villas, once so neat and pretentious, were falling to pieces while their present occupants, numerous and cheerful, sat at peace on what remained of the stoeps. Even the *Mairie*, painted cake-icing pink, was in a state of decomposition, its gardens a mess, the inside looking as though it had been taken over by squatters. And yet the effect of all this, on me at least, was to raise questions about the proper goals of life. Were the claims of Africans that theirs was a man-centred society that rejected the false ends of western materialism true, or merely a cover for laziness, or perhaps both at once? The truth in human affairs is rarely pure and never simple.

My hotel was a large pre-war Belgian establishment whose concierge was transfixed by the flickering pictures of the television – he had one of the twelve thousand sets in the whole country. My room was vast, with a wide brick arch leading to an alcove as large as most hotel bedrooms. The bath was built for a race of giants, though the water supply was now insufficient for a small enamel bowl. As far as I could tell, little or no work had been done on the hotel for many years, with the possible exception of the removal of furniture, of which very little remained.

On the corner of the street was a pavement bar and café. There I watched evening come to Kisangani. It was the time at which the sons of the Lebanese and Greek traders of the city showed off on their motor-bikes and in their cars, tearing through the main streets at high speed and with maximum noise. From their madcap antics I imagined their lives of bored desperation. As I sat, two young vendors of newspapers and pamphlets approached me. Their newspapers were uninformative and truthless, except about football; and their pamphlets, written by a Jesuit, concerned human rights under the Zairean constitution.

'I didn't know there were any,' I said jokingly.

The vendors did not understand. They were illiterate and did not know what they were selling.

I was not able to stay long in Kisangani. A boat, the *Colonel Kokolo*, was about to depart for Kinshasa. On the way upriver it had been stranded on a sandbar and was two weeks late. No-one knew when there would be another boat.

But first I had to change money. It so happened Zaire had not long before followed the prescription of the International Monetary Fund and devalued its currency – the Zaire – to its true value against the dollar. Whatever the economic benefits of the I.M.F.'s advice, such as a lower standard of living for the Zairean people, for the traveller the devaluation was an unmitigated disaster. It destroyed at a stroke the black market for dollars. Instead of changing his money in two minutes with a black marketeer, he was obliged now to treat with the bank. Anyone who has dealt with an African bank will appreciate what this means.

I arrived at the bank before opening time which, in the event, was rather later than the time advertised. I was the only customer in the large, echoing 1950s banking hall. I was faced by fifteen clerks and secretaries, all of whom were polite and cheerful, greeting me with a happy *bonjour*. None of them was competent to change my money, though none was overburdened with work: it required someone from the office upstairs. Fortunately, I had brought a book with me to read. Eventually, the right man arrived, charming and apologetic. He required a virtual biography – my antecedents, profession, present and future whereabouts – all entered in what appeared to be septuplicate. If Mr Kurtz were to return to the Heart of Darkness he would exclaim 'The forms, the forms!' rather than 'The horror, the horror!' I suppose that is progress of a kind.

Two hours and a half later I emerged with a bundle of notes. Some were crumpled like a paper handkerchief, others new and freshly-printed. Whatever the inefficiency of the bank, I was surprised there had not been the slightest hint at an illicit payment, unless the delay itself was such a hint and I was too obtuse to realize it.

I had now to buy a ticket for the boat. The offices of ONATRA, the state-run shipping line which was one of the I.M.F.'s targets, were down by the quayside. A large and excited crowd had already gathered for the afternoon departure, and a market had assembled. Rows of women sat by their mats on which they displayed food for the journey: fresh and dried fish, fresh and dried meat, starchy roots and vegetables wrapped in banana leaves, kebabs and doughnuts, and baskets of black fried caterpillars.

My late request for a cabin caused some consternation at the ticket office, already besieged by requests for deck space. Only the *capitaine* could authorize it: the *capitaine* not of the ship but of the office, who also had nautical rank. I found him upstairs in his office, drinking tea. I explained what it was I wanted.

Before him on his desk lay the plan of the cabins on the boat. I saw that they were not all taken, and he saw that I saw. Nevertheless, he slid the plan into a drawer and shook his head lugubriously. What I asked was difficult, if not impossible, especially as the boat was about to sail. It would take time to arrange, success was not assured, he would have to ask others . . .

I'll wait, I said, and took out my book to read. My reaction disconcerted him, as was my intention. He had nothing to do, and shuffled the papers on his desk guiltily. He jumped up, then sat down, then jumped up again and examined minutely an old circular from headquarters pinned to the wall. He must have thought I was very slow on the uptake. I was still reading patiently: I had decided that while I was prepared to *pay* a bribe, I was not prepared to *offer* one. This was, no doubt, a less than rigorous moral distinction, one which might be hard to defend philosophically; it was a priggish distinction, inasmuch as I had not experienced the *capitaine*'s conditions of life; but such, at any rate, was my state of mind at the time.

The *capitaine* shuffled his papers some more and then could stand it no longer.

'There is a reservation fee, monsieur!' he exclaimed.

He asked for 200 Zaires ($3.20). This was a very small proportion of the total cost of the ticket, a modest demand to which, in the circumstances, I willingly acceded: for without paying it I might have been stuck two weeks in Kisangani.

The *capitaine* gave me a piece of paper to take to the booking office. There, a single clerk behind a wire grille faced a seething mass of would-be passengers, waving their money over each other's heads to attract his attention. The more desperate and urgent they became, the slower he worked. But as soon as he saw me he invited me into his office that I might be served immediately and in comfort. Had there been an orderly queue I should have hesitated to take advantage of this flagrant racial discrimination (in my favour); but since everyone was using whatever advantages he had – height, reach, penetration of voice – to be served out of turn, I accepted my chance gratefully. Once in his office, I gained a clerk's eye view of the customers. A hundred faces, concentrating on him alone, pleading for attention, struggling to reach him: I understood at once his urge to be disobliging.

I had my ticket in no time at all. No resentment seemed to have been aroused by my intrusion: it was merely part of the natural and immemorial order of things.

I boarded the *Colonal Kokolo*. It was a large and fairly new river ferry, five storeys high and of shallow draught, which looked as though a single wave would topple it. Attached to the bows by steel rope was a flat metal barge with cramped catacombs of cabins in two layers. Lashed to the starboard side of this barge was yet another barge, similarly incommodious. But the passengers in those barges were privileged, compared with those who slept on the lower decks and had no cabin at all.

The departure of the boat was a festival of trade and laughter lasting several hours. Passengers and their relatives passed back and forth over the gangplank, baskets of fish and eggs and caterpillars were hauled into the boat from pirogues – simple hollowed-out tree trunks, pointed at both ends – that came to meet the boat from the other bank of the river (dominated, architecturally, by a mission station), and fishwives with laser-beam voices gossiped from ship to shore and shore to ship. All was animation, and I thought with mounting disgust of the statement of a French intellectual I had read, to the effect that matters could deteriorate no further in Zaire, for the simple reason that the government was already the worst possible. Dishonest fool! He preferred to believe the beautifully consistent theoretical schemes he had constructed rather than the evidence of his own eyes, with all its inconsistencies. For him, Mobutu's lack of intellectual coherence was the worst possible crime, even though the twentieth century incontestably proved it was possible for a government – and often an intellectually coherent one – to crush all animation and laughter out of its subject population: something which Mobutu, for all his corruption and misdemeanours, had self-evidently failed to do, or even tried to do.

I looked for the chief steward, who had the key to my cabin. I found him on the lower deck at the stern of the boat, carrying a bucket of water. He was keeping moist the ten-foot-long gavial, a crocodilian with a long, narrow snout, that lay immobile on the deck, its legs, tail and jaws tied up with rope. The gavial was his, and tenderly he threw the bucket of water over it. The gavial blinked languidly with its translucent nictitating membrane, and looked philosophical.

> How cheerfully he seems to grin,
> How neatly spreads his claws,
> And welcomes little fishes in
> With gently smiling jaws.

The chief steward was taking the gavial to Kinshasa, to be sold as a delicacy. There he would fetch more than 5000 Zaires ($80). He patted it complacently upon its scaly head.

I returned to one of the upper decks. There I met a pale and thin young Englishman, surrounded by travelling cots, water filters, cardboard boxes of prepared foods, and a baby walker. He looked harassed and hot. He was a protestant missionary from further down the river who had been paying a visit to his mission headquarters in Kisangani. He apologized almost at once for travelling first class, but said he had his wife and two young children with him and it was more a matter of safety than of comfort. Sanctity was evidently identified in his mind with discomfort. As we talked, another Englishman came on board. He shook my hand in no very friendly fashion, and asked me what I was doing. I said I was travelling only, that I was a doctor and also something of a writer.

'Not another one,' he said with real bitterness. 'Aren't there enough books already?'

'And what do *you* do?' I asked.

'I'm a missionary.'

'Not another one,' I said with what I thought was gentle irony.

It was a case of a soft answer not turning away wrath.

'You've never met any missionaries,' he said with fury.

'On the contrary, I've met them all round the world.'

He turned from me and addressed only his fellow missionary, who was called John. He said John's wife was waiting for him on the quay and that as he was pressed for time he wished to say goodbye to them both straight away. John asked me whether I should mind guarding his things, and I said of course not. Actually I was not pleased to be associated with the impedimenta of domesticity – a packet of cornflakes and a teddy bear were protruding – so redolent of cramped suburbia: the more so as I was under the observation of a tall thin Dutchman who was clearly contemptuous of the smallness of European domestic existence.

John returned with his wife, Jennifer. She carried their new-born baby, and was followed by their daughter of three. It is a curious fact, one that is perhaps inexplicable, that missionary wives often have an appearance in common: a pointed chin, thin and bloodless lips, a complexion preternaturally pale (considering they live in the tropics), and dry neglected hair. They seem often to be holding themselves in, as though a wild, party-going, dancing sensualist were trying to escape from the whalebone corset of mission life. As for missionary children, they too are pale and often come out in pink blotches: though I daresay no more frequently than other young white children in the tropics. All the same, Jennifer's children were *very* blotchy.

I left them to settle in their cabin, knowing we should have plenty of opportunity to talk in the days ahead. Next, I met my neighbour in the cabin adjacent to mine: Peter, a big, healthy Australian of my own age who lost no time in telling me he was taking two years off to travel luxuriously round the world to escape the attentions of the Australian Inland Revenue. Peter was disarmingly honest, even when boasting. He was rich; he owned the most profitable commercial radio station in Sydney; he made $900,000 last year. He had a beautiful house overlooking Sydney Harbour, the most beautiful view this side of Paradise; Australia was rich, it couldn't go wrong, Australians had the highest disposable incomes in the world; Australian food and wines were the best on the planet; his girlfriend was so beautiful she could have had any man she wanted, but he knew she would wait for him; he had bought Japanese yen travellers' cheques before leaving Australia and the yen had appreciated by 50 per cent soon afterwards; Sydney Opera House was the eighth wonder of the world.

In anyone other than an Australian, all this boasting might have been irritating: but with him, it was related with such innocent pleasure in his own good fortune that it had quite the reverse effect, and one felt almost a participant in his joy.

In no time at all he had effected a remarkable transformation of his cabin. He had brought flowers with him, he pinned a map of Africa to the wall, he covered the chairs and bed with striking African blankets, he set up his portable stereo system: the cabin was no longer a dismal cube of anonymity.

Peter had waited two weeks in Kisangani for the boat and while he was there he had got to know Paul, the Dutchman. Paul was a long-term traveller too, though just now he was on his way to Brazzaville to catch the cheap Aeroflot flight to Amsterdam, via Moscow. (The Soviet airline charges half as much as other airlines, presumably to gain foreign exchange; and all the wanderers of Europe seem to use it). Paul was a believer in Good Causes in general: he was against war, pollution and exploitation, and in favour of peace (for which he had demonstrated in Amsterdam), justice, democracy and squatters' rights. He was *pro* Africa and *anti* the system.

'What system?' I asked.

The system that had plundered Africa and returned the wealth to a few multinational companies.

'It is nevertheless the system that allows you to travel round the world for nine months of every year without doing any work whatsoever,' I remarked.

To do Paul justice, he laughed. It was the first of several verbal fencing matches. He was travelling in one of the cramped lower cabins, and whenever the noise, filth and overcrowding became too much for him he would climb to our deck, where the engine noise did not reach and from which the boat seemed to glide unpropelled through the water with the utmost serenity.

Peter and I toured the boat and its satellites before we departed. Peter was dressed in long white shorts, a blue floral shirt, sunglasses and espadrilles, for whose cleanliness and general welfare he was much concerned if we tarried in what he called 'the lower depths'. On the way downwards, we passed a man carrying two large lizards, mottled yellow and black, that were also to be sold in Kinshasa as delicacies. Later in the journey he cut off their heads and stored their bodies in the ship's cool room, but now they were still alive, if profoundly lethargic and indifferent.

The bottom deck was home to all those who paid least for their tickets (or perhaps did not pay for them at all). They slept on mats, propped against steel pillars or baskets of produce, or contorted into shapes that filled odd corners. For the deck was not merely home, it was a business premises as well, a thriving market that supplied all the needs of the people who lived along the banks of the river from Kisangani to Kinshasa. The boat did not stop at many villages, but every village sent out a flotilla of pirogues (even in the dead of night) to bring fish or antelope, bales of smoked monkeys or hunks of smoked elephant, baby crocodiles or bush pig, bananas or pineapples, to exchange for the modern necessities the jungle did not provide: soap and salt, tape cassettes and pills, dresses and injections, mosquito coils and hurricane lamps, margarine and beer. To reach the moving boat in an unstable, narrow pirogue was not without its hazards, and though manoeuvred with the utmost skill we saw in the course of the journey many of them go under, and a Zairean told me that the boat never completed its journey without two or three villagers at least being drowned in their efforts to board it.

The market was not homogeneous, but divided informally into sections. The fish and meat were on an open stretch of the deck under the bridge; passing through a corridor of latrines, dark and rusted, awash with urine and shower water that leaked from all directions at once, there was the 'indoor' market, so crowded with goods and stalls and passengers (and goats grazing on cardboard and greens in fragments of space) that it was a struggle to walk through. There were merchants of cloth and merchants of jeans; there were trinkets, stationery, soap, oil, tinned food – particularly sardines; and there was a whole section of the market for pharmaceuticals, in which I took a special interest.

Not surprisingly, the pharmacists' wares were a gallimaufry of preparations, from the lifesaving to the lifethreatening, from narcotics to placebos. De Witt's Kidney and Bladder pills were everywhere, and sold well; there were a thousand vials of Vitamin B12, a substance often given by doctors in Africa to patients who feel they need something powerful (for it is a striking pink colour), when they have no strictly medical need for any treatment at all. There were little polythene packets of what in Tanzania is called *rangi mbili* – two colours. This was tetracycline, in red-and-yellow capsules, in which form it is to be found all over Africa. Its ability to cure certain forms of tropical venereal disease, as well as a host of other infections, has given it a reputation as practically a panacea. In Tanzania in times of shortage, there is a lively and lucrative black market in tetracycline. But in the quantities in which it was sold on the boat, a few capsules at a time, it might well have done more harm than good, allowing germ resistance to emerge. Worse, there were single vials of injectible antibiotics for sale, unlikely in almost any circumstances to be of any therapeutic value if injected only once: and they were sold with syringes and needles, either used or unused, according to purse. With the spread of AIDS, to say nothing of hepatitis B, used needles were a menace; but in Zaire's economic circumstances, and with a population convinced by precept and example of the superiority of injections over other modes of treatment, it was unlikely the practice of re-using needles would quickly be abandoned. Perhaps saddest of all were the tubes of skin-lightening creams to be found at the pharmacists' stalls. All advertisers and salesmen exaggerate the powers and properties of their products, of course, but there was something particularly poignant about the suggestion, insinuated by the pictures on the cartons, that if only Africans would lighten the colour of their skin, a sophisticated life of dining by candlelight, sipping dry martinis in tuxedos and glittering evening dresses, would be opened unto them. What depths of self-hatred and cultural confusion the producers of these creams prey upon! Some countries in Africa have forbidden their sale, perhaps rightly; unhappily, one does not legislate the underlying confusion away.

Continuing our tour of the lower decks, Peter conceived an increasing distaste for what he saw (one of his boasts having been that Australian plumbing was the best in the world). He wanted to take a shower, he said, as we passed a freshly beheaded goat. The turtles and baby crocodiles no longer charmed him. By now, the public address system was in full working order, and relayed Zairean popular music at an eardrum-tingling volume. It was impossible to complete a sentence of thought in one's head. Zairean music, highly favoured in much of Africa, struck me very soon as numbingly monotonous: monotonous as to rhythm, monotonous as to melody, and monotonous above all as to emotional pitch. Perhaps it is by its very insistence that it achieves its effects: a trance-like state, the mind having emptied of all thought or recollection, pleasant or unpleasant. The music was to play all day and every night until the small hours, and for those in that region of the boat there was no escaping it. Entertainment was for them not only available, but compulsory.

'Let's get out of here,' said Peter, turning pale.

Our route of escape included a bar, where enormously fat grand-mothers, worthy of respect, kept up their weight with snacks of greasy fried starch, mothers breast-fed their babies, and soldiers quaffed beer, all happily shouting above the music. The temperature in the iron-walled room was decades of degrees above that of the tropical rain forest outside.

'Jeeze, what an inferno!' said Peter when we had regained our own deck. But it was as I had always suspected: hell was much happier than paradise.

We cast off late in the afternoon, to the cheers of the passengers and the crowd on the bank. The captain had been unable to say when we would depart, even ten minutes before we did so; as to the date of our arrival at Kinshasa, it was so shrouded in mystery that he would not like to hazard even a *week* of arrival. It all depended on so many factors. Besides, he found our desire to know these things rather puzzling: we were on the boat, weren't we? we wanted to go to Kinshasa, didn't we? the boat was going to Kinshasa, wasn't it? Therefore, what more was there to be asked?

We glided past the bank on which important Belgians had built their villas, all now in virtual ruins. Soon the light softened, and glowed warmly on the calm surface of the water. The red disc of the sun drifted down to the horizon and beyond. Silhouettes of people began to appear against the reddish sky, dancing on the roofs of the barges. They danced not with or for others but alone and for themselves, just for the joy of life. I thought again of the French intellectual who said all was for the worst in this, the worst of all possible Zaires.

A gong, in the form of a plate struck with a fork, called us to dinner. It was meat and potatoes, as it was to be throughout the entire journey, lunch and dinner. Peter refused the hunks of murderers' meat, and took only potatoes.

'I'm a vegetarian,' he said. 'I've been one ever since 1976. I thought it would be good for my karma.' He ate a potato, overboiled and tasteless. 'Since I gave up eating meat I've become a millionaire.'

After dinner we went up on to the highest deck, the roof of the whole ship. The engine noise was a faint hum, the Zairean music a distant murmur, the shore a different shade of black. From the bridge the powerful beams of two searchlights cleaved the darkness, probing for hazards. Peter wondered why they didn't have sonar, like all Australian yachts. Then he told me he was an amateur numerologist, and offered to tell my fortune from the numbers in my date of birth. He discovered I should be a success in life, more through persistence than talent.

We stared into the tropical void.

'Jeeze,' he said after a long silence. 'I wish I had some John Lennon. Instant karma.'

I woke early next morning, but not as early as the passengers on the lower decks. Many of them were dipping tins into the river to draw water with which to wash themselves: despite the overcrowding and the enforced squalor, their personal cleanliness was impressive.

I toured the boat again. Once had been enough for Peter, whose appetite for local colour was easily satisfied. And Paul, who ate and slept amongst it, was only too eager to escape from it. The noise and the lack of privacy quickly eroded his determination to travel native, and he fled to our deck and our company. Besides, he needed somewhere to smoke his marijuana in safety, and he used Peter's cabin for this purpose. He smoked it fervently, as though it were a duty rather than a pleasure. He called it *feeding his head*; 'I need to feed my head' he would say about four times a day as he disappeared into the cabin. I think he despised all those who found plain, unfuddled consciousness quite enough to be getting on with; but the only evidence he ever showed of having reached a higher plane was a certain red-eyed vacancy with occasional fits of girlish giggles at seemingly banal objects and events.

All day pirogues joined us from the riverbanks. They tied up to the *Colonel Kokolo* and were often strung like a necklace around it. They brought fish to trade, mainly; large and often grotesque, with huge scales and mouths with fleshy appendages or sometimes vicious teeth, fish that looked as primaeval as coelocanths. There were large and repulsive catfish too, that had to be soaked in fresh water for twenty-four hours to remove the taste of mud that impregnated their flesh.

I made friends with a young Zairean from the lower decks who took to visiting me three times a day. He had an intelligent, sensitive face, and was often content to say nothing as he leant over the rail watching the bank slip by. He was a petty trader, on his way to Kinshasa: he too wanted to escape to privacy and quiet, though these were not, he said, often desired by Zaireans. And almost before I knew it a young cripple called Michel, with one leg withered by polio, had attached himself to me. He possessed no caliper so that at every step he had to bend low and support his knee with his hand. He had an unaggressive, pleasing manner and a plausible hard-luck story: his parents had died and he had had to abandon his education, and now he lived from hand to mouth, his dream of a career shattered. Since it is difficult to turn down a direct request from a man you know will have a disability for the rest of his life, I was soon giving him money for his meals. When not speaking to me, he read the New Testament, apparently with intense concentration and deep devotion; he once asked me to pray with him for the safety of the ship and I was too cowardly to refuse. Was his piety, I wondered, part of a calculated act to engage the sympathies of gullible western tourists? Was it, in fact, a trade or profession?

'If you have Africans around you,' said Peter, 'it usually ends up costing you a lot of money.'

Later, Michel showed me a photograph of his young wife and baby; he also told me he was a poet who had had three poems on the subject of love published in Kinshasa. From the point of view of an act, if that is what it was, this was a mistake, for it showed him to be not quite so helpless and abandoned as I, in my sentimentality, had assumed. But by then, the pattern was established: I paid for everything he wanted.

Peter, now in a pink floral shirt, spent much of the day on the roof deck with a textbook and a self-instruction tape of the French language. Even allowing for his partial befuddlement by too many beers, he made less progress than I should have thought possible. His powers of mimesis were virtually nil. After several weeks of study, to say nothing of two years' instruction at school, his 'bonjour' was still greeted by French-speakers with puzzlement as to what he was trying to say. He needed me to translate 'yes please' and 'no thankyou'.

I turned to the missionaries. Their daughter of three tended to grizzle – 'a typical whingeing Pom', as Peter had it – and they took it by turns to reward her for it with their full-time attention, leaving one of them free to speak to me. They had been two years in Zaire and spoke their local language fluently. Jennifer had actually been born in Zaire (the Congo as it was then), just before the civil war. Her father was a printer who had suddenly felt the call, and he went out to a mission on the river to print its tracts and hymnals. He returned to Britain after the outbreak of war and was now a suburban pastor.

Jennifer struck me as colourless not only physically but in character. An abstract goodness had, by an effort of will, replaced and made redundant all other aspects of her personality. When she spoke to Africans she adopted a tone of implacable sweetness. She had expunged from her speech all metaphor, hyperbole and understatement, as being inimical to the telling of the Truth. I asked what she and her husband did at the mission.

He was a maths teacher, she the school administrator, though she had been to Bible College and had qualified as a theologian and Sunday school teacher. The pupils at the school came from miles around, from far distant villages and settlements. Their thirst for knowledge and instruction, she said, was insatiable.

I asked about general conditions of life in their part of Zaire. Was there, for example, much malnutrition?

'There's none in the villages,' she said. 'But they get it sometimes when they come to school. Some of them suffer terribly.'

Was I hearing correctly? I looked at her: she was staring expressionlessly at the river bank.

'Do you mean to say . . .?'

'When they arrive at the school they're given tools and a plot of land. They have a year to develop it. If they are lazy in that year they suffer later.'

John arrived, carrying the baby, with the daughter trailing discontentedly behind. Jennifer took over their care and John sat beside me. He had been a computer programmer in Colchester when the urge to Serve the Lord came upon him. Jennifer's background made the choice of mission field an easy one. He didn't regret his decision, though life in Zaire was far from smooth or straightforward.

For one thing, the mission had been indigenized. This had led to a lowering of standards. In the old days it had been difficult for an African to become a Christian – perhaps too difficult. When whites ran the mission, an African had to go to Bible class at five o'clock every morning for a year, and if he missed so much as one morning without adequate reason he had to start all over again. A Christian in those days was a real believer who had suffered for his faith. But these days a would-be convert had only to attend Bible class once a week, and that irregularly.

Nevertheless, Zairean pastors enforced some discipline on their congregations. For example, you could be expelled from the church for adultery, drinking, gambling, swearing or quarrelling and refusing to make up. The social consequences of expulsion from the church in a protestant village were considerable. It could ruin a man, if he were a trader; if he were a farmer, he might have difficulty in finding fertilizer or selling his produce. Another offence for which a man might be expelled was witchcraft, but here the church wavered a little. The trouble was that even pastors believed in their hearts in witchcraft. In a village nearby their mission, for example, a man had unexpectedly died. The pastor went into the forest and shot a monkey: from the way it fell from the trees he knew the man had died of witchcraft. He told his congregation, who took four suspects and tortured them (one method they used was to put chillies in their eyes) to make them confess. One of the suspects died under torture and the three others, when released, complained to the *gendarmerie*. The Zairean state is opposed to both witchcraft and accusations of witchcraft; but in a murder case, no prosecution under the law can be brought unless the head of the victim's family lays a charge. The victim in this case was the pastor's father and the pastor was now head of the family; and he laid no charge that would incriminate himself. So the murder went unpunished and the pastor continued his fight against adultery and swearing.

In other respects, too, life in Zaire was difficult. Until recently, the postage on a letter to Europe was more than a post office clerk's weekly wage, with the result that the clerk in John's village had not only steamed the stamps off his letters, but had tried to sell John back his own letters. The clerk's exactions had grown less since his weekly wage was increased to four letters to Europe, and *some* letters had of late even been known to reach their destinations.

The soldiers had become more reasonable ever since they too began to receive their wages. The government's previous method of paying them was to enact a sudden regulation with which it was impossible for the population to comply, thus giving the soldiers the opportunity to exact 'fines'. It was once decreed overnight that thenceforth all motor vehicles must carry a fire extinguisher, at a time when, of course, fire extinguishers were completely unavailable in Zaire. For some weeks the soldiers enjoyed a large income from this source alone: until people started painting aerosol cans red and pretending to the dumb soldiery that they were fire extinguishers.

John's mission was in Mobutu's home province and the people there were fiercely proud of him. That he had become one of the world's richest men was a cause for celebration rather than for recrimination. It showed he was a great leader. If he had a luxurious villa in Geneva, apartments in Paris, houses in Brussels and bank accounts in Zurich, it was all to the greater glory of Zaire. At least there was one Zairean of whom the world took note; and the Zaireans, not long ago the most despised and humiliated of people, lived vicariously in the deference accorded their leader – knowing nothing of the laughter he evoked behind his back.

On the third day out from Kisangani, we steamed into Lisala, the small town near John and Jennifer's mission. Lisala was Mobutu's birthplace and he had decided to honour the town by expropriating the villas of its prominent citizens that overlooked the port from a small green hill. He was going to build a palace for himself. Compensation had been promised but was as yet unpaid, and work on the palace had not begun because the project was not as dear to Mobutu's heart as the transformation of Gbadolite, a hundred and fifty miles to the north, on the border with the Central African Republic. Though born in Lisala, Mobutu's ancestral home was Gbadolite and, as everyone knows, Africans are deeply respectful of their ancestors. Therefore, Mobutu had decided to transform Gbadolite from an obscure settlement into the Las Vegas of equatorial Africa. In honour of his ancestors, an international hotel and a five star casino-hotel had been constructed; it only needed a clientele to complete the scheme.

The missionaries were welcomed back by pupils from their school: formal education being a prolonged and uncertain process in Africa, they were of every age between ten and thirty. Could it be that the weedy and undernourished-looking children would grow into the strapping and magnificently-muscled young men who jumped confidently into the water and swam out to meet the pirogue that took the still pale missionaries from the boat to the landing stage?

I waved goodbye to the missionaries from the lower deck, more for the sake of social convention than for any intimacy that had grown between us. We had not discussed religion directly, but they were sensitive to the odour of scepticism. Meanwhile, the chief steward refreshed his gavial with a bucket of water aimed between its jaws, and checked it for signs of life by poking it in the eye with a stick.

The Congo River, it has been said, inspires two things: fine writing and boredom. The two, of course, are intimately connected.

The width of the river, its slow, inexorable progress through a flat, steamy, monotonous landscape upon which Man even yet has had little impact, serves as a continuous reminder of one's physical insignificance. The climate, the vastness, the inactivity both enforced and voluntary, raise the 'big' questions in any mind in the slightest inclined towards them. Minds uncluttered by an illusion of purpose, or by the surface froth of mere existence, readily turn to the ultimate but unanswerable questions of philosophy. On the Congo, even a prosperous pork butcher would ask, 'What is it all for?'

The boredom of the Congo of fine writing is deep and penetrating: ontological in its implications. Yet my Congo was different from that of the three famous novels in English about it: *Heart of Darkness*, *A Burnt-Out Case* and *A Bend in the River*. I was not sufficiently alone: *en route*, the *Colonel Kokolo* had picked up two more satellite barges, rotting and rusting hulks, and the resulting ensemble was more like a floating slum than a mere vessel. All around, from dawn until deep into the night, was evidence of concentrated effort and high endeavour: loading and unloading, cooking and washing, turtle and fish-eviscerating, bargaining over dried snake, the portage of huge baskets squirming with fat, black-headed pus-coloured grubs the size of a thumb, the drying of goatskins stretched over the grille of the engine room – the 'big' questions held no fascination for the great majority of the passengers. And Peter, my principal companion, was not of a philo-sophical bent. The coffee in the morning, which tasted of nothing I had ever tasted before (but could be compared with diluted fish soup), might have provoked a sombre man to morbid reflection: but it merely reminded Peter of the espresso machine he had lately bought at home for $2000, not because he drank a lot of coffee, far from it, he drank only one cup a week because he was afraid of cancer of the pancreas, but for the sake of his friends who might drop by.

In the evening, when the sky turned the colours of a fine opal (an Australian stone), and the river was transcendently calm, and the banks on either side were a mile away, and the little islands of water hyacinth bobbed gently on the faint swell, Peter and I did not talk of Man's Redemption, of appearance and reality, of Platonic essences and Pascal's bet: we talked of *Côte d'Or* chocolate. For, as everyone knows, Belgian chocolate is particularly good; and Peter maintained that, as a former Belgian colony, it must be available at every provincial town. Mind you, he warned, not all *Côte d'Or* chocolate is of the same quality: it has varying percentages of cocoa solids; and, speaking for himself, he would only buy that whose percentage was greater than thirty. In its own way, our conversation was serious.

Not that I escaped philosophy altogether. The boat had taken on board a group of young trainee officers in the Zairean armed forces. They travelled second class, while the already commissioned officers travelled first. The trainees were a studious lot, spending all their day reading on the topmost deck. Before long I was engaged by two of them in conversation, one called Abondombo who, alone among them, had a stupid face, the face of a man one could readily imagine committing an atrocity on orders from above, though he was just as ready to be friendly; the other, Abecoli, an intelligent and sensitive-looking man who, to my amazement, was reading Descartes.

'A soldier who reads Descartes?' I said.

Abecoli had no vocation as a soldier. But he had studied politics at university, and it had convinced him that in Africa only the military could effect change and modernization. Democracy as it was known in America and Europe was not possible in African conditions: the people were too parochial and ignorant. They were too easily swayed by demagogues who promised them the earth. Therefore, in Africa the army would have to rule for a long time to come, which was why he had joined up. He was interested in politics, not war.

'So I am speaking to the future president of Zaire,' I said.

A faint smile fibrillated on his lips.

'Perhaps,' he said.

I had guessed his ambition and he admitted it.

'But why Descartes?' I asked.

'I must prepare myself from first principles.'

'I am president, therefore I am rich?'

Abecoli laughed. Abondombo looked bemused: he couldn't follow our conversation, which perhaps was just as well. He would have made an excellent sergeant. He drifted off for a time.

Of course, Abecoli wanted only to save his country.

'From what?' I asked.

The usual things: poverty, ignorance, disease.

'And Mobutu?'

He said he was too young as yet to think of the presidency in any concrete way. First he must graduate as an officer.

We were joined by an air force lieutenant, a tall, lean man with Nilotic features. The future president saluted him with a stamp of the feet, relaxed and then shook him warmly by the hand. They were friends: but I noticed how, among soldiers throughout Africa, the impersonal, cold imported European salute was always followed by a handshake, as if the soldiers wanted to remind themselves that they were Africans first and members of an alien institution only second.

The lieutenant also was a highly intelligent man, whose face was quick and mobile. He was a trained radar engineer, though there was no radar to speak of in Zaire. He was too highly-specialized to have any hope of promotion, especially as he had no personal or tribal connections to help him on the upward path. He wanted to leave the air force to start a civilian business, repairing videos and the like; but he would have had to buy himself out and he had no hope of accumulating enough money on his air force pay. When not actually laughing, his face had a rather melancholy cast.

He had done four years' professional training in France.

'So you are as much French as Zairean,' I said.

He was greatly flattered. Among other things, he had learnt how to eat in France. The Zaireans ate to fill their stomachs, the French to be transported to paradise. It was something of which he had ceased to speak to his fellow-countrymen, for they were incapable of understanding unless they had seen and tasted for themselves.

I asked him whether he had been well-treated in France, fearing that he might recall only humiliations. On the contrary, his eyes lit up: he had had no difficulty in finding women, and he had been paid more by the French government than they paid French nationals of the same rank.

'So you came home a rich man,' I said.

He shook his head and then laughed.

'We Africans are not like you whites. We do not think of the future. We think only of today.'

It was a strange echo of the most banal of expatriate judgements on the African character. He regretted his insouciance now, his foolish belief that his good fortune was deserved and would continue for ever; but at least he had happy memories, and he laughed some more.

He had once been married, with six children, but had divorced and shortly afterwards his wife died. My professional curiosity was aroused as to the cause of her death.

'Tuberculosis,' he said.

I expressed surprise, and said I had treated a large number of cases: nowadays only a very small proportion of consumptives died. His wife, however, had not sought any kind of medical treatment until she was on her deathbed. The wasting nature of the disease, the slow melting away of her flesh, the night sweats, had persuaded her she was the victim of magic, and for eighteen months she had gone from one witch-doctor to another.

I said I was sorry to hear of such an unnecessary death; to which he replied that many Zaireans were still very primitive.

We were joined by another group of trainees, and in the course of mutual interrogation that results from such encounters, the subject of religion was raised. Most of them were protestants, two were catholics. I said I had no religion.

'But you believe in God?' they asked anxiously.

I didn't like to sound dogmatic, so I said: not really.

The trainees and the lieutenant grew excited and bombarded me with arguments. I could hardly make out what they were saying, but the strangeness of my situation struck me forcibly: I had never expected a theological debate with Zairean soldiers on the river. They argued as though their lives depended on it.

The lieutenant managed to quiet the hubbub, and decided the Socratic method was best.

'Take this boat,' he said. 'Do you think it assembled itself?'

I recognized his line of thought at once: my old friend the Argument from Design.

How much more wonderful and intricate was the Universe, he said, than this boat, how beautifully and unfailingly does its mechanism work, how miraculous that everything for our sustenance and enjoyment should be found on just one little planet! Did this not speak of Design and Intention? And if a boat had a boatbuilder, did the Universe not have a Universal Architect of infinitely greater skill, wisdom, beneficence, etc.?

'But the boat,' I said, 'was not built by one man. If the boat is an analogy with the universe, there is a pantheon, not one God alone.'

The air force lieutenant pointed to a pirogue approaching the steamer.

'That was made by one man,' he said.

'So!' I exclaimed. 'Now you compare the whole of the Universe with a pirogue.'

He laughed, but admitted that he was.

As is usual with such discussions, it lasted a long time – more than two hours – the search for Truth being strictly subordinate to the desire to win. From theology it was but a short step to the supernatural, and here again I played the part of the sceptic. If these soldiers had ever wavered in their belief in God, their belief in spirits and the supernatural was as solid as a rock. It was something for them self-evident, requiring no proof, as real as the rain or the earth. The lieutenant adopted a tone of careful reason.

'I have been to France,' he said. 'I am qualified as a radar technician. Radar is a very advanced science. I have mastered it and I understand its power. But I am also an African, and I know there are things which your science cannot explain.'

I agreed.

'There will always be such things,' I said. 'But take your wife: because she was ignorant she believed her illness was caused by magic. In fact, anything we can't understand can be explained by magic. There are many Zaireans who would think your radar was magic, but *you* know it is not magic.'

'You whites are very clever,' he replied. 'But why is it you always deny us Africans our own special kind of knowledge? We admit your science, but you deny what *we* know.'

His speech met with general approval. There was something agonized about it, a desperate plea for recognition. I should have let the matter drop; but in my eagerness for dialectical triumph I said something wounding.

'You say Africans have special knowledge of the supernatural?' I asked. 'And they know how to make use of it?'

'Yes,' they all eagerly agreed.

'Then how is it that Africans are the poorest and most powerless people in the world?'

My words had the effect almost of an electric shock. I regretted them at once: but I was impressed by the calm and dignified way in which they were taken, the initial impact over. After all, I expected African intellectuals – and these soldiers *were* intellectuals – to be as prickly and defensive as their politicians.

'What you say is true,' said the lieutenant. 'But still we know what we know. We have knowledge that others do not have.'

Our discussion was brought to a timely end by two choirs which formed on the deck to sing hymns as the sun went down. They took up opposite corners of the deck and soon established themselves as rivals. One was a protestant, the other a catholic, choir, and they sang different hymns at the same time, producing a musical effect that was less than pleasing. The catholics had an advantage: not only was their choir larger, but they had a tambourine and were permitted to dance as well as sing, a frivolity the protestants forwent. The officers and I, tired by our intellectual exertions, went in search of beer, whose bottle tops the female sellers removed with their teeth; and by the time we returned to the deck the protestants had left the field to the catholics, whose singing now had the timbre of triumph.

The river grew ever wider as we sailed downstream. Sometimes the far banks were nothing but faint green lines dividing the river from the sky; at others we were close enough to watch the villages, the children splashing in the river, the women preparing food, the men out in their pirogues. Sometimes a passenger, seeing his home village, would dive off the boat and strike out for the bank, even if it were a mile away. Their swimming seemed somehow full of joy and overflowing good spirits.

At times we passed through floating islands of water hyacinths, the bows of the boat tearing cruelly through the gentle, silent green archipelagos. The water hyacinth is an attractive plant, with an elegant mauve flower. It adds a pleasing dash of colour to a landscape whose restrained palette becomes a trifle monotonous. But at one time this prolific aquatic weed threatened by its luxuriant overgrowth to halt entirely the traffic, and therefore the commerce, of the river. I was told the hyacinth was not native to the river, but had been introduced by a European who had a villa on the banks, and who thought some water hyacinths would be nice. Within a few years they had spread hundreds of miles up and down the river, clogging the navigation channels.

More significantly than whether the story is true, it is *believed* to be true. It symbolizes the almost casual irruption of Europe into Africa, and the profound and lasting effects that even the most vapid and banal of European actions has on a continent in some ways still as vulnerable as a new-born child.

After a few days on board we began to feel a desire to have the solidity of land once more under our feet. A stop at Mbandaka, formerly Coquilhatville, just above the confluence of the Congo and the Oubangui, gave us the opportunity. The *Michelin* map, by far the best, marks the town in bold upper case, leading the uninitiated to expect something of a metropolis: which it no doubt is, by comparison with other settlements between Kisangani and Kinshasa. Peter and I scrambled over the barges to reach the quayside where a crowd had gathered, the arrival of the boat being an event in an otherwise eventless town. We were avid for fresh fruit and vegetables, of which we had seen none save some sour oranges since leaving Kisangani, and also for *Côte d'Or* chocolate, the desire for which we had raised to a ruling passion by repeated musings upon its manifold fine qualities. Peter was even thinking of starting another business to import it wholesale into Australia.

Turning back to look at the boat from the quay, Peter thought it would make a good photograph. As he put his camera back into its case I said:

'Now you'll probably be arrested as a spy.'

Sure enough, as we were leaving the quay for the town, a young man dressed all in black and wearing dark glasses interposed himself between us and the exit.

'You took a photograph,' he said.

'So fucking what?' asked Peter.

'It is forbidden to take photographs in the port,' said the man in black.

'Tell him I only took a picture of the boat. You can buy postcards of the boat.'

But the man remained adamant that photographs were prohibited, and added they could be useful to an enemy of Zaire, though he did not specify how.

'Give him fifty Zaires,' I advised Peter. 'That's all he's after.'

Peter was incensed.

'Tell him he's not getting any fucking bribes out of me, so he can fuck off.'

Translation was not really necessary.

'Who the fuck is he anyway?'

I asked him who he was, and he said he was a member of the security service. I asked for proof of his identity: he had none but said he would take us to his chief. I repeated my advice to Peter to end the affair with fifty Zaires; the higher up he went, the more expensive it would become.

'Fuck, no!' exclaimed Peter, and stormed back to the boat to return his camera to his cabin, leaving me with the secret policeman.

His chief, as it happened, was strolling along the quay. He wore a grey safari suit, stretched at the front by a paunch. When he heard what had transpired his face took on the aspect of a man assuming a heavy responsibility.

They boarded the boat together while I remained on the quay. I watched them searching for Peter's cabin, they by now having attracted a comet's tail of followers. From a distance it was like a scene from a thriller. When they found Peter there was much gesticulating and, from the look of it, much mutually incomprehensible shouting too.

I rushed to the boat to see whether I could smooth things over, but by the time I reached the scene Peter had so antagonized the two men that the situation was irrecoverable. They were removing the film from his camera with expressions of grim patriotic determination.

'It's got all my pictures of pygmies and volcanoes,' said Peter, now much distressed. 'If they take it I might as well not have been there.'

I alternately tried to bribe the chief in the safari suit and demanded to see his identification. But I carried no conviction, and the two men walked off the boat with the film.

'Pigs! Half-brains!' shouted Peter as they departed.

After that, our little promenade in Mbandaka gave Peter not much pleasure. He brooded on the loss of his film. Had they *really* thought we were spies? And if they did, to what end did they think we could put a picture of the *Colonel Kokolo* at Mbandaka quayside? Or had it been, as seemed more likely, merely an attempt to extract money from us? Was it their failure to do so that angered them? (Peter forgot his manner had been less than conciliatory). He derived some consolation – but not much – from their inability to have the film processed, since it was of a special, supersensitive type.

The sleepy, decaying colonial streets of the town did not charm him, neither did the pleasant atmosphere of drowsy immobility sweeten his bitterness. There were few fruits or vegetables for sale – some ready-squashed tomatoes, small onions, chili peppers and rambutans, closely resembling the lychee but not so good. We also found chocolate in an Indian store, kept in a padlocked refrigerator. It contained only twenty per cent cocoa solids, but Peter bought it all the same.

We returned to the boat.

'The moral of the story,' I said (apart from never to take photographs in Africa that anyone could conceive as being of strategic importance, and always to treat officials as though they performed difficult tasks with great skill), 'is beware of Africans in safari suits or dark glasses.'

There was a large crowd to watch the boat leave Mbandaka. When we were three hundred yards from the bank a pirogue with two men raced towards us. In the bubbling swell created by the churning engine of the *Colonel Kokolo* as it changed direction, the pirogue overturned and the two men were thrown into the water. They thrashed about for a considerable time, trying to find their submerged pirogue. The passengers and the crowd along the quay watched with mounting excitement as the men grew desperate. Encouragement was shouted, and not very useful advice. It seemed the men might drown but suddenly they found their pirogue, turned it right way up and climbed into it with evident relief. Great was the cheering from the boat and quayside.

'Boo!' shouted Peter. 'Shame! Boo!'

The river was soon so wide it was difficult to believe it was a river at all, and not a lake. But the pirogues continued to join us with their wares, the bales of smoked monkeys looking like Peking ducks with human shrunken heads attached. A woman with a single chicken to sell, who rowed her pirogue alone, capsized. She panicked, not for herself but for her chicken, which was not a strong swimmer. She screamed, though whether from grief or to give the chicken instructions, I cannot say. At any rate, the passengers found it highly entertaining. In the end, she salvaged both her chicken and her pirogue, swimming to the latter with the former held high above her head, squawking in terror. There was tumultuous applause from the boat and her panic turned to laughter in an instant.

Michel, the cripple, called a photographer with a Polaroid camera to take our photograph together. He wanted one, he said, because our journey had been for him *inoubliable*. In that case, I said, he didn't need a photograph, but my argument was not accepted. Not surprisingly, it was I who paid for this souvenir. Then, as we were only a day's journey from Kinshasa, he asked me to give him the only warm clothes I had with me. It would represent no hardship for me, he said; as a European, I could just buy some more; but for him, it was the chance of a lifetime (at least until the next boat sailed). Once more he asked me to pray with him, but I said my French was not up to it.

As Kinshasa drew near, Abondombo – the stupid cadet officer – began to hover round. I felt rather like a rich uncle who, fatally ill, begins to receive visits from his nephews.

The forest gave way to savannah, miles of rolling grassland without evidence of cultivation. I took a last tour of the boat and its appendages on the evening before our arrival. When I returned to my cabin I found Peter, rather drunk, and Paul, the Dutchman, deep in anxious conversation.

Paul, it appeared, had felt the need to 'feed his head', and had used Peter's cabin for the feast. Two army officers had smelt it as they passed, and entered the cabin. At first, Paul denied it was marijuana. Then he admitted it and had paid them 200 Zaires. Peter had come along and abused the officers in broad Strine, with such good effect they felt obliged, they said, to take the matter further. They said they would have Peter and Paul arrested on arrival in Kinshasa. Peter was too drunk to grasp the situation fully – he swayed as though the boat were in the Bay of Biscay during a storm – but Paul said he thought nothing would come of it, though his face told another story. The prospect of several years in a Zairean gaol was not, to put it mildly, alluring.

I told Peter to go to bed, and Paul drifted back anxiously to his quarters. The two army officers knocked on my door. They wanted to talk to me about my friends. Smoking marijuana was a crime in Zaire, they said, and foreigners were not exempt. But it was Peter who puzzled them. Why was he so insulting? They were educated men, their fathers held responsible positions, they were not fresh out of the jungle, they had been to Brussels and Paris.

Yes, yes, I said, I could see that. The trouble was, Peter was drunk. He didn't know what he was saying. Besides, Australians – here I faltered a little, for linguistic and other reasons – Australians were famed for the directness of their speech, sometimes a little too vigorous perhaps, but not without its charm, and when one got to know them they were the kindest and most generous of people.

The young officers looked sceptical. We'll see in the morning, they said.

We steamed through the Stanley Pool, where the river is fifteen miles wide, and the skyscrapers of Kinshasa gleamed white in the distance, strangely sepulchral. The officers wished us good morning, and smiled as though nothing had happened. They were happy to be 200 Zaires the richer.

SIX

Kinshasa and Congo Brazzaville

While struggling to alight from the boat and hemmed in by people and luggage, Peter had a gold pen taken from his shirt pocket. He shouted, but to no avail. The theft was executed with almost admirable skill, the thief waiting for his victim's moment of greatest immobility.

Kinshasa is quite unlike anything else in Zaire. Its central boulevards, where foreigners and the Zairean élite live, are clean and spacious. The roads are not potholed. The modern architecture, while in no way distinguished, is far from unpleasant. The colonial villas that remain have been maintained. The gardens are well-kept, even the public ones. Muhammed Ali's remark – 'Zaire's got to be great, I've never seen so many Mercedes' – seemed for a moment a shade less fatuous.

But Kinshasa is a city of three millions, not many of whom live in air-conditioned, marble-faced villas. Abondombo, the stupid-looking cadet officer, offered to show us a hotel that was both reasonable and clean, somewhere away from the city centre. It was in the ring of slums that, apart from the river bank, encompass the city. No doubt an enthusiast for progress, for whom it was a simple matter of potable water, vaccination and more schools, would have been appalled by the visual and olfactory evidence of urban deprivation; but the sight of children relieving themselves in what would be gutters if roads were constructed, no longer surprises me or causes me to itch with a town-planner's passion for sensible sewers. In spite of all the statistics proving their wretchedness, these people obstinately refused to *look* miserable. Even the street hawkers, armed with half a packet of Marlboro or a few sticks of goat kebab, who should have been seething with anger at this waste of their lives, smiled as I turned down their merchandise, and laughed among themselves. It was most irresponsible of them. Impressions can, of course, be very misleading.

Abondombo, rather surprisingly (and suspiciously), decided to stay in our hotel which, though cheap enough, still charged a not inconsiderable proportion of his monthly salary for a stay of only one night. One night was all he wanted to stay: and sure enough when he left I discovered my camera and $550 in travellers' cheques were gone.

Meanwhile Peter and I wandered the city. We found groceries with an odd selection of luxuries, including asparagus from South Africa and Pilsner from the German breweries of Luderitz in South West Africa. Most of the customers were white, the wives of aid workers and diplomats, and many brought their houseboys with them to carry their purchases to the car outside. Except for the presence of an occasional member of the Zairean élite with a taste for refined foods, the shops might have been the grocery in the fictional town of Luc in *A Burnt-Out Case*:

> The high vexed colonial voices, each angry about something different, rose around him, competing for attention . . . 'But you simply must have potatoes,' a woman's voice was saying. 'How dare you deny it? They came in on yesterday's plane. The pilot told me.' She was obviously playing her last card, when she appealed to the European manager. 'I am expecting the Governor to dinner . . .'

Peter had two problems to solve in Kinshasa. The first was to change money and the second to obtain a visa for Cameroon. His joy at having bought Japanese yen the month before its spectacular rise in value changed to chagrin by the time we reached the sixth bank in the city that did not take yen.

'But it's a major world currency, you dodos,' said Peter to the bemused bank clerks.

Eventually he found a bank that seemed willing to accept the all-conquering yen. Peter signed a cheque for 50,000 ($300), but at the last minute the bank decided it did not, after all, accept them. The rate of exchange published on its notice board was for theoretical information only.

'What the fuck am I going to do with this cheque now?' asked Peter of the uncomprehending manager.

His luck at the Cameroonian embassy was not much better. It was an impressively modern building, as befitted one of the most successful of African countries, but the lady in a canary yellow suit deputed to answer enquiries moved as though her joints were excruciatingly inflamed. She was not in the mood for giving visa application forms and she asked Peter, through me, why he did not apply for a visa in Paris.

'Because I've never been to Paris. I'm Australian,' he replied.

This did not strike her as a cogent reason at all. She suggested Peter went to Paris and apply there. Apparently the call in Cameroon's latest five year plan to encourage tourism had not yet reached her.

'But I've got a ticket for Cameroon,' said Peter, as she picked up a magazine to read.

Visas, she reiterated, could be granted only in Paris: and anyway, it was time for lunch. It was lucky for her there was a strong counter.

Out in the street I suggested to Peter he try again next day, when her mood might have changed for the better.

'Jeeze no,' he said. 'I'm sick of these half-brains. I think I'll go to South America.'

He found a flight to Rio, via Lisbon. But even then his troubles were not over. The plane, which had come from Johannesburg, was hijacked to Lusaka. Fortunately, no-one was hurt, except for loss of sleep; and in a postcard from Rio after the event, Peter told me he was on Portuguese television for a day. 'I was the handsomest passenger they had on T.V. footage,' he wrote.

I decided to move to the Intercontinental for a day or two. Large, impersonal, luxurious and usually vulgar international hotels (with no greater gesture towards geographical location than a portrait of the president in the lobby and an ethnic artifact or two) play a disproportionately big part in the lives of undeveloped nations. They are generally truer centres of power, where more real decisions are taken, than the rubber-stamp national assemblies. They are also a focus of ambition and a model of how life should be lived. Since Kinshasa is not a city that attracts tourists, there were two classes of guest at the hotel: businessmen and American marines. Perhaps the latter were there to test whether they could withstand the torture of continual background music; while the former met rich Zaireans over lunch to carve up the country's wealth between them.

Ties are no longer worn by Zaireans, not even by the élite. In the name of authenticity, a new national dress has been designed, like a safari suit but with a high collar. In ordering this change of dress Mobutu by implication compares himself to Mao and Nehru. The desired connotation of the Mobutu suit is presumably national and egalitarian: but there is all the difference in the world between the foodstained variety, shiny with wear, unwashed for months, worn by the poor clerk, and the beautifully-tailored variety, of the finest cloth, set off with a matching cravat and handkerchief of Italian silk, worn by the élite.

It is not only money, in quantities too vast for even the average millionaire to understand, that Mobutu has appropriated. He has appropriated the symbols and cant of revolution. His party – the only permitted party, of course – is called the *Mouvement Populaire de la Révolution*. He has made every African abandon his European name and adopt an authentic African one; but, mixing his metaphors as it were, he decreed they should address one another as *Citoyen*. Mobutu wears leopardskin hats and sometimes feathers for authenticity, but goes to Paris to buy them and when he has a toothache he flies to Europe in a special jumbo jet, because there are no dentists in Zaire worthy of treating the presidential teeth.

I discovered the theft of my camera and money while in the Intercontinental. I let out an exclamation of rage which my hermetically sealed and soundproofed room reduced to a strangled sob. What irked me most, after the initial shock, during which I vowed never to befriend anyone again, certainly not in Africa, was that I should now, for insurance purposes, have to report my loss to the police: a process which I anticipated would be as timeconsuming as it was futile.

I went to the local police station as directed by the lordly and disdainful hotel doorman. There were three policemen there, their equipment consisting of a table and two chairs. They were pleasant, indeed sympathetic, but hopelessly drunk. They would gladly have provided me with a report, had I brought them a pen and a piece of paper. They suggested I return next day with the requisite stationery; but I decided instead to go to the *Bureau de Recherches* of the *Guarde Civile*, a division of the army. By then, I was almost reconciled to my loss by the excuse it gave to see inside an army installation and even began to think of the affair as a small adventure without which the crossing of Africa would have been incomplete.

The *Guarde Civile* was located in a fortress next to the market, down streets in which Lebanese traders hawked all kinds of electronic gadgetry – the new beads of Africa. At the gate of the fortress stood a man with an Uzi, whose weapon had quite replaced his larynx, inasmuch as he communicated entirely by short, sharp jerks of its barrel. The passing crowds did not linger outside the *Guarde Civile*. A Japanese sports car, driven by a senior officer, went through the gates and I took the opportunity to slip inside. The senior officer received salutes from everyone and then shook hands with them. He came over to me to ask what I wanted. As he spoke a column of recruits went trotting by, their hands held on their heads. This division of the army looked less of a disorganized rabble than I had expected: though whether they would have disintegrated under fire I could not, of course, say.

I was directed to an office down a corridor in which civilians and soldiers strode with purpose. There was much clicking of typewriters, and everyone carried a file. In the office, however, things were more relaxed – the purposiveness had been for show. One wall was covered entirely by a soothing photograph of a Canadian maple forest in the fall, golden-leaved on a golden afternoon. The eight occupants of the office, all in civilian clothes, appeared to have nothing to do and bade me welcome. They cleared a place for me and told me an official report of the theft would be completed as soon as their commanding officer returned. In the meantime, the youngest of them said he wanted to practise his English, which he had been learning at night school for two years.

'Do you know Shakespeare?' he asked.

'A little.'

'*Antony and Cleopatra*? We learn *Antony and Cleopatra*.'

I quoted a few lines:

> The barge she sat in like a burnished throne,
> Burn'd on the water: the poop was beaten gold;
> Purple the sails, and so perfumed that
> The winds were love-sick with them; the oars were silver,
> Which to the tune of flutes kept stroke, and made
> The water which they beat to follow faster,
> As amorous of their strokes.

His eyes glistened with pleasure. He was nearly ecstatic. Had I committed all that to memory, he asked? English was a wonderful language and he wanted to read its literature. I said that French was also a wonderful language, with an equally wonderful literature. No, it was English he wanted to learn, he said, and Anglophone African authors he wanted to read (as well as Shakespeare). French for him was unimportant.

I had no time to investigate how he had come to this strange conclusion, or how an ordinary Zairean soldier had conceived a passion for Shakespeare (a very impressive phenomenon), since his commanding officer, a slight and stern man in a black velvet jacket, entered, whereupon everyone stood to attention. In no time at all the requested report was in my hand and, after an exchange of addresses, I was once more in the military parade ground. There, another column of raw recruits fresh off the streets, some of them barefoot, was being made to crawl over the concrete ground, under imaginary barbed wire fences. The gates swung open to let me leave, and the passing crowds of shoppers, hawkers and idlers looked nervously in.

Along the boulevard leading to the hotel I bought, in a bookshop frequented only by expatriates, a biography of Chekhov. There were no books about Zaire, its history, geography, flora, fauna, past, present or future; but it so happens that when I travel I wish always to read about somewhere quite other than where I am. I suppose it is yet another manifestation of the restlessness that causes one to travel in the first place, a restlessness that is never satisfied and often consumes uselessly all other passions. But Chekhov's life is an inspiration wherever one is. The question of how a character of such rare beauty (to say nothing of his genius) could have emerged from the physical and moral squalor of his childhood is one that will never be answered. It gives muted hope in an age when governments wish to involve us all as accomplices in their crimes. But whether whole nations or continents can by effort of will emerge from physical and moral squalor, as Chekhov did, is uncertain.

At my next stop, to collect my visa from the embassy of the People's Republic of the Congo, I noticed on the table a letter from the Ethiopian embassy to the Congolese ambassador. It was addressed to *Comrade His Excellency the Ambassador*. Here was another confusion visited upon Africa by the adoption of European conventions. As I waited for my passport, I had great fun in imagining an agonized meeting at the Ethiopian embassy to decide whether *Comrade His Excellency the Ambassador* or *His Excellency the Comrade Ambassador* was the correct form of address. I imagined all the power of convoluted Marxist dialectics – the sovereign method of proving whatever it is that has to be proved – being brought to bear on the question, and the punishment as Enemies of the People of those who plumped for the wrong answer. The letter was probably an invitation to dinner.

On my last night in Kinshasa I watched television. I had one of the country's 12,000 sets all to myself. There was a re-enactment in dance of the 1984 presidential election which Mobutu won with unsurprising ease. From that date, most buses and taxis sported a sticker: *Zaire dit Oui au Maréchal*, Zaire says Yes to the Marshal. With its usual firm grasp of local reality, the IMF had insisted on the election as a condition of a much-needed loan. The method of balloting was, however, distinctly curious. Not only was Mobutu the sole candidate, but a vote in his favour was recorded by depositing a yellow card in the ballot box, a vote against him by depositing a red card. Just in case the presence of the security police inside the polling stations was not sufficient reminder, at many locations only yellow cards were made available, the red ones being delivered after the election was over. Mobutu 'won' the election with a higher percentage of votes than ever. The IMF was satisfied, and agreed the loan.

The dance recaptured the Marshal's famous victory. Swaying ladies with vast wobbly breasts in tee-shirts tore up the red papers while athletic young men advanced rhythmically towards the ballot box, two steps forward and one back, climactically recording their votes for the Marshal. The dancing was accompanied by the ululations of a choir. A caption rose from the bottom of the screen: 'Zaire: A Happy People Who Dance and Sing'.

Every hour from eight in the morning till four in the afternoon a ferry crosses the river from Kinshasa to Brazzaville. Gone are the good old days when the two cities were not on speaking terms, when it was easier to go to Europe than to cross the river, and when, inspired by ideological differences, the two countries nearly went to war. Armed incursions were now the private prerogative of soldiers of either country disgruntled by the non-payment of their wages, who compensated themselves at the expense of the peasants on the other side of the river.

Entering the compound of the ferry terminal, a young man in casual clothes demanded to examine my passport.

'And who,' I asked, 'are you?'

He showed me a plastic identity card.

'Don't you have secret policemen in England?' he asked.

'Yes,' I replied.

'*Eh bien,*' he said, in the tone of one who, against the odds, has proved a difficult Euclidean theorem. 'I am also a member of the C.I.A. Follow me.'

He led me to a small tin hut containing the Anti-Fraud Squad, in the person of a plump girl stretched the length of a bench, who was not asleep but not quite awake either. It was very hot in the tin hut.

'Search his luggage,' ordered the secret policeman.

'Must I?' she asked.

'Yes.'

'Why?'

She struggled to raise herself a little, but invisible bands kept her tethered to the bench.

'Please open your bag, monsieur,' she said feebly.

I opened my bag and she let her forearm drop into it. She tried to stir the contents, but the resistance was too great. She was still lying down.

'Are you ill?' I asked. 'I'm a doctor.'

'Tired, monsieur,' she replied.

'Why?'

'Too much work.'

She said I could close my bag now. The secret policeman wished me *bon voyage* and said he hoped I would return soon to Zaire. This was seconded by the Anti-Fraud Squad who said I was very kind.

I joined the queue waiting to board the ferry, which was now approaching the Zairean bank. An official was not satisfied with the queue, which looked perfectly orderly to me, and waved a baton at it angrily to get it to move elsewhere – all except me, that is, who was permitted to stay where I was. The resulting chaos established the importance of the official beyond doubt, and he was mollified. Then another official came to search the queue for Zairean currency, whose export was forbidden. There was a loud argument over a Malian refugee's (allegedly) last ten Zaires (fifteen cents), an argument resolved in favour of the official who took possession of the money in the name of the *Mouvement Populaire*, and presumably spent it in his own name. The boat by then had docked, and a Zairean in a smart Mobutu suit, with dark patches of sweat spreading under his arms, drove his brand-new Mercedes with tinted windows on to the car deck, there to be much admired by the barefoot passengers travelling second class. The owner sat next to me on the upper deck with his attaché case on his knees, which he opened to take out a gold pen. Neatly packed solid inside his case were bundles of 500 Zaire notes, crisp and freshly printed.

The ride across the river was smooth. As the half-American skyline of Kinshasa receded, the greener bank of Brazzaville, less pretentious, drew nearer. In the middle of the river were some small islands, upon which were beached scores of rotting hulks. As we drew into Brazzaville's small port, a vast red hoarding came into view. It claimed the Revolution had given the Congolese people complete serenity of heart and mind. Originally it had claimed much more than this, but unhappily several of the hoarding's panels were missing, leaving only the skeleton behind and an unfinished exclamation: Glory to . . .

The complete serenity of heart and mind had recently been disturbed by student riots in Brazzaville, when an undisclosed number of students were shot dead. The government, in response to IMF pressure to reduce the number of its employees by more than a half, had withdrawn the guarantee of civil service employment to graduates, and replaced the automatic system of grants to students by competitive examinations. However sensible the measures were from the abstract economic point of view, they did not meet with universal acclaim; and it was odd to see how two African countries with ideologies as different as Zaire's and the Congo's came to the same point. In Africa, ideologists propose, but the IMF disposes.

The people getting off the boat and those getting on seethed like two immiscible liquids heated up: there was a lot of movement, but not much progress. An official in a drab blue uniform grew angry at the sight of me, and snatched my passport from my hand. Having established himself as a man not to be trifled with, he became only moderately unpleasant. I was relieved to see, however, that he did not treat his returning compatriots with much greater friendliness.

Brazzaville, in atmosphere if not in population, is still a small city, with a few incongruously large modern buildings. In fact, the Congo is one of the most urbanized countries in Africa: more than half the population (of only two million) lives in the capital or the port of Pointe Noire; and the proportion increases daily. No blandishments or appeals to patriotic feeling have been able to reverse this urbanization, despite food shortages in the cities and a plenitude of land with which to rectify them.

My first evening in Brazzaville I went to a Russian restaurant I had noticed, called *Raspoutine*. There were tables on the pavement and a large, crudely-drawn bear painted on the window. The proprietress was seated at the bar, on a high stool, laughing loudly. She was a peroxided blonde, heavily made-up in garish colours, broad shouldered and hipped, her women's wrestling champion figure squeezed into tight clothes and a miniskirt short enough to have been fashionable twenty years before (when she was a young woman). She spoke in Russian.

It was she who served me my meal.

'Excuse me, madame,' I said, 'but I am curious as to how a Russian comes to live in Brazzaville.'

She sat down at once at my table. I guessed that melancholy underlay her barmaidish jollity; but then I am predisposed to see melancholy everywhere.

'I married an African,' she said.

'A student in Russia?'

'The Ukraine.'

Of course, the marriage had been a disaster. It had broken up when they returned to the Congo, where her husband, despite all his prior protestations, expected her to be a true African wife, subordinate and incurious as to his long absences from home. They had a daughter, now fifteen. I caught a glimpse of her behind the bar: she too was frozen in the mode of the mid-sixties.

The proprietress was still a Soviet citizen. I asked her why she did not return to the Ukraine. She shrugged her shoulders, insofar as her lingerie permitted.

'I'm used to it here,' she said. 'When I go back to Kiev, everyone is rushing about, I can't do it any more. I haven't been back to Europe for several years.'

She spoke of Europe as though its divisions were insignificant by comparison with the gulf separating it from Africa.

'But aren't you lonely?'

She shrugged again.

'Of course,' I continued optimistically, 'you have all the people at the Soviet embassy.'

'They never come here. They never speak to me.'

'Why not?'

She gave me an old-fashioned look. Was she an agent of the KGB, I wondered? Was Brazzaville a centre of international espionage, like Istanbul during the war? She changed the subject by asking me what I was doing in Brazzaville. I told her I had practised as a doctor in Tanzania and was now returning home by travelling across Africa.

'So you are not staying here?'

'No.'

'I thought so,' she said in a language more expressive than mere French. 'The good ones go, the shit stays behind.'

She roused herself to go to an African customer who, having studied in Russia, wanted to practise his Russian. He was completely fluent, able to enjoy backslapping jokes in it, laughing with the deep bass laughter of an African big man. From time to time, she glanced across from his table to mine.

The potency of three beers surprised me when I got up to leave. In spite of a certain unsteadiness, however, I felt mellow. Fortunately, the streets of Brazzaville at night are quiet and unthreatening. I passed a café where expatriates gathered each evening to drink the beer of boredom, and I heard English spoken there. I wanted to ask the whereabouts of a Scottish engineer I had known in Tanzania who had come to the Congo to build a road, but I was too shy to interrupt. (Later I learnt the engineer had long since gone: the project had been abandoned for lack of funds.)

I continued past the Soviet embassy, a colonial mansion down a tree-lined avenue. On the railings was fixed a glass-fronted noticeboard for propaganda photographs. I stopped to look at them. In mid-winter a group of Africans in overcoats and fur hats stood on some Moscow steps with a short, plump and rather bored-looking Russian. The caption read: 'A Meeting of Militants of the Soviet-Congolese Friendship Society'. How, I wondered, did one go about being militantly friendly? The next picture provided a clue. In a Kiev street a large lady of the tractor-tyre-changing type, in Ukrainian national costume, heavily made up with white powder and lipstick, had grabbed a small African and was dancing with him forcibly in the street. He looked bewildered, she faintly disgusted. She was, in short, being militantly friendly.

Across the entrance to my hotel was slung a long red banner:

WELCOME TO BRAZZAVILLE LAND OF PEACE AND DEMOCRACY

The delegates to a conference on Peace and Prosperity in Africa had arrived. They were emerging from the restaurant, where *nouvelle cuisine*, at $30 a head without drinks, was served. They were dressed in Islamic boubous or Italian suits, all beautifully tailored. To mark the occasion of the conference the reception were selling a record called *For Peace in Lebanon*. It was not disclosed how exactly the sale of this record would bring peace about, or to which faction fighting for peace the proceeds would go. In any case, sales were not brisk. The delegates stood in little knots in front of the very large photographic portrait of the President of the Republic, who used to call himself *Comrade* and wear battle fatigues and dark glasses, but has now graduated to *Son Excellence* and wearing natty double-breasted pin-striped suits and having his photo taken while resting one hand delicately on a mock Louis XV escritoire (the fulfilment, perhaps, of another condition laid down by the IMF?) The delegates talked of Peace and Prosperity while, working their way between them, prostitutes offered by unmistakable gestures to perform fellatio for them.

Fellatio for peace? It made as much sense as the posters of doves in the lifts.

I went next morning to buy a railway ticket to Mbinda, on the border of Congo with Gabon. Outside the station is a huge and hideous concrete statue of an African with short legs and a vast torso, his arms held high above his head and broken chains hanging from each wrist.

In general I mistrust rhetorical statuary, subject as it is to humbug. But the history of the Congo would excuse rhetorical excess. The territory was won for the French by an Italian count, Savorgnan de Brazza, who was personally beloved of Africans for his unusual sense of justice and fair play, which explains why there is still a Brazzaville but not a Léopoldville. Nevertheless, it was Brazza who unintentionally led the way to the holocaust that soon engulfed the territory. He grossly overestimated the wealth to be gained from a sparsely-inhabited rain forest, whetting appetites for unrealistic gain; and equally grossly underestimated the capital required to develop and administer the colony. The result was the French government refused to spend money on it (in 1900 there were 30 administrators for an area larger than

France); while concessions were granted to forty companies to exploit the produce of vast tracts of land. This they did with a viciousness that *Heart of Darkness* does not begin to convey. In some areas the population is thought to have halved within *two* years of the company regime. This policy was not even commercially successful: most of the companies never made a profit and sank without trace, except for one which survived until 1935.

I went to the British embassy, but the *chargé* was on leave, and the post was not of sufficient importance to make a *locum tenens* necessary. On the way there I passed a memorial to Lenin, a now-derelict brick wall with a statue in front of it, around which children played games. Nearby was the mausoleum of Marien Ngouabi, a radical president assassinated in circumstances still unclear, who thus achieved the status of a Martyr, his remains worthy of a perpetual, goosestepping guard. His tomb is a fine example of the socialist realism school of mausoleum architecture, betraying not the faintest glimmer of any recognizable human emotion, but only a coldhearted attempt to overwhelm the eye with the massiveness of rectangular granite and the power of the state.

A young post office worker out for a stroll attached himself to me. He was, as the Tanzanians and Nigerians say, *not on seat*. We chatted, and among the interesting things he told me was that the store in the President's home village, in the north of the country where few of the people but all of the government come from, sells caviare and champagne instead of the otherwise ubiquitous beer and sardines.

Near his place of work, to which he was regretfully returning, I noticed a painted slogan: 'Everyone Must be Worthy of His Salary, His Daily Bread.'

'And you,' I asked my post office friend, 'are you worthy of your daily bread?'

He laughed and laughed.

To enter the People's Republic of the Congo one needs a visa. To leave it one needs another visa. This system has the merit of creating work for clerks who might otherwise, as the educated but unemployed, conspire against the government. One peculiarity of the system is its inflexibility: exit visas are not granted more than a day ahead of the proposed exit, and their validity does not last for more than twenty-four hours. This precision is, of course, considerably in advance of that of transport timetables, and thus causes the traveller some anxiety, until he recalls that he can probably bribe his way out of any situation.

I did not learn of the need for an exit visa until after I had bought my train ticket. I arrived at the immigration department five minutes too late to hand in an application that would have given me a visa to coincide with my train journey. I explained my predicament to the clerk: unless he helped me, I should have to change all my arrangements.

'*Dommage*,' he said with melodramatic indifference.

'I hope you die a slow death of starvation as you deserve,' I muttered as I left. This was not quite fair: as a doctor I knew all too well the urge to disoblige an ever-importuning public.

And of course, an extra day in Brazzaville did me no lasting harm. I tried to look on it as a chance to overcome the self-imposed tyranny of time. But still in my heart the indifferent *dommage* of the clerk rankled. It outraged me that a single word from this semi-educated man of no talent – as I took him to be – should change the course of my life for a day, or even a minute.

I caught the express train from Brazzaville to Pointe Noire, along the famous – or infamous – track of which it was once said it cost a human life per sleeper to construct. At the end of the 1920s the French still used forced labour, and 15,000 labourers died. Armed with this knowledge, I felt – as the train meandered slowly towards its destination – I should experience exquisite emotions and reflect profoundly on history. But the little girl next to me used my ribs as a target for her elbow, and the other passengers seemed more preoccupied with the price of segments of *La Vache Qui Rit* processed cheese than with any historical associations of the train ride.

Brazzaville was more extensive than I had suspected: the shacks accompanied the railway line for many miles. But once we had left Brazzaville the land was deserted: an open heath unexploited by man, forested only where a river cut a valley through the land. As a feat of engineering, the line seemed minor. Why had so many died constructing it? Disease, cruelty, neglect and disorganization rather than any inherent difficulties in the terrain.

I alighted at a village called Monte Belo, to catch the branch line train going north. It was mid-afternoon, overcast but not likely to rain, and the village was depressingly familiar in its ugliness. The track divided it into two. On one side was the market, selling the universal trade goods of Africa, with a couple of Indian shops with slightly more substantial stocks. The market stalls were made of rough black poles and crude thatch. Though trading was over, many people remained in the market: their merchandise was now gossip. In such a place, gossip is not a vice, but a necessity of life, like air or water. On the other side of the track were ordinary mud houses.

As I waited for the train I was befriended by the school teacher. He invited me to his hut, surrounded by an area cleared of vegetation to keep the snakes at bay. Nearby were several large, dark-leaved mango trees that gave shade in the heat. He brought chairs from his hut and we sat outside.

Though young, he was a man devoid of ambition, content to teach in this backwater for the rest of his life, to take his ease each afternoon after school watching the chickens peck and scratch the dust, the pigs root among the fallen mangoes, and the children – always with running noses – play with torn cardboard boxes or other household detritus. Was it not boring, I asked, for an educated man?

'Why do you ask?' he replied. 'Are *you* bored?'

I protested that I was not, but my protestation sounded hollow. It was impossible now to ask him what was the point of education in such a place – especially French education – other than to drive the young into Brazzaville to live on the margins of a marginal economy, while harbouring unrealistic hopes and ultimately a resentment that would blight their lives. Why not teach them instead to grow two ears of maize where one grew before? Alas, that would be regarded as a very second-rate kind of education, never leading to a government white collar job.

The train came, not very late, and we exchanged addresses. What if all the people to whom I had given my address wrote to me? I waved, and hoped he would forget me.

The journey northwards was accomplished mainly in the dark, the engine's searchlight sending a sharp yellow beam into the black void. We were crowded and uncomfortable, and surprisingly cold considering we were virtually at the equator and at no very great altitude. There was forest outside, but the feeble glimmer of the carriage lights illumined only the nearest trees, and then so faintly they seemed as insubstantial as shadows. For no clear reason I felt uneasy during the journey, as though we might be attacked by bandits or the train might break down and we be prey to marauding animals; or as though there were some less tangible malevolence travelling with us. The passengers were silent and subdued; but it was late.

At villages along the way – Makabana, Mossendjo, Moungondo and Mayoko – many of the passengers descended, so that by the time we reached Mbinda, at one in the morning, there were few left on board. The station was bleak, the station master's office untidy and full of sacks, and the only bench already occupied by passengers waiting for the four o'clock train. But there was nowhere other than the station to stay in Mbinda, and I made the best I could of a stretch of concrete next to a wall, impregnated as it was with urine. Sleep came for a couple of hours and then I was woken by the rising passengers for the early train, who once more impressed me deeply by their good humour at an abominable hour in the morning after a short night's sleep. When the train was gone I was on my own. I thought to conquer tiredness and discomfort by reading the life of Chekhov under the reddish glow of a paraffin lamp. As a strategy it was only partially successful.

The dawn came, and no doubt it was all topaz and amethyst, but I was in no condition to appreciate it. Mbinda was some distance from the border of Gabon – as usual, estimates of its distance varied – and I set out to walk. The first sign of life in the little town, with its broad, dusty main street and its stubby memorial obelisk to independence, was the delivery by bicycle of freshly-baked *baguettes*, a taste for which is one of the most enduring and widespread legacies of French colonialism. The bread was still warm and the more delicious because I had not eaten since the previous morning.

Another early sign of life was the operation of the overhead cable railway which brings manganese from mines deep in Gabon to the railhead at Mbinda, for transportation by train to the port of Pointe Noire. It is the longest cable railway in the world, a proof, if such be needed, of the power of capital to ignore distance and conjure up marvels in the remotest places. For sixty miles the railway cuts a perfectly executed and parallel swathe through the hilly forest, the steel supports striding confidently from hilltop to hilltop, while the suspended black buckets pass to and fro with inhuman regularity, every four seconds, as though with a purpose of their own. The railway brings incongruous bustle to the still world of the equatorial forest.

Once out of the town, the forest was quiet and fragrant. The road curved round the hills and for the first two miles I felt much refreshed. Then my bag began to grow heavy. Fortuitously, a young woman and a child of three appeared from the forest. She laughed at my weariness and took my bag as though it weighed nothing. It was clear she expected white men to be feeble. She chuckled as we strode along towards her 'village', a collection of four huts in a small clearing. There she refused any payment other than thanks and wished me *bon voyage*.

Shortly afterwards I had a lift in a pickup truck taking three soldiers to open the border post. They were late, but it mattered little, since I was the only person wishing to cross the border. Their post had two rooms and a verandah, with a bamboo flagpole in front. Fifty yards away was the Gabonese post, its flag – green, yellow and blue horizontal stripes – already raised.

Before they could attend to business, the guards had first to raise the Congolese flag, a rather forbidding blood red and black emblem. We all stood to attention as it was raised, the three guards rendering the flag a rigid salute. Their patriotism was formidable. Afterwards, they brought a table and chairs from the office on to the verandah and sat down to play cards and to chat, having decided that my passport, being unusual for these parts, required inspection by the *chef de bureau*, whose arrival was expected at any moment.

Affixed to the wall of the office were two posters. One bore passport-sized photographs of the Central Committee of the Party, clustered round a bigger photograph of the martyr-president, Marien Ngouabi; the other an exhortatory slogan: 'The Betterment of the Conditions of Life of the Masses Is to Be Obtained by the WORK of EACH and EVERYONE in all sectors'. In spite of this, the guards continued with their cards. They put their pistols on the table because their holsters, when sitting, were uncomfortable. From time to time I asked when the *chef* was coming; they always replied 'soon'.

After two and a half hours, I asked:

'Soon in relation to what?'

But soon for them was an absolute, not a relative, concept.

Eventually the *chef* arrived, driving a Land Rover as though there were a national crisis. He jumped out. The men saluted him, then shook his hand. He stamped my passport without delay. As I walked towards Gabon, he settled down to play cards with his men.

SEVEN

Gabon

At the Gabonese border I found a guard reading a French illustrated magazine, his *képi* hung up on a peg behind him. There too was a picture of the Gabonese president, El Hadj Omar Bongo, giving a speech behind a lectern that looked about to overwhelm him by its size (only later did I learn of Bongo's extremely short stature). A brief inspection of my passport persuaded the guard that the responsibility of stamping it was far too large for him, and so he took it next door to the *chef* for his decision.

I settled down to read a three-year-old French news magazine. Was France still a Great Power, it asked anxiously? The guard returned, read a novel in pictures, and then went out for his lunch, though there seemed nowhere for him to go.

An hour later, my magazine read and re-read, I went to see how far the *chef* had progressed in his complex deliberations over my passport. I found him with his head resting on the table, fast asleep, my passport held at arm's length, open at the page with my photograph. I underwent something of a personal crisis: was I so boring that the mere sight of my photograph put people to sleep?

Above the sleeping officer was a notice: 'He who has nothing to do poisons everyone'. Should I wake him and restore him to useful life? Would it be *lèse-majesté* to do so? My mind was made up by the arrival of a truck at the border going in the direction of the next town, Bakoumba. It might have been the only vehicle through that day, and I had no desire to spend the night at the border. I woke him.

In his confusion and anxiety to return to his natural condition, he stamped my passport without further ado, and I had my lift.

It was twenty miles along a red earth track to the town. We did not pass another vehicle on the way, or see a human habitation in the forest, but

only caught glimpses of the overhead railway, with its unceasing procession of steel trolleys. Bakoumba was in a large clearing in what had become
an eroded heath. It was strangely centreless having, like Topsy, just
growed. We pulled up at the police station and as I climbed out of the cab a
young policeman in a blue uniform, who was developing a paunch that
would one day proclaim him a man of importance, approached me and
said:

'You have been to South Africa. You are a spy.'

It is difficult to prove a negative, though in a sense he was right. I had
been to South Africa, ten years before, and I was not merely a casual
tourist (of whom there are practically none in Gabon). But if the South
Africans wanted to send a spy to Gabon, would they not have sent him on
one of the many flights between Johannesburg and Libreville? Would they
not (do they not?) use their large agricultural aid project outside Franceville, very near Bakoumba, for the purpose? And did not the policeman
know that much of the meat he ate came from South Africa? That, in short,
Gabon and South Africa maintained close and lucrative relations?

He led me into the empty police station, gave me to understand I was
under arrest, and locked the gate while he went for a stroll – not for the
exercise, or because he had someone he wanted to see, but precisely
because he had *nothing* to do, thus impressing upon me both his power and
my insignificance. But it was very hot and strolling in the sun was
uncomfortable. He quickly decided to return to the shade of the police
station to continue his interrogation of me.

'When did you come from South Africa?'

'I didn't come from South Africa.'

'Where is the South African stamp in your passport?'

'There isn't one.'

'Why have you come to Gabon?'

'I'm a tourist.'

'There are no tourists in Gabon.'

'I'm not surprised.'

'Are you armed?'

He took my word for it that I was not: it was, as I have said, very hot and a
search of my bag would have required at least minimal effort. He took my
passport and, with a frown of intense concentration, scrutinized it for
incriminating evidence. But even this proved too arduous for the climate.
Talking was as much as he could manage.

He asked me my occupation and I told him I was a doctor. From that instant his manner changed. He became respectful, deferential even, and produced a chair for my better comfort. Then he walked round me admiringly and declared:

'You have much paper in your head.'

It was the highest compliment of which he could conceive. I knew it was a preliminary to a consultation. The policeman had venereal disease and needed advice. I wrote a prescription and seriously thought of poisoning him. A dozen digoxin taken at once would certainly make him very sick. In the end, I opted for more conventional therapy.

I wanted to go on to Moanda and the policeman, who had now set me free, went in search of a pickup taxi. A very rusty specimen was procured, with a drunken driver. The policeman threatened to arrest him unless he charged me the proper fare and not an inflated one. I was a doctor, he said.

The motto of the driver, much disgruntled by this missed opportunity to overcharge, seemed to be *Better never than late*. It was strange after so many delays – I had been three hours in the police station – suddenly to risk all for the sake of a few extra kilometres per hour. Our path did not always exactly coincide with that of the road, and the driver showed a marked tendency to overcorrect for his errors, but we reached Moanda safely. It was larger than Bakoumba and had a French-run hotel on a low hill a little way out of town. I felt I needed a drink and went to the bar. It was empty – the hotel was principally a weekend resort for expatriates from Libreville. In the corner was a television. There were two Muslim preachers, one an African dressed as a Palestinian, the other in a flashy cream-coloured suit. Be good, they said, don't fornicate, don't be selfish, and work hard (but not for your own sake).

I was furious. I wanted to pick up the television and hurl it against the wall. In fact, I wanted to scream.

Next morning, I had to wait an hour or two outside a bakery for transport to Lastoursville, a hundred-and-twenty miles away. For once the back of the pickup truck was not overloaded, and it was very pleasant to travel through the jungle in the open air. My two fellow passengers were a young woman and a young man who discussed for half the journey the relative positions of men and women in society. The discussion was largely for my benefit: whenever one of them made a particularly telling point he or she turned to me for approval. And unlike in other parts of Francophone Africa, French seemed their natural means of communication.

The discussion turned on whether men or women had the harder lives.

'Men divorce us if we don't have enough children for them,' said the woman.

'Women live longer,' said the man.

'I don't believe it. We do all the work.'

'Are there more widows or widowers in your village?'

It continued in this vein for a long time, but there was another difference between them: the woman was arguing from conviction born of experience, while the young man, with his hat placed at a rakish angle upon his head, argued from a playful contrariness and desire for argumentative triumph. One had only to look at the expressions on their faces to know that truth was on the woman's side.

At a small settlement two more passengers got on. One of them was a great fat woman, a trader, the other an adolescent with spindly, malnourished limbs. The youth was not quite all there: he sat staring, his mouth wide open, liquid snot dripping from his nostrils, reacting with terror whenever a remark was addressed to him. Unusually – for Africans are generally tolerant of deformity and mental aberration – the others taunted him. They told him to wipe his nose, but he only had his shirt, already far from clean, and he used that, which brought further taunts and laughter at his stupidity. He knew only that he was being laughed at and struck out feebly at the young man, who turned away the blow with ease and further taunts. The weakminded youth was close to tears. I wanted to give him some comfort, for I felt somehow that the others would not have behaved like this had I not been there: they would not have felt a need to draw a distinction between themselves and him. But he *was* repulsive and I was too cowardly to upset the others with an ostentatious display of disapproval: so I just watched.

The fat woman trader bought up all the bananas for sale by the roadside, until the truck was piled high. She was the local Nelson Bunker Hunt of bananas, trying to achieve a monopoly to drive up prices. She also bought a very large dead rodent, about two and a half feet long, like a cross between a beaver and a rat. It was a prized local delicacy, and in Libreville would fetch $30.

We reached Lastoursville at lunchtime. It is a small town, taken in at a glance, that runs for a few hundred yards along the left bank of the Ogooué River. This river, though broad, is not navigable and was a great disappointment to Brazza, who hoped it would prove a highway to the heart of equatorial Africa. He did, however, have the honesty to admit the illusory nature of his hopes: unlike the more famous but less admirable Livingstone, who harboured similar hopes for the Zambezi but never renounced them, all evidence to the contrary notwithstanding, and thus lured expeditions of gullible followers to avoidable deaths.

There was a small hotel in Lastoursville and I decided to stay. It was run by a French couple who, though I was the only guest, seemed far from pleased to see me and showed no curiosity as to where I had come from. The *patron*, rather plump, consoled himself with constant top-ups of *Ricard*; his wife, emaciated, thin-lipped and amazingly pale, was inconsolable.

The restaurant was in a covered verandah overlooking the river: a pleasant spot. The tablecloths were dazzlingly white and crisply starched, and somehow reassured me that life was worth living and there was order in the universe. Absurd, no doubt: but let he who laughs travel through Africa and then belittle the comfort to be derived from clean table linen.

In the corner worked an old African woman in an apron as white as the tablecloths, which she was ironing. I ordered a plate of *charcuterie* and to my amazement a selection of salamis, pâtés, terrines and smoked hams, far superior to anything to be had in a large English provincial town, was brought forth. Here was no concession to climate, to isolation, to geography, to anything; if it was folly, it was magnificent folly. Perhaps it was the neverending struggle in this tiny town for good *charcuterie* that had embittered the patron's wife.

After lunch, in the full heat of the day when everybody else was asleep, I went for a walk. There was a new bridge across the river and here I was able to contemplate the brown waters in silence. Only an occasional truck, bringing huge hardwood tree-trunks ten feet across out of the forest, disturbed my thoughts. Were they heedlessly hacking down the forest for quick gain, I wondered? Probably. I had brought Camus' *L'Etranger* with me, and I read it leaning over the rails of the bridge. Was it possible for any human being, even a French intellectual of the 50s, to be quite so indifferent and disillusioned as Merseult? In Lastoursville, perhaps. Still, something about him didn't ring true: there is some fundamental dishonesty, some lack of frankness, lurking somewhere in the book. After all, it is not possible to go through life without *some* kind of preference, even if it is for death. As for the etiolated comfort offered at the end of the book, it is about as heartening as a sorbet in the Arctic. Did not Camus (here I am identifying him completely with his creation) feel the faintest flutter of fear in the instant before his car crashed and he was killed?

That night, as every Saturday night, there was a disco near the hotel. Green and pink lights flashed, the whole town came, everyone danced, the Africans for joy, the whites to forget. And round my bed, the mosquitoes also had their dance.

Next morning, a local shopkeeper found me a lift with a man going all the way to Libreville in his pickup piled high with goods. He was a roadbuilding technician and the truck was his own, but he asked me not to draw the conclusion he was a wealthy man, at least not by Gabonese standards. In his job he saw the fantastic corruption of the élite, but he played the idiot and pretended to notice nothing, much less *do* anything about it. If the big people – *les grands* – overheard you remarking on the corruption you had witnessed, it would be very much the worse for you. Stupidity was the safest policy.

For the first fifty miles of the journey (it was three hundred and sixty in all) the road followed the Ogooué River and also the track of the new Trans-Gabonese Railway. This line connects Franceville with Libreville and was for a long time the largest construction project in Africa, costing two billion dollars, or two thousand dollars per head of Gabon's population. This scale of building is completely beyond the resources of most African countries, but Gabon is by far the richest state, thanks to its oil, in sub-Saharan Africa.

The forest was not flat, as one somehow always expects jungle to be, but stretched over rolling hills. From the vantage point of the brows of these hills it was possible to see the vastness of this green ocean, reaching to the horizon in all directions, the road a thin red scar, a seemingly pathetic token of Man's presence. Could it really be, as the conservationists have it, that a forest of this unimaginable size and density and exuberance, with its monumental trees, is so threatened by human greed that within a generation or two nothing of it will remain? The statistics say it is so, therefore it must be so; but it is hard to believe it when, as an insignificant individual, you look around you and see nothing but the forest's canopy, blue-green in the distance, for twenty miles in all directions.

The forest did not extend all the way to Libreville, however. Suddenly we reached an area of dry upland heath with a blast-furnace climate. We stopped at a village, Ayem, for lunch. It was exactly on the equator, and utterly desolate; but even here it was possible to find pâté, a sign, I suppose, that despite corruption the oil prosperity has trickled down everywhere in Gabon. The driver took two bottles of Guinness in the belief – supported by advertisements in English throughout the country – that Guinness is good for you. I was not so sure, for every crash barrier along the treacherous road had been broken, usually with the twisted wreck of a vehicle in the gulley below. But the driver suffered no ill-effects, apart from a certain lethargy and sleepiness half an hour later; and he stopped at a small stall to revive himself with some kola nut.

I had read of the kola nut in African literature: of how it was split and offered to visitors in a ceremony of welcome and peace, of its deep symbolic significance in West African culture. It is also the Cola of Coca-Cola, imparting the caffeine that gives the drink its 'lift'. But I had formed the wrong impression of both its appearance and its taste. I had conceived of it as the size of a papaya and the taste of a cashew. But the kernel itself is the size of a chestnut and as bitter as quinine. An acquired taste, certainly: but one which, once acquired, can lead to mild addiction.

We entered the forest once more, and it was forest all the way to Libreville. A hundred miles from the city the road was surfaced, but this proved a delusive advantage: it invited the incautious driver to accelerate, and then jolted him violently with wonderfully camouflaged potholes. Another hazard in the dark was unlit vehicles; but to have seen the noble trees of the jungle silhouetted against the golden sky of the dusk was nearly worth the risk of untimely extinction.

We stopped to buy palm wine fifty miles from Libreville. It was much cheaper here than in the capital, the driver said, and of better quality. He had brought a plastic bucket with him for the purpose: he bought two gallons. He bade me try the still-fermenting white liquid with a stale, sour smell. I found it difficult to disregard the insects trapped in the grey froth on the heaving surface, but nevertheless I drank – or rather, as an alcoholic patient once said to me to prove his problem was not a serious one – I *sipped*.

We reached Libreville late. The driver took me to a merchant friend of his, to whom he had to deliver the goods in his pickup. The merchant was a prosperous man in his thirties, just developing the glossy *embonpoint* of West African affluence. The front door of his house opened on to a large living room, brassily decorated and furnished *à la* Farouk. All the chairs were focused on a large video screen. The breezeblock of the walls, however, showed through. From the door to the kitchen came a procession of women and children, at least eight of them, all of whom treated the head of the household with great deference. I didn't discover how many people lived in the house, but it was evidently many. The living room was kept in a state of cleanliness and almost clinical good order most unusual (in my experience) in Africa. On the shelves of a wall-fitting were some large volumes bound in cheap imitation leather: an encyclopaedia of Marxism published in Moscow.

The merchant took me to a hotel, the best, he said, in Libreville. It was a palace of bad taste, with tuneless soothing music as inescapable as air-conditioning. There is something profoundly depressing about the ultramodernity of a few years ago. The colour combinations, once thought bold and daring, now looked only garish. Yet the hotel set the tone of Libreville society, it was the place to be seen. Not long before, it had been the location of the annual gathering of Gabonese ambassadors abroad. They were addressed by the Foreign Minister. He told them that the price of oil, on which Gabon was almost wholly dependent for exports, had fallen sharply; and therefore, at a time of greatly reduced government revenues, it was essential as never before that Gabon had value for money from its foreign missions. He hinted darkly that he suspected *some* missions were not giving value for money.

'And now,' he said, having concluded his address, 'I cordially invite you to have a glass of champagne with me in the bar.'

It was ten o'clock in the morning. Since a bottle of mineral water costs $5 in the hotel, I hesitate to guess the price of champagne. I never found out, because the next morning I left in search of a more modest establishment.

Libreville is a strange city. It was founded in 1848 by the French on the model of Freetown in Sierra Leone as a haven for freed slaves. Nothing of that era remains. The modern city was founded on oil wealth, which it was once believed would increase *ad infinitum*; and also on the vanity of El Hadj Omar Bongo (Albert-Bernard until his conversion to Islam), who spent more than $1,000,000,000 on beautifying the city for the 1977 conference of the Organization of African Unity, practically bankrupting the country in the process despite its oil revenues. There is no unifying aesthetic principle in the city's architecture; it looks as though a score of architects have been allowed to act out their fantasies free of fear of retribution. The Presidency, an establishment of such size one would imagine Gabon were a world power, is a starkly modern building of stone and glass, except for one corner, cream-stuccoed and colonnaded somewhat in the style of Nash. The Central Bank of the States of Central Africa (the customs and monetary union of Gabon, Cameroon, the Congo, Chad, the Central African Republic and Equatorial Guinea, of which the last four are bankrupt) is in the shape of an elegant arc six storeys high, tapering towards its top, with hanging plants cascading between its filamentous piers. It is by far the finest building in all the city; but, as I walked down the *Boulevard Triomphal El Hadj Omar Bongo* in which it is situated, there was the unmistakable smell of open sewers.

Gabon now has many more French residents than it ever had as a colony, and Libreville has a quarter known as *Petit Paris*, where there are boutiques, cafés and *épiceries* as expensive, if not as elegant, as any in Paris. Here the gilded youth of Libreville – the children of oil company executives and of the Gabonese élite – pass their days in sophisticated boredom, and housewives in *crêpe de chine* search for something with which to amaze their guests for dinner. Here Africa is relegated to the sale of souvenirs at roadside stalls, and the three post boxes outside the central post office are eloquent testimony to Gabon's virtually colonial status: there is one box for Gabon, another for France, and a third for *Abroad*.

Yet even here the real Africa would make its appearance through the veneer. I went to buy stamps at the central post office, and was told there were none. An elegantly dressed secretary from an oil company behind me had brought some letters for registration, and knowing the shortage of stamps often encountered at the post office, had brought a sheet of stamps with her. The man behind the counter at once offered to buy them: a curious reversal of roles between the post office and its public. She refused, however, and merely gave him enough stamps to cover the postage of her letters. She handed both letters and stamps to the clerk. As soon as she was out of sight, he sold the stamps to me. They were not of the right denomination, but that didn't seem to matter much: for the postage on my letters varied with each time of asking.

I walked along the corniche beside the Gabon estuary, a channel wide and long enough to be the outlet of a far mightier river than the tiny and insignificant Mbé; past commercial bank where Muslim traders from countries to the north discharged millions of francs from under their robes for payment into their accounts, and travel agencies offering holidays in Disneyland. Armoured cars of the French garrison in Gabon ground by; and officers of that garrison, hard, ruthless and intelligent-looking men, went by in limousines.

At the end of the corniche was an exhibition ground with a Chinese trade fair. It was opened a few years previously by President Bongo. He, his cabinet, the presidential guard and the diplomatic corps (in that order) had walked through it. There was not much in the fair of interest to the diplomats, most of the exhibits being the cheap and shoddy trade goods of African commerce; but there were some fine carpets which one diplomat's wife made enquiries to buy.

'I'm sorry,' said the Chinese manager, 'but all the carpets have been sold to cabinet ministers.'

'In that case,' said the diplomat's wife with asperity, 'I hope you got your money first.'

The terrible truth began to dawn on the manager, who was new to Africa.

'But they are all rich,' he said. 'All millionaires.'

'Because,' continued the diplomat's wife pitilessly, 'if you give them the carpets before you've got your money, you'll never see it.'

Meanwhile, the Presidential Guard, in crimson robes with sabres, fell on the Chinese buffet prepared for the diplomatic corps and left rather less than a plague of locusts might have done, inasmuch as some of the plates went missing too. The Chinese were bemused; the diplomats were hungry.

As in most African countries – or at least capitals – one cannot for long escape the name, thoughts, deeds and speeches of the president. For eighteen years, Bongo has been president in Libreville. I heard several French businessmen, long-term residents of the country, say 'He is a good man'; meaning, of course, he lets them alone to make their money.

In the same breath they said he had eaten people, or at least parts of them, in accordance with magical rites in which, despite his conversion to Islam, he was still a believer. But this story, apocryphal or not, did not affect their estimate of him, tinged as it always was with condescension – a good man, *for an African*. Anthropophagist or not, he had brought peace and stability to his country.

President Bongo is not a tall man, barely five feet tall even in the built-up shoes he always wears. He is sensitive about his stature, and chooses his cabinet not by ability alone (some say he prefers his ministers stupid), but by height, or lack of it. The use of the word *pygmée* is not encouraged in Gabon. And whenever he is photographed, which is many times every day, it is either alone, when there is no-one about with whom to compare him, or when others are sitting or bowing. I saw scores of photographs of President Bongo: it was impossible to conclude from any of them that he was not the tallest man in the world.

He had just been 'chosen' as the presidential candidate of the only legal party, the *Parti Démocratique Gabonais*, in the forthcoming presidential 'election'. He was, of course, the only candidate. The announcement of his candidacy was treated by the press as a matter of surprise and delight, and it showed a picture of *le Grand Camarade*, as he is known, posing coyly on the presidential lawn, as modest as a world-famous soprano receiving a totally unexpected ovation. The change in his party title from Secretary-General to Founder-President inspired similar paroxysms of journalistic gush. As for the election itself, he must have been very satisfied: he won with 99.97 per cent of the votes, an improved performance on the last election when he won only 99.96 per cent.

Even on the days when *le Grand Camarade* is not entertaining the visiting Zambian Minister of Telecommunications or the Bulgarian Deputy Minister of Fisheries, his thoughts provide the newspaper with much-needed copy. An article on the role of universities in Africa quotes the President *in extenso*:

Economics cannot be the sole measure of Man. Our development must be founded on what we are at the deepest levels of ourselves, that is to say, our culture; a culture which is not merely derived from the genius of other peoples; a culture which asserts itself, and blossoms by returning to and preserving our most authentic traditions and values while at the same time remaining open to foreign currents . . .

Unfortunately, he does not give practical hints as to how the worlds of dugout canoes and jumbo jets, of manioc and *nouvelle cuisine*, are to be reconciled. Gucci spears, perhaps, or Givenchy feathers?

In a Libreville bookshop I found a comic-strip biography of *le Grand Camarade*. He was an Infant Prodigy, of course, clearsighted and brilliant from the first, as well as unselfish and hardworking. There was no mention of his later exploits as a womaniser, when uncomplaisant husbands of women upon whom he had set his sights displayed a marked tendency to early retirement or worse; or of his wife's similar effect on the spouses of those she favoured.

Yet Gabon does not have the atmosphere of a totalitarian state. Ministers are summoned to the Presidency by public radio message. And unlike *le Grand Camarade*, they are not immune from criticism. Once a year each minister has to face a panel of interrogators on television to give an account of their ministry's work during the previous twelve months. It is a terrible ordeal, with questions that range from 'Why was such and such a public work not completed?' to 'Who was that woman I saw you with last Thursday?' The annual baiting of the ministers exposes them to public ridicule, and makes them therefore less of a threat to the president.

Le Grand Camarade is too interested in making money to be a true totalitarian. He has guided his country through an era – coming to a swift end – of unexampled prosperity. A nation of simple forest dwellers has been the recipient of tremendous wealth it did nothing to create. That it has not ended in disaster is a measure of his leadership: for sudden wealth is to simple societies a heavier burden than poverty.

Le Grand Camarade owns the largest supermarket in Africa, along his *Boulevard Triomphal*. Here, at great profit to him, the wives of the men who *really* run Gabon buy cheeses and pâtisserie and fruit flown in daily from Paris. I bought strawberries. There is a French manager, of course.

I met an employee of a large French construction company who was both an engineer and a lawyer. He was responsible for drafting contracts all over Africa. At the signing ceremony of one such contract in Libreville he met *le Grand Camarade*.

'I like this contract,' the great man said. 'It is a very good contract.'

The lawyer-engineer, his heart sinking, waited for the pious truisms about developing the country, helping the poor, training the workers etc., he had heard a hundred times before.

'It will make me an even richer man.'

As the lawyer-engineer said, it is rarely one finds an honest man in Africa.

Lambaréné is probably the most famous place in Gabon. It has its beauty (perhaps *charm* is a better word), though it takes a certain connoisseurship of monotony to discern it. But it is not for the landscape that a little stream of people makes its way, pilgrim-like, to Lambaréné. As everyone knows, or used to know, it was here that the doctor-organist-theologian, Albert Schweitzer, spent most of the last fifty-two years of his life. The settlement had seen other distinguished residents – if more temporary ones – such as Mary Kingsley, the eccentric English gentlewoman turned river trader, icthyologist and anthropologist, and Trader Horn, whose book *The Ivory Coast in the Earlies* went through scores of impressions but is now scarcely read; but for every person who has heard of them, a thousand must know of the Doctor, whose features, like those of Einstein, were once an icon of the age.

His stock, however, has been falling. Very few are the secondhand bookshops without a dusty shelf of his unsaleable books, or of works about him. In an age when it is as necessary to knock down heroes as to set them up, his philosophy has been declared null and void, his rendering of Bach wooden and eccentric, his attitude to Africans demeaning and paternal-istic, his hospital a disgrace, his personality unattractive and dictatorial, his treatment of his family unfeeling, his disdain of publicity another form of self-advertisement, and his knowledge of medicine thoroughly exiguous. Above all, he committed the mortal sin of not moving with the times.

Thus the erstwhile saint, whose perfect goodness went without saying, has been transmuted into the very opposite: the selfless man an egomaniac, the brilliant scholar an ignoramus, the humble worker for the poor an oppressor. Of Dr Schweitzer it seems still impossible to write, *on the one hand . . . on the other hand . . .*

Some of his medical ideas were undoubtedly odd. He believed to the end of his days that the slightest exposure to the rays of the tropical sun was very harmful to a white man, especially if the rays fell on his head. Thus:

Mrs Faure had, without thinking, walked a few yards in the open without anything on her head, and was now prostrate with severe fever and other threatening symptoms. Truly my fellow traveller . . . was right when he said that the sun was our great enemy . . .

A white man, working in a store, was resting after dinner with a ray of sunshine falling on his head through a hole in the roof about the size of a half crown: the result was a high fever with delirium . . .

The skipper of a small merchant vessel had to make some small repairs to the keel of his craft . . . While working at them he bent his head so far that the sun shone upon his neck below his helmet. He, too, was for a time at death's door . . .

Schweitzer never questioned his belief, though on the very next page he wrote something that might have given a less dogmatic man pause to consider:

Following the advice of an experienced colonial doctor, I treated the sunstroke as if it were complicated with malaria . . .

I asked the way to Dr Schweitzer's hospital of an old lady, bent with age, who was smoking a short-stemmed pipe.

'Doctor *who?*' she asked.

Eventually, I found the point at which pirogues called to ferry people across the river. It was past an old Catholic church of crumbling red brick built in the 1880s, in which there was a ten-foot high statue of an African Christ carved from a single piece of wood; and past a luxury hotel built to cater for weekenders from Libreville.

The pirogue was paddled by a wiry old man, the fare being 100 francs (30 cents). I had seen many pirogues capsize, but I still had not appreciated just how unstable they are: the act of turning one's head is sufficient to cause a perceptible rocking, which it is then natural to try to correct by turning one's head in the other direction which, of course, only makes matters worse. My admiration for the skill of the boatmen of the Zaire increased.

On the far bank of the river was the famous hospital, a collection of long, low buildings roofed with tin that even from a distance looked somewhat higgledy-piggledy. Our progress towards it was held up for a time by a sandbar, on to which we had glided with a loud scrunching noise from the keel. We were not, fortunately, held up long; in a stationary canoe on the Ogooué, the thoughts of a man who has read

Mary Kingsley soon turn, whether reasonably or not, to crocodiles. But we were soon once more afloat on the water, which looked like a vast stream of tea, into which the milk had not yet been properly stirred.

I had read that Dr Schweitzer's hospital was not a model; that he had made do with poor hygiene on the grounds that Africans would be intimidated by too much cleanliness, and thus not feel at home; that there was no sanitation to speak of, and that animals were free to roam at will. Nevertheless, it still came as something of a shock. Admittedly it was no longer in use as a hospital, and the ramshackle collection of wooden, tin and cement buildings was now inhabited by hundreds of families. Yet there was something in its basic design that seemed positively and deliberately to *preclude* the possibility of hygiene, that embraced filth and chaos as good in themselves. In the early days of the hospital there may have been no alternative; but later, when Schweitzer was one of the most famous men in the world, could not something better have been built? There was no lack of funds: and a new, modern, hygienic hospital (staffed by Europeans) has in fact been opened, a little above the old hospital, on a hill. It is soulless, perhaps, but one would prefer to have one's appendix out there, rather than in the old hospital. I was reminded of Chekhov's remark vis-à-vis Tolstoy: 'Reason and justice tell me there is more love of man in electricity and steam than in chastity and refusal to eat meat . . .'

I walked up the alleyways between the wards, past the pharmacy with its famous notice that all medicines were to be paid for at once and in cash, towards Schweitzer's house. There I found a group of casually – but fashionably and expensively – dressed Germans. The men had beer bellies, the women hibiscus blooms over one ear in their hair. They were the crew from *Südwestfunk* making a film about the life of Schweitzer. They had evidently found reality somewhat unsatisfactory, as far as filming was concerned, and had constructed a wooden set, spick and span, in the midst of which sat Dr Schweitzer in dazzling white ducks and pith helmet. I arrived just in time for *Südwestfunk*'s lunch: the arc lights were switched off, and Dr Schweitzer ambled off in the direction of the very ample buffet. Later in the day, an African in a battered Toyota saloon gave me a lift. He was an actor from Libreville, chosen to play the part of Joseph, Schweitzer's African assistant. He seemed a rather washed-up man, and he said it was difficult to be an actor in Gabon. I asked him what he thought of all this fuss about Schweitzer: he thought it was very good, because it gave him work for a month and the Germans paid well.

I left Lambaréné with the feeling that Schweitzer was an enigma without resolution. Why does a man give up a brilliant career – two brilliant careers – to immure himself in a primitive and (from his point of view) cultureless jungle? Can massive egoism be the whole answer? Or for that matter, burning love of mankind? There is a splendid little speech by the Administrator Leblanc in Gilbert Cesbron's play *Il est minuit Docteur Schweitzer*: 'He's chosen the worst district . . . these birds nest only in the most uncomfortable trees . . . When he dies he'll ask God as a reward for permission to build his wards in Hell . . .'

I returned to Libreville where, unfortunately, I had to stay for several days: unfortunately, because Libreville is undoubtedly one of the most expensive cities in the world. But it was necessary to procure visas for the countries ahead, and so I stayed.

I made things more expensive still for myself by eating in the *Pescadou*, whose French *patron* was evidently a connoisseur of his own food. Squeezed into a brilliant white chef's tunic and apron, he bulged like water in a balloon, and his shoes squeaked as he went majestically – like an archbishop bestowing blessings – on a tour of the tables, secure in the knowledge that his dishes were the finest possible. Complaint was not to be contemplated: he was an artist who created only masterpieces in that most important but difficult medium, food. In benighted Africa he, too, was a missionary of sorts.

I whiled away the days with the English, American, Gabonese and French newspapers. I had read no news for several weeks, and felt vaguely guilty, as though I were failing in some public duty to worry about what I could not affect. In any case, nothing much had changed. I read also one of the most famous works of Francophone African literature, *L'Enfant Noir*, by Camara Laye. I wandered the city reading this poetic and lyrical account of a village childhood in Senegal, beautifully and simply written. The author's viewpoint is clear:

I don't know where the idea comes from that rusticity – taken in its sense as a lack of finesse and delicacy – belongs to the country: the forms of civility are better observed there than in the town; one sees a ceremoniousness and mannerliness there that the town, in its rush, does not know. Life, it is true, is simple there, but the relations between men are more strictly regulated, perhaps because everyone knows everyone else. I noticed a dignity in everything that was done in the country that I never encountered in the town . . . in truth, an extraordinary concern for the freedom of others . . .

This is all, of course, quite true; but is it – was it ever – the whole truth? Using the book as a foil, I thought of counter-examples. I remembered the village in Tanzania where once a fortnight I did a clinic. The villagers had somehow got it into their heads that an old man was performing magic in his hut to kill everyone in the village. Three villagers stole into his hut one night and beat him to death. A little while later his son, who had been away, returned; and hearing of his father's murder went to the police, who arrested and locked up the three murderers. The villagers clubbed together to collect money; and with this money they went to a doctor at the nearest government hospital to buy a death certificate for the old man, saying he had died of natural causes. This they showed to the police, to prove the three imprisoned men had no case to answer. But even when the police received an order from higher authority to release the men, they refused to do so without a bribe.

Of course, Laye was writing of a different country at a different time. Surprisingly, he does not mention the evils of colonialism. His Africa is unspoilt, prelapsarian; it has undergone a fearful and rapid deterioration. However, I am sceptical of golden ages, both past and to come.

I left the bright lights and open sewers of Libreville without very much regret. I took a communal taxi to the little town of Cocobeach, on the southern bank of the estuary of the Rio Muni. It was from here that I hoped to take a pirogue to Acalayong, a village in Equatorial Guinea.

The town clustered round a tiny bay along a coast fringed with palm trees. The water lapped the beach gently in a never-ending series of caresses. On the beach the morning's catch – little piles of small silver fish – aroused the villagers' interest. Across the estuary were the low hills of Equatorial Guinea. The principal edifice of Cocobeach was its concrete water tower, with the words *Ville de Cocobeach* in incongruous neon lettering around it.

I went to the border post, another dreary two-roomed construction with a small verandah overlooking the sea. There were two sheepish young Africans, barefoot, waiting there. They told me the officer was out and it was impossible to say when he would return. But return he soon did, at half past eleven, though only to announce it was time for lunch and to suggest angrily that I should return at three o'clock. I asked for special consideration as I wanted to cross over to Equatorial Guinea as soon as possible, but the request only enraged him further; he snatched my passport, slammed the door of his office shut behind him, and locked it loudly. He was in his early twenties, developing an official's paunch, and his expression was brutal and stupid. My hands trembled with impotent rage as I tried to read *Moby Dick*.

A few minutes later, he re-emerged but strode straight past me. He returned to his room with a pillow and large cassette recorder, which he played very loudly – disco – for about half a track, and then switched off. His snores soon caused the whole building to vibrate.

'Monsieur,' one of the barefoot Africans urged timidly. 'Monsieur.'

'Yes,' I replied, my temper on a short fuse.

'Can you give us some money, monsieur?'

He was meek and submissive, but I was in no mood to be charitable.

'Why?' I asked sharply.

'We are hungry.'

I exploded at last. I strode up and down the verandah gesticulating wildly.

'Who shows me consideration? Who? Why should I be nice to others? Why?'

In my heart of hearts, I was enjoying myself.

'We are under arrest, monsieur, we are not officials. We haven't eaten since yesterday morning.'

I looked at them: I began to grow ashamed of myself. Was I not becoming like the officialdom I despised, using my power to give or withhold in any way I chose?

They explained they were Togolese without money or papers, on their way to visit their parents who lived in Libreville. (Gabon is a promised land in this part of the world: for the Gabonese import labour rather than perform menial tasks themselves.) The two young men were arrested as they tried to enter the country, having walked all the way from Togo. They repeated they were hungry, having been given nothing to eat since their arrest.

Their poverty was plain to see. They had the wiry bodies of people who never eat too much, and often too little. They had no belongings, their clothes were tattered, their feet were dusty and hardened.

'How much do you want?' I asked.

'A hundred francs, monsieur.' (30 cents)

I found the modesty of their request touching. Only truly poor men could have asked for so little or set their sights so low. I gave them twice what they asked.

One of them bounded off joyously to the nearest shop. He returned with a few cigarettes.

'I thought you were hungry!' I exclaimed, my anger rekindled by their improvidence.

'A hundred francs for cigarettes, monsieur, a hundred francs for food this evening.'

Who was I to tell men who had come with nothing all the way from Togo how to spend two hundred francs sensibly?

During the long wait till three o'clock, I wandered into the office that was still open. On the wall was a cyclostyled notice from the general of the *gendarmerie*, complaining of the level of absenteeism in the force. Recently the general had gone on a tour of inspection and found only one man out of thirty at his post. In future, he thundered, absenteeism would be severely punished. While I was reading this notice a little man in yellow check trousers entered and accused me of spying, and threatened to have me deported to Equatorial Guinea. I said I was trying to go there anyway, but this did nothing to placate him. I simply waited for him to become bored with his own fatuous accusations, which he soon did.

At three fifteen sharp, the officer emerged, shirt and trousers unbuttoned, groping his way through a fog of sleep. He called me to his room, which smelled of stale sweat, and started to look through my passport. Suddenly he jumped, as if shocked by electricity.

'You are a doctor?' he asked.

I admitted it.

'I have a problem.'

He smiled at me beatifically, as though he had always been my best friend. I had no difficulty in guessing the kind of problem he had: he had had it a long time. I wrote out a prescription for him.

'Togolais!' he called. 'Togolais!'

The two prisoners came to him.

'Take this to the pharmacy,' he ordered.

They turned to go.

'Run! Hurry!'

They trotted towards the pharmacy.

'Run! Run!' he shouted after them, and they accelerated.

With the laboriousness of the newly-literate, he wrote something in my passport, extruding his tongue with the effort. It was too late now for me to cross the estuary that day, and he asked me, his day's work done when he handed me back my passport, to have a drink with him. As we went off towards the bar I noticed the Togolese running back from the pharmacy.

'Wait at the office,' ordered their captor.

The bar was a low flat cavern built of wood, designed to trap the heat. All the uniformed men – police, soldiers and others – of Cocobeach came to join us to refresh themselves after a hard day's extortion. I was introduced as the immigration man's 'friend', he by now having forgotten entirely his initial reception of me, and expecting that I had too. The beer flowed and then the corn spirit, which tasted fierce and chemical. Some of the spirit was infused with a local bark, good, so I was told, for the bowels.

'Just as well,' I remarked, tasting it.

We had to shout above the music: Africans like it loud. The men joked about the scantiness of each other's beards, a joke that lasted several rounds. My 'friend' suddenly announced he would like to go to another bar, and it was then I discovered the drinks had all been on me.

The other bar was a wooden shack where the corn spirit was, if anything, viler still. I excused myself: my friend's eyes were by now quite red and drinking had obviously set in for the night. Merely to look at him was sufficient to give one a hangover.

My room for the night was a small box of black planks, without a window. For the use of this I paid 5000 francs to the owner, a large woman who sailed rather than walked (though she was often becalmed), whose buttocks trailed far behind her.

As dusk came to Cocobeach the neon letters on the water tower lit up:

ILL DE COCO EACH

I walked round the village. Children danced outside bars where music played, while others kicked a ball of their own devising round a piece of grassy land. Some men in uniforms lolled in deckchairs outside a small barracks and neither slept nor talked nor moved. Time stood still in Cocobeach.

I passed the border post, from which the sound of the water lapping the beach was audible. Perhaps it was this soothing rhythm that enabled the Togolese, still waiting on the verandah, to stay calm and to all appearances contented. They waved to me. I waved back, wishing I had half their philosophy.

EIGHT

Equatorial Guinea

I took a pirogue with an outboard to Equatorial Guinea early next morning. One of the Togolese, seeing me from afar, ran to carry my bag the last few yards on to the boat. Even the immigration officer, who looked as though he had not been to bed that night and as though blocks of concrete were hailing down on the back of his head, was there to wave me goodbye.

It was an hour to Acalayong. The estuary was wide at first, with forested hills on either side; but soon we turned into a narrow creek in a mangrove swamp, with its smell of rotting vegetation, black waters and the mangroves themselves that rose above the mud on a tangled latticework of roots.

It was raining slightly when we arrived, and the village presented a far from enticing aspect. We landed at a beach of black mud, over which little mud fish laboriously crawled, using their fins as desperately inefficient levers. For some reason I thought of party members after a revolution. A policeman came down on to the beach to meet me. Equatorial Guinea having been until 1968 a Spanish colony, his uniform was of Spanish cut. We shook hands and he said he would take me to the *jefe*.

The village was simply two lines of delapidated wooden buildings stretching less than a hundred yards along a road of thick red mud, the forest looming immediately behind. There was one concrete shell of a building, dated 1949, which had been neither finished nor demolished.

The *jefe* was in a small office and was dressed in yellow football kit. I knew at once I should have difficulties with him: he replied to my polite *buenos días* with a filthy scowl, and snatched my passport angrily. The merest glance at it threw him into a towering rage: he let forth a stream of invective, banging the table with my passport, pointing with venom to my

Nigerian visa (of which I had, till then, been rather proud, since everyone had predicted – wrongly, as it turned out – great travails in procuring one). I hadn't the faintest idea what his rage was all about; whether, for example, it was all a histrionic performance in pursual of a bribe. A soft answer – several soft answers – did not turn away wrath. He said I should have to return to Gabon, I could not enter Equatorial Guinea. The policeman ushered me out on to the rickety verandah, from which I had a view of the fine misty rain falling on the village and the forest behind. I should wait here, he said; in the meantime he searched my baggage as the *jefe* had commanded. He found an empty notebook and asked for it; a request which, in the circumstances, I felt unable to refuse, whatever my true inclinations.

In the meantime, the *jefe* had emerged, having changed into a pair of well-pressed fawn trousers, a freshly laundered shirt, and some very expensive shoes, worth more than the rest of the village put together. He then paraded up and down the village street, ostentatiously greeting the otherwise bedraggled villagers with *abrazos* and engaging in cheerful, animated conversation. With the quick paranoia of the slighted, I assumed that his affability, in such marked contrast to his previous irritability, was directed at me. I asked the policeman, considering him to be – comparatively speaking – my friend, whether it would be politic to offer the *jefe* a bribe.

'No sé,' he said – I don't know.'

I waited for five hours on that verandah, during which my reflections on Africa and Africans were far from favourable. In the meantime, several pirogues full of Guinean residents in Gabon arrived, and the *jefe* treated them with relatively little obstruction. This increased my bitterness, and I considered whether I should not, perhaps, take matters into my own hands and just walk down the jungle road, away from the village. But while such a course of action would have provided momentary gratification, it would have turned me into a fugitive; and with the next village fifty miles down a mud track, one with little chance of escape.

Fortunately, another *jefe* arrived: everyone in Acalayong, it seemed, was a *jefe* of some description. He was polite and after a lengthy explanation of my presence said he would get the first *jefe* to stamp my passport. Unfortunately, it was now his siesta. I had only another hour to wait, however; and then, with a face of thunder, and with a reluctance that spoke of an opportunity lost, the first *jefe* affixed an ancient and practically illegible stamp on the page.

'*Muchas gracias*,' I said, trying hard not to sound sarcastic, and hating myself for the pusillanimous effort: but then I come from a country where, when a man steps on one's toes, one apologizes to him.

There were two pickup trucks that came to carry arrivals from Gabon to Bata, the largest town on the mainland territory of Equatorial Guinea, once known as Rio Muni. (The other part of the country is the island of Bioko, formerly Fernando Po.) There were many customs examinations and re-examinations to go through, and loadings, unloadings and reloadings, and organizations and reorganizations, before we could depart. I was befriended by a large matron, to whom I confessed I was hungry. From the size of her, she was *always* hungry, and she took me to a wooden shelter on the estuarine beach where another large matron of her acquaintance sold lukewarm fish stew that tasted of mud and pepper out of a giant, never-empty pot. She ate hugely, and it was assumed, with as much confidence as that the sun would rise again tomorrow, that I should pay: which I did.

We left the dispiriting little village with only an hour or two to dusk. The rain had stopped but the road, deprived for years of any maintenance, was pudding-like in consistency, with potholes and ruts three and four feet deep, and red lakes of muddy water whose depth it was impossible to foresee. Many times we had to alight to push, and before long were all caked from head to toe in a film of henna-coloured earth, dried and cracked into lizard-scales.

Our progress was slow. The land had few inhabitants. There were clearings in the forest from time to time with a few wooden houses, neat enough and with flowers growing round them, but I saw no land under cultivation. Some of the houses had fetish statues outside. Twice we stopped to buy porcupines and monkeys, the latter strung up like hanged criminals.

As night fell, fever entered the blood of the drivers. They entered a deadly competition, racing along the narrow forest track side by side, almost touching, each trying to forge ahead of the other. The vehicles slithered and skidded, often just escaping the embrace of giant trees on either side of the road; miraculously we escaped accident, but I was in the truck that eventually lost the contest, the driver recovering his sanity as suddenly as he had lost it.

The journey of eighty miles took ten hours. At eleven o'clock we passed through a village with a military road block. The driver thought first to ignore it, crashing through the barrier and driving on; but just as he had lost his nerve in the race, he lost it again now, stopped and reversed meekly to the roadblock, where the reception of the soldiers was far from friendly. We were now highly suspect to them, and they insisted upon searching all our luggage by very dim torchlight. They demanded to see not only my passport but my vaccination certificates, buried deep in my bag. This was pure vindictiveness, for they were only semi-literate and had no idea of the meaning of the certificates. I thought to taunt them by feigning ignorance and asking for how long my yellow fever card was valid; but wiser counsel prevailed.

Before we continued the driver had to pay for the broken barrier – a branch of a tree flung across the road.

We reached Bata at two in the morning. The roads were, if anything, worse than in the forest. The few lights that shone in the darkness illuminated no great prosperity. We churned and skated in the mud, labouring up the faintest inclines, and sometimes slithering Sisyphuslike to the bottom.

The driver knew of a cheap hotel: he stayed there himself. My room was another windowless box, about the size of a coffin; but I was tired and one can, after all, sleep well in a coffin.

The hotel, I discovered next morning, was in the muddiest part of town. The mud sucked at one's shoes; people walked gingerly if they were shod. The unshod were at a great advantage in Bata after the rains.

I asked the way to a bank, but the first people I asked either did not know what a bank was or denied knowledge of one in Bata. After several inquiries, I found a man who not only had knowledge of *two* banks (he mentioned that there were two with civic pride), but offered to take me to them.

The first, while technically open to the public, in the sense that the doors were not locked, was deserted. It was a ghost bank: no transactions had taken place there for a long time. There were not even any papers left. The second, on the sea front, was an attractive colonial-style building with dark shutters and a tiled roof. Its façade had been recently whitewashed, though only its façade: the side walls were decaying. But it looked a better hope and I waited for it to open.

It was only after I had changed $100 there that I learnt how fortunate I had been to do so. For lack of ready money, the bank sometimes shut its doors for two months at a time. I met a Spaniard who had once seen a simple and naive rural Guinean deposit his life savings in the bank. The Spaniard wanted to warn him against such a course of action, for once the money had disappeared into the maw of the bank's accounts, it was quite likely never to be seen again. But the Spaniard did not do so, for in the present climate he might have been accused of economic sabotage.

Equatorial Guinea was, in fact, going through a severe liquidity crisis occasioned by a sudden switch from its own worthless currency, the *bipkwele*, which it had produced for years like confetti, to a currency, the CFA franc, which was freely convertible at fifty to one to the French franc. The printing presses were able no longer to disguise the poverty of the country with a shower of coloured paper, for it was no longer master of its own money. (That distinction had passed to the French.) So short was Equatorial Guinea of banknotes that wages, when paid at all, had sometimes to be paid in ten franc coins; while for a time it was possible to exchange a 10,000 franc note for eleven 1000 franc notes because currency smugglers found the large denomination notes more convenient.

Bata was a town more dilapidated than any I had seen – and I had, in a sense, made a special study of the subject since coming to Africa. It was nearly seven years since the coup that brought an end to the insane regime of Macias Nguema; a regime that killed or forced to flee over a third of the population; that reduced agricultural output to practically nothing; that turned the country into a forced labour camp; that closed it to the world; that left even the capital city without electric power; under which every installation fell to pieces if it were not deliberately smashed; under which it was dangerous to own a single book or even a page from a book, such ownership marking one out as an intellectual and plotter to be slaughtered; a regime that revived illiteracy in a country with previously the highest literacy rate in Africa; that unleashed a savage army to loot and rape at will; in short, a regime that was one of the worst in this, the century of such regimes. Seven years ago it had fallen, but Bata was still suffering its effects, and perhaps would never recover.

The roads in the centre of the town had once been paved but, after years of neglect, most had either been churned back into mud or, at the least, were so cracked and crevassed that they were a menace to any vehicle – not that there were many. Two piers were crumbling progressively into the sea. The balustrade along the sea wall had collapsed, and the lamps that once graced it had toppled on to the beach below, there to rust into oblivion. Along the beautiful beach, littered in places with broken light bulbs (with barnacles and mussels grown on to them), were former Spanish villas, their roofs caved in, their doors gone, their windows smashed. A once luxurious hotel, the *Panáfrica*, over-looked a stretch of the bay without equal; at first sight empty, most of the furniture having been removed, and the windows either cracked or smashed, more careful observation showed it was open, if not exactly for business, then for members of its staff to lie asleep on the few chairs remaining in its lobby. Between the buildings the undergrowth of the jungle was creeping back. The market was near the monument to the 'martyrs' of the 1979 coup who died *por una Guinea mejor* – for a better Guinea, the words that appear at the bottom of all official correspondence, like the *Yours in Christ* of evangelicals. It was a poor affair, scruffy and almost without fresh produce, though with plenty of imported tinned sardines and Scotch.

Amazingly enough, one good restaurant and bar had survived in Bata, to which all the expatriates repaired, in some cases as often and for as long as possible. On the bar counter was a telephone; suddenly it received a tug from behind the bar and went crashing to the ground. The barmaid swore violently, and lifted the culprit by one arm from below: a mischievous baby chimpanzee who had been caught in the nearby forest. She smacked him and banished him to his cage outside.

A Spanish expatriate at the bar spoke to me. He had drunk a lot of *tinto* in his life and had grown so enormously fat that breathing was no longer something he could take for granted. He had that strange growth of stubble, never more but never less than three days, that always gives a man – however blameless his life has been – an appearance of desperate dissolution. He had been in Guinea all through Macias Nguema's time, a feat of true escapology, for the dictator had been a violent hispanophobe and not above killing foreigners. He was reluctant to speak of those times, both from natural recoil from dreadful memories and from fear. Fear was not yet ended in Guinea: the man who had led Macias' overthrow was his nephew, Teodoro Obiang Nguema, who had for long served in Macias' army as an officer; and many of the men who were powerful under Macias were powerful still. One talked, if at all, in whispers.

To illustrate how far Guinea had sunk, he pulled the telephone directory off the bar to show me. It was a slim volume of forty-eight pages with very large print: there could not have been more than a few hundred subscribers in the entire country. It was the preface to the directory to which he wanted to draw my attention:

The outstanding work undertaken by the Government of National Reconstruction and its irrevocable ideal of a BETTER GUINEA has made possible the publication of this first TELEPHONE DIRECTORY FOR EQUATORIAL GUINEA, which satisfies such an imperious necessity and whose appearance would have been utopian in the first decade of independence.

Therefore, the National Telecommunications Service can do no less than dedicate this modest work to His Excellency the President of the Republic, OBIANG NGUEMA MBASOGO, as a sign of recognition of the impulse and new direction he has given to the Nation in general and to the improvement in our telecommunications in particular.

He slapped the directory back on the counter.

'What are you doing in Guinea?' he asked.

I explained that I was *en route* through Africa, and that I wrote.

'You mustn't let them know you are a writer,' he said.

'Why not?'

'Because they would kill you.' He drew a horizontal line across his throat to indicate a cut. 'They would cut you up and throw you in the sea. No-one would know. They wouldn't tell anyone. They don't like writers.'

His earnestness was a little alarming. But how would they find out I was a writer? I had my diary with me, of course . . . Gradually, alarm gave way to another emotion: pride. I had never been important enough to be worth killing before. The threat of death, faint as it was, gave new significance to life.

It rained that afternoon, throwing drapes of grey over the town. Towards evening, as the rain subsided, Bata rang with the sound of military music, not terribly well-played to be sure, but with a certain swagger that proclaimed the army's lordship over all it surveyed. Lined up in the streets were ranks of thin looking conscripts – such men are dangerous –

harangued by officers in khaki capes who picked out culprits (or scapegoats?) to stand with their hands on their heads.

I didn't display excessive interest in the cavortings of the army: in Africa they hardly draw distinctions between curiosity and espionage. Besides, I didn't want to add to the self-importance of the officers. Who, I wondered, was this army ever going to fight, except perhaps itself and civilians?

I went to a bar next door to my hotel. There were two from which to choose: I elected for the one without pink and green lighting and with a lower decibellage of music. There, over a Cameroonian beer, I met a teacher at the *Politécnico* and we started talking. He had been a refugee in Spain for many of the Macias years; though, like many Guineans I met who had been refugees, he preferred to say he had been a student all that time. When he learnt I was a doctor he told me about his wife who was in Bata hospital. She had had fever for two weeks: treated several times for malaria, she had failed to improve. She had never had a blood test in all that time to determine whether she really had malaria or not: they just went ahead and treated her for it anyway. He asked whether I should like to visit her and I agreed, on condition I was not expected to interfere with her treatment.

It occurred to me as we walked the unlit streets that he might be leading me into a trap. He wasn't. We arrived at the hospital: the first building was whitewashed and well-lit, semi-classical in design with a large *porte cochère*. It gave no indication of the numerous and gloomy barracks behind, the wards with faintly glimmering lights, like the dying embers of a fire, escaping from between the slats in the shutters.

His wife was in a ward for medical cases. There were six patients in a white-tiled room of more than adequate size, and only one patient per bed – something by no means universal in African hospitals. Many of the tiles were missing from the walls and were now irreplaceable, of course: during the Macias years, Bata's hospital – which before then had been one of the best in West Africa – was closed down and looted. But even after all that it was in better condition than many I had seen.

His wife was on a pallet, surrounded by her belongings. There were beads of sweat on her brow, her lips and mouth were dry, and when she spoke – faintly, for she was weak – her teeth seemed prominent, as in a skull. She greeted the appearance of a white stranger with exhausted indifference. Her husband explained nothing and said little. In the bed opposite was a young man whose flesh had melted to the bone and who was too weak to raise his head from his pallet; he was all too evidently dying. A nurse with a cigarette in his mouth was trying and failing to set up an intravenous infusion into the skeletal arm of another patient.

I remarked that the sight of such a ward gave me the urge to start medical work again. Why then not take a job in Bata, my companion urged. The foreign doctors in the hospital were well-paid and in fourteen years – he was quite specific about the time it would take – I should return to Europe a millionaire. I did not like to go into why I thought I could not spend fourteen years in Bata.

We left his wife, whether to recover or die I do not know. His concern for her seemed less than all-consuming; perhaps, I thought, he was a man who kept everything inward. But as soon as we were out of the hospital he asked me whether I wanted a *chica* for the night.

The chica he had in mind was the fattish owner of a bar in a hut, with four bottles of spirit and a single light hanging by a wire draped over the thatched roof. By this light she was removing the lice and nits from her young daughter's hair and crushing them between her thumb-nails. I left my companion to enjoy her favours.

On the morning of my departure from Bata I went to the cathedral, a very Spanish building, the columns and walls of whose cool and dark interior were painted mottled brown to imitate marble. It was deserted. Around the architrave was a painted message of very hispanic piety: 'Blessed be the hour in which the Most Holy Virgin came in mortal flesh to Zaragoza . . . 1954'. It was a message from an age as bygone as that of the Romans. Macias Nguema had hated the church and tried to destroy it in Equatorial Guinea: even when it was not political, it was a mute contradiction of the dictator's all-embracing pretensions. The building itself had suffered neglect and decay. Upstairs in the balcony the wood rotted, windows were cracked or broken, in the corners were dusty giant cobwebs of the kind seen in tombs in horror movies. What, I wondered, would remain of this church in twenty years?

To reach the island of Bioko (called Macias Nguema when Macias Nguema ruled, and before that Fernando Po, after its Portuguese discoverer) I resorted for the first time on my journey to an aeroplane, since there was a ship only once a month between Bata and the island

and no-one – certainly no-one at the national shipping company – could say when next it would sail.

The airport, along a road of quite extraordinary muddiness, was under renovation. I had noticed earlier in the day that the balustrade along the sea front was also under repair; and in the prevailing atmosphere of inspissated inertia, it was clear something very unusual was about to take place in Bata. It was: in less than two months' time, the heads of state of the *Union Douanière des États d'Afrique Centrale* (to which Equatorial Guinea had just acceded) were to meet there. As a general rule, if something is under repair in Africa, a head of state is about to go by. Among the visiting heads of state was to be the then current chairman of the Organization of African Unity, Denis Sassou-Nguesso; and so that his and the other presidential buttocks should not be unduly bruised by the unevenness of the airport road the *South Africans* had been asked, as the only people on the continent capable of doing it in time, to resurface the road. Furthermore, they – the South Africans – had built the only comfortable accommodation in town for the presidents, at a cost of $600,000 (the road was going to cost much more): the presidents therefore would not have to stay in the disgusting *Panáfrica* and would be able to issue their denunciations of apartheid in tolerable comfort.

At the airport I met a young South African vet called Piet. He was on his way back to Bioko from Gabon, whither he had accompanied another South African injured at the model cattle farm the South Africans were trying to establish on the island after the destruction of the Macias years.

Although the South African project was, as I later discovered, by far the most successful of the 131 foreign aid projects in operation in Guinea, since its staff worked not only for a tax-free salary and pension, but for a cause, whether good or bad, namely the reduction of South Africa's isolation, Piet did not wish to stay much longer in Guinea and was doubtful of his future in South Africa. An Afrikaner who spoke English with a certain hesitation, he had considered moving to England. He said his government was offering too few concessions too late; and he was prepared to stay in a black-ruled South Africa, providing only it had not been preceded by a bloodbath.

We flew the short distance to Bioko in an ancient aircraft that had belonged previously to Air Madagascar. Bioko is volcanic, one of a chain of volcanoes that stretches hundreds of miles from Mount Cameroon in the north to Principe, Sao Tomé and Annobon in the south. It rises to ten thousand feet, a forest-covered, dark green mountain that emerges seemingly sheer from the sea, its peak more often than not obscured by a chaste veil of thin white cloud that hovers around it, and like most such veils creates an inordinate desire to see what lies behind. When we landed, however, we had a clear view of the peak; more unusually still, we had a clear view of Mount Cameroon, thirty miles away across the straits that separate the mainland of Africa from Bioko.

Piet knew an aid worker for an international agency, a Briton fluent in French, Spanish, Catalan and Portuguese, with whom he was to stay the night, and he suggested I came along too. Phil, the aid worker, lived in what can only be described as the aid quarter of Malabo, the capital city (formerly called Santa Isabel, and for a time, during British occupation, Clarence). Phil asked me to stay.

His house was on a little estate of ten modern houses built at great expense by his organization. From time to time, when the government was host to a conference in Malabo and needed decent accommodation, these houses were requisitioned, a crate of whisky and champagne would appear in every room, and later the houses were returned in a post-orgiastic condition.

The recycling of aid money is undoubtedly the principal economic activity of Equatorial Guinea. More than half the vehicles in the country are connected in some way with aid projects, and organizations voluntary, national, bilateral, international, charitable, religious, political, medical, agricultural, of every conceivable hue, have descended like vultures on the carcass of a country that until 1968 had a *per capita* income second only to Libya's and Gabon's on the African continent. But it is an ill wind that blows nobody any good; and Equatorial Guinea's misfortune (an inadequate word) had turned it into a land of opportunity for the perpetually disgruntled cosmopolitans of the international aid fraternity, whose need to help those less fortunate than themselves is happily compatible with their need for large tax-free salaries. As far as I could tell, the greatest economic effect of the multifarious United Nations agencies had been to increase the turnover of the well-stocked shops in Douala, just a short weekly chartered flight away in Cameroon. The prayer of the aid workers must have been, 'Lord, rehabilitate Equatorial Guinea's economy, but not just yet.'

The prayer was not really necessary since the Guinean economy was proving highly refractory to rehabilitation. At independence, the country exported 40,000 tons of some of the best cocoa in the world, and 8,000 tons of coffee; Macias Nguema reduced it to nothing; and now, seven years after the coup that removed him, only 5,000 tons of cocoa of variable quality, and no coffee at all, were being exported.

The lack of progress was at least partly caused by government incompetence and corruption. The entire cabinet, with the exception of the powerless prime minister and the illiterate minister of works, came from the same village (the President's). No enterprise in the country could hope to succeed, or be allowed to exist, without the participation of the President in its profits. There were no effective property laws, except for members of the government: what they wanted, they took. When an international aid agency announced it was providing funds for the 'rehabilitation' (a word much used in Guinea) of cocoa plantations, many of them were confiscated from their owners, not in the desire for a productive asset, but in the hope of laying hands on the aid money to squander at once or deposit abroad. To raise a little extra revenue, the Guineans had resorted to selling the same consignment of cocoa to three different buyers, a ruse that was likely to work only once or twice before destroying their trade completely. And on the eve of Independence Day, when the President promoted himself, much moved, to general (the next step up being to *mariscal*, marshal), the last thousand dollars was removed from the treasury so that the government could throw a party for itself.

Those aid workers, amongst whom Phil was one, who took their work seriously were doomed, therefore, to frustration. It was for that reason, Phil said, that weekends in Malabo tended to be wild. We had arrived late on Friday afternoon and the evening started at nine o'clock with drinks in his house for friends. There was, to my surprise, much champagne, and of good quality; champagne being one of the few commodities not in short supply in Guinea.

After a couple of hours we went on to a party at the house of a Spanish planter, once a big game hunter in central Africa, who had bravely (or foolhardily) staked his future on the recovery of the Guinean economy. His house was a large colonial building with high-ceilinged rooms and crumbling plasterwork. Most of the guests were Spanish expatriates. Once more the champagne flowed, from desperation, according to Phil.

Under the surface gaiety of the guests, he said, lay a profound unhappiness and dissatisfaction; but it would have taken a psychologist to distinguish between this melancholy gaiety and the true variety.

They sang and danced without any of the foolish inhibitions that so cripple the British in such situations. They each had a fund of songs which all of them knew, learnt as children and never forgotten. I awaited with terror the awful, inevitable moment when they would ask for an English song, or that I should dance. I dreamt up excuses: laryngitis, an old knee injury. What an ungracious, antisocial culture I came from! How could I explain that it also had its attractions (though I couldn't for the moment think what they were)?

The bank manager, fat, unshaven, tipsy from champagne, stood up to sing a flamenco song, melancholy, wistful, *emocionante*. His tenor voice had an impassioned vibrato. Did he sing so movingly because his bank had all but collapsed, or because of the vanity of all human endeavour? Whatever the reason, it was difficult to imagine a British bank manager singing anything less anaemic and non-committal than *Happy Birthday to You*, and even then only in chorus. After his brief and passionate excursion into the realm of song, however, the bank manager fell back on to the sofa to resume his consumption of champagne.

The dancing lasted until the early hours. From there some of us went on to *el Bantú*, a low dive, a bar-discothèque, and haunt of prostitutes. Here the gaiety was definitely forced, as bachelor expatriates sought desperately to persuade themselves they were not wasting the best years of their lives in a wilderness bereft of purpose. The prostitutes were alternatively utterly exhausted or provocatively pouting for custom.

Beyond *el Bantú*, with its own generator for stroboscopic lights, the city lay in darkness. The President had left Malabo for Bata, and so the electricity supply had been switched off. Across the water was the faint pink glow of the oil wells in the Bight of Biafra.

Later that morning Looksmart, Phil's Ghanaian houseboy, arrived to clear away the things from the drinks party of the night before. A name like Looksmart had all but destined him for such a job. Not that he was complaining: he had come to Guinea from Ghana having heard it was a land of opportunity, and he had indeed found work there. Probably there were Guineans in Ghana who had heard the same of Ghana, for Africans are not immune to the idea that things must be better elsewhere.

But for Looksmart, the *real* promised land was what he called 'the White Man's Country'. He had taken a second job, that gave him only six hours a day free, to save for his fare. He undoubtedly thought of white men as superior beings, effortlessly endowed with wealth who, moreover, behaved with an everyday decency and honesty not to be found amongst Africans. His experience was, of course, limited to whites of the aid community who, whatever their shortcomings, are educated men who behave with a certain circumspection. I had not the heart (and an odd racial pride made me reticent) to tell Looksmart that there was poverty and ignorance too in the White Man's Country, that he might not be welcome there and that he might encounter prejudice, rejection, cold and misery.

But he, who had been born five years after Ghana's independence, was unshakeably of the opinion there was no hope for Ghana (or the rest of Africa) until the white man returned to rule. Was he saying it to please me? I asked him what had led him to his conclusion.

'Our rulers are corrupt,' he said. 'They think only of themselves. They don't think at all of the small people like us.'

'And if you were a ruler,' I asked, 'would you too be corrupt?'

'Yes,' he replied. 'Corruption is in the black man's blood.'

As if to prove his point, he stole a considerable sum of money from Phil's attaché case two days before Phil left Equatorial Guinea for good, and made off with it. With considerable cunning Looksmart must have observed Phil as he used the combination lock of his case: and until he took the money, he had never shown any sign of dishonesty but, on the contrary, devotion and loyalty. Yet even so, I cannot find it in my heart to condemn the truly poor when they know their theft will make little difference in the long run to those from whom they steal.

Looksmart had discovered from my passport that I was a doctor. He took the opportunity to consult me about his asthma, an attack of which he had suffered every night for fifteen years without benefit of regular treatment.

'I am happy with myself,' he said. 'Only my chest . . .'

He could not play football with his friends and that worried him. He had been in hospital many times in his life, and to many different hospitals, but always as a last resort. I wrote a list of medicines for him, should he ever find himself in a country where they were available. Then he asked me whether I had anything to give him to make him taller and stronger. He was good-looking, but only five feet six tall.

I told him that at his age he would have to accept his height as God-given. As for the injections about which he had heard to make him more muscular, I had no doubt that he would find doctors to give them for a fee, but my advice was studiously to avoid them.

'In any case,' I asked, 'why do you want to be taller and stronger?'

'So that people will respect me.'

Phil also had a Ghanaian night-watchman called Bernard: not that there was much crime to be guarded against in Malabo, or that Bernard, who slept a lot on duty, would have been of much use had there been any. Phil first noticed him and then employed him because of his brilliantly white teeth. One day Phil asked him how he kept his teeth so very white.

'Vim, sir.'

Fernando Po once had a fearful reputation as the most fever-ridden location along the West African coast. Whole garrisons of Spanish soldiers were wiped out at a time, and Sir Richard Burton, who was consul in Fernando Po between 1863 and 1865 (and detested it) wrote of his consulate that it was a 'corrugated iron coffin or plank-lined morgue, containing a dead consul once a year'.

Now that fever holds fewer terrors than it once did, one can appreciate the beauty of Malabo.* Architecturally, it must have improved immensely since Burton's and Mary Kingsley's day, for it is now a charming Spanish town, whose delapidation and slightly *ersatz* quality only please the connoisseur of unusual atmospheres all the more. Fine roads one may see anywhere; but the potholes in the roads of Malabo have become small gardens of wild flowers and even of small shrubs, living in peace and undisturbed by zealous municipal road-repairers. There are ornate *fin-de-siècle* baroque buildings, in a condition so parlous you think they must crumble to dust if someone tries to climb the stairs – until you see four people appear, chatting nonchalantly, on the elaborate wrought iron balcony. In the squares and other open places are benches decorated with Spanish tiles depicting African life as a kind of genteel pastoral idyll, all black nymphs and shepherds. Unfortunately, many of the tiles have been broken or have faded, never to be replaced. The town, built on

*Nevertheless, in the year I visited Equatorial Guinea, approximately one tenth of its expatriate population died. There was an air crash in which a Spanish transport aircraft dived into the sea with eighteen aboard. No-one will ever know the cause, though rumours abound. Others died of malaria, or in road and other accidents.

the classical grid pattern, has charming colonnaded streets, a grandi-loquent cathedral, and a mock-splendid former governor's palace, re-cently refurbished for a visit by President Mobutu, who cancelled at the last minute because of a crisis at home. And from the verandah of the *Hotel Bahia*, now practically devoid of services, is one of the most beautiful views I have ever seen, a beauty so moving that the general state of decay all around is all the more poignant. A perfect little bay, enclosed in cliffs a hundred feet high and ringed with palms, has water of pure sapphire.

There was a single large vessel in the port, a Spanish cargo ship whose captain was temporarily under arrest. The drowned body of a Ghanaian stowaway had been found floating in the sea nearby; and according to his companion who survived, the captain of the ship, on the discovery of the two stowaways, had ordered they should be beaten and thrown overboard, despite the pleas of the drowned man that he could not swim. According to the captain, the two men had jumped overboard of their own accord on being discovered: but that did not account for the signs of a severe beating on the survivor's head. The incident had entered the complex realms of politics and diplomacy, with the Spanish consul affecting to find the survivor's story self-evidently absurd; and in the end, predictably, the matter was resolved not according to justice or evidence, but according to power, Spain being the largest single aid donor to Guinea.

Down in the bay was a small grey gunboat, a gift of China to the government of Macias, which was scuttled in the 1979 coup. The sea lapped round its deck cabin, atop which a radar antenna stood motionless. Tied to the shore was the new Equatorial Guinean navy, another grey gunboat, this one a gift of Nigeria, which was used by the crew – so rumour had it – for a little private piracy.

Along the road leading down to the bay are some man-made caves dug into the rock face. A short passage, through which it is necessary to stoop, leads to two small, dark caverns. These repositories of empty Coca-Cola tins were once the slave caves from which the slaves were shipped across the Atlantic. The scene, no doubt, of innumerable barbarities, it seemed somehow frivolous that I should so fastidiously avoid, for the sake of my shoes, the slime created on the floor of the caverns by the continuous ooze of water through the rocky walls.

One of the less attractive buildings in the town was a featureless, greyish-white block that occupied two of the squares of the grid. The slatted, shuttered windows on the upper floor revealed nothing, yet somehow one sensed the foetid disorder – the unmade beds, the dirty mosquito nets – within. It was permitted to walk along only three of the building's four sides, for it was the barracks of the President's Moroccan guard, and Moroccan soldiers, with guns they looked only too willing to use, shooed one away from the barracks' main entrance with gestures of unmistakable hostility. The President did not trust his own countrymen to defend him, a common enough phenomenon in Africa. As tough and sinewy as old meat, battle-hardened (it was said) in the deserts of the Western Sahara, with black teeth and mean reddish-brown faces, the guard looked as though their hobby was disembowelling grandmothers with bayonets. I was told the Guineans went to considerable lengths to avoid these Moroccans, who terrified them: and one look was sufficient to understand why.

Malabo market was unimpressive, except for the quantity and variety of imported drink. There was little fish, and that little, having been caught in Guinean waters, frozen aboard Spanish vessels, and taken to Spain, was then brought back to Guinea. The pathetic little heaps of thawing fish, with black clouds of flies hovering above them, seemed somehow to symbolize Africa's plight. But no matter: there was more laughter even in Malabo market than in Harrods.

I was a week in Malabo. The town seemed mysteriously to sap my will, as though it were the final, irrefutable argument for the vanity of all human purpose. Phil's project to rehabilitate the cocoa farms had come to a temporary halt for lack of funds: the treasury was empty and the government was unable to put up its agreed share of the costs.

There were three restaurants in Malabo. One on the shore was now deserted, though until recently the best in Malabo (not a difficult distinction). The owner had been killed in a fire the week before. A small man, he had conceived it his duty to rescue an air-conditioner from a burning house he was passing. It fell on him and crushed him to death. I don't think I've ever heard of a more absurd demise. I patronized both restaurants that remained in business. The first was owned and run by a large African woman of violently changeable mood. At one moment she would laugh with her customers and dance with them; at the next, for no discernible reason, she would grow angry and – in mid-meal – close the restaurant down and go home. In any other town, but not in Malabo, her behaviour would have long since bankrupted her.

The other restaurant, called the *Beyrouth*, was owned by a misanthropic (or painfully shy) Lebanese, who every night of his life ate in his own restaurant, but always completely alone. The restaurant had a large courtyard strung with coloured lights, but it would have taken more than these to enliven the gloom prevailing among the United Nations and other expatriate patrons. It was at the *Beyrouth* that someone played a locally celebrated practical joke on a former American ambassador. Taking advantage of the restaurant's name and atmosphere – one could imagine Humphrey Bogart playing a hard-bitten spy there – the joker called the ambassador and, affecting a Russian accent, told him his Soviet counterpart wanted to meet him at the *Beyrouth* to tell him something of the utmost importance. Thinking perhaps to score a striking coup in a post of otherwise not vital importance to his country, the ambassador duly appeared at the appointed time and waited – and waited. Everyone laughed. Nevertheless, the ambassador was not entirely foolish: for the Soviet embassy has more than fifty personnel, not all of whom could be occupied with cultural relations and the promotion of trade and tourism.

At the Ministry of Information, an office scarcely humming with activity (Equatorial Guinea does not, for example, publish a newspaper or a magazine), I found some books – five, to be exact – about the country, all of them dedicated, like the telephone directory, to the President. Waking the man at the desk, I purchased a novel called *El Reencuentro: El Retorno del Exilado*, by Juan Balboa Boneke. It was not so much a novel, actually, as a tract: at every opportunity the characters proclaimed the necessity of hard work and sacrifice to rebuild their shattered land. The author had spent the long Macias years in exile in Spain, and had become so European that he was much preoccupied as to how he would become African again. He was worried also about his children. He wanted them to reject the superficiality of Europe, its cult of 'welfare always unsatisfied', its 'anxiety always to earn more and more'; he talked of Europe's 'career that finally ends in the dehumanization of Man, the empire of THINGS, of luxury and ostentation, slowly separating itself from other values that are much more transcendental, spiritual and ethical'. He wanted his children to appreciate the 'humanistic and cultural resources of the Bubi' (his tribe, much persecuted by Macias), 'the philosophical richness of their ancestral society'. Above all, he wanted them to reject what he called Europe's *presentism*.

I think I understood what he meant, and I sympathized. Nevertheless, it struck me that here, once again, was an African author being not wholly honest about African society as it now was. Instead, he was comparing Europe with a pre-contact Africa of his mind, that may or may not have existed. The alleged philosophical superiority of backward societies is a common psychological defence against the onslaught of an overwhelmingly more advanced material society. And what are African élites today if not ostentatious, and what is Mobutu's and the President of Equatorial Guinea's behaviour if not *presentism* writ large? The problem for Africans is that a distorting mirror image of Europe has entered their souls, and remains there whether they like it or not.

On Sunday I was invited to 'lunch' at the house of the Spanish people to whose party I had gone. It was more an important social event than a mere meal, lasting ten hours. Once more the *sangría* and champagne flowed, and the food itself was prepared with wonderful care of ingredients not often seen in Malabo. Once again I could not but compare the fun-loving nature of the Spanish with the lugubrious, mortgage-obsessed, rain-sodden temperament of my own nation. Nevertheless, when it came to a discussion of the merits of our two languages, I defended my own. The chief argument produced against English, propounded with passion by a young Spanish woman of stunning attractiveness, with dark eyes beyond the powers of any language to describe, was that English is virtually devoid of the diminutives in which Spanish is so rich, and with which anything from love to contempt can so succinctly be expressed.

'That is because,' I explained, 'the English have no emotions.'

– ¡Exacto! – exclaimed the young woman.

On another day I went to the South African cattle station, high up in the centre of the island. From Malabo the island had seemed a single volcanic mountain; but going inland I discovered to my surprise that there were several peaks, all jungle covered. We passed the little bay of Luba where, in Macias' time, the Russians had a submarine station. We climbed to several thousand feet, to one of the wettest regions of the globe, where four yards of rain fall every year, and rare is the day that does not have its inundation. The night and day of my visit was not one of them, and the open grassland, which appeared as a sudden unexpected break in the jungle, was thoroughly sodden. It was a world of emerald and grey.

There had been a cattle farm here in Spanish times, but Macias had plundered it until there were very few cattle left, and those were starving. The South Africans, five of them, were there to revive the farm, and in this they had achieved some success. As to their ultimate motive in being there, it was something we did not discuss, but it was unlikely – I surmised – to be the mere assurance of a supply of dairy products to the Equatorial Guineans, however deserving they were of butter and cheese. At any rate, they did not live in great state like other aid workers; their conditions, if not primitive, were certainly not luxurious. Their wooden house was cold and damp; I slept on the floor, next to the parrot stand, on which the parrot, a one-bird guano factory, screamed on waking in the morning: ¿Que pasa? ¿Que pasa? ¿Que pasa?

I spoke to Enrique, one of the farm's Guinean workers. Unlike most of the Guineans to whom I spoke, Enrique was willing to talk of the Macias years. He was a Bubi, one of the minority tribe disproportionately persecuted in that era of institutionalized paranoia. He himself had been subjected to forced labour without pay for many years. I asked how he had kept alive, and he replied that, like thousands of others, he lived as an animal in the forests, gathering whatever was edible. Even now, when life was a little easier, bananas were not cultivated in Guinea but grew wild, as a gift of nature. His hut had been raided many times by soldiers and his few possessions taken. The faintest glimmer of rebellion or dissension against this tyranny had not only been useless but fatal, for the soldiers, often drunk, had thought no more of killing a family than of walking on ants. He had been lucky to survive at all.

Enrique had an intelligent, immediately likeable face; but when he smiled – which was often – there was still a melancholy withdrawal in his eyes. He had been to the depths of hell, and no joy could ever be unalloyed for him again.

I asked him about the Spanish days. They were good, he said; no-one had any idea of the cataclysm that was coming. They had been happy, for though wages were low, you could buy everything. But it was useless to think of those days now, for they would never return.

And how did he find the South Africans? He had no complaints. They were friendly, they were not rude; they paid wages regularly, on time; when the workers were ill, they gave them medicines free of charge. What more could one ask, especially in Equatorial Guinea?

I had been a comparatively long time in Malabo, and though I had sometimes been reduced to reading the classified advertisements of a two-month-old *Daily Telegraph* or the share prices in an even older *Financial Times*, I was strangely reluctant to leave. Perhaps doing nothing is my métier. But eventually I booked for the short flight to Douala, with pangs of guilt about once more resorting to aircraft in defiance of my resolution not to.

The flight was not until after the great weekly event in Malabo, the arrival of the *Iberia* flight from Madrid. Half the town's population, and all the expatriates, come out to the airport to greet it. For the latter, it is reassurance that the outside world continues to exist. Since there are no instruments at Malabo airport, and since the island is very often shrouded in cloud, the flight has not infrequently to return whence it came, to try again soon. When this happens, a temporary but profound gloom settles over the expatriates, who have longer to wait for their life-giving letters and supplies.

On this occasion, however, the sky was blue and the flight not much delayed. There was a large, excited crowd; the airport bar – owned by the President's wife – was doing a roaring trade before noon. The aircraft landed, to more excitement still: no-one who has not seen a modern jetliner in complete isolation, against an exotic tropical background, can appreciate the majesty of these magnificent machines.

It was at the airport I met a man about whom I had heard much, Bill-From-Princeton. He was called Bill-From-Princeton because that was how he had introduced himself when he first arrived in Malabo: *Hello, I'm Bill from Princeton.*

Bill-From-Princeton was a professor of economics who had been seconded to the Guinean government as an adviser, and was paid an enormous salary by an international agency. Rumour had it that his first act on arriving in Malabo was to go to the President to ask for a salary *reduction* of $30,000 a year, on the grounds his salary was not justified. If this interview ever took place, I am surprised he came out of it alive:

exalted integrity and honesty being the last kind of example the President would wish him to set.

Bill-From-Princeton was the tallest, cleanest-cut, handsomest thing that had ever been seen in Malabo, the living embodiment of a high-fibre, low-cholesterol diet. Brilliantly intelligent, he was also good at sport. His particular field of knowledge was corruption in the Third World. I had read a chapter of his forthcoming book on the subject, the typescript of which happened to have been in Phil's house. It was about why Pakistani milk-sellers adulterate milk and it was thirty pages long. I had thought you didn't need to be a Princeton professor to know why Pakistani milk-sellers adulterate milk, but there was more to the matter than I suspected. It was all a question of inadequate flows of information, apparently.

Our meeting was unfortunately brief. I should have liked to hear more of his *strategies*, as he called them, for reducing corruption in countries like Equatorial Guinea. One of them, I heard, was to go to the President to explain why corruption was a Bad Thing.

'I see,' the President will say. 'I never realized. In that case, I'll close down my Swiss bank account and sell my villa in Majorca.'

I wished Bill-From-Princeton luck with his strategies and boarded the aircraft to Douala.

NINE

Cameroon

I entered Cameroon after the short flight without the difficulties of which I had been forewarned. ('Difficulties' meant bribes.) A Cameroonian diplomat returning home on leave, who wore heavy gold rings like knuckledusters, experienced even fewer difficulties: he simply pushed past the crowds and entirely ignored the lesser officials of his republic. I followed in his slipstream.

Suddenly in Douala I felt a loss of confidence in my journey. I had written about an earlier journey across South America and been criticized for lack of moral purpose. I still had none, unless curiosity was moral. Nor was I any more of a humanitarian than I had been then (another criticism): although a doctor, I was still able to see poverty without bankrupting myself to relieve it. What I had taken as a lack of humbug, my critics had taken as almost psychopathic detachment.

And Douala sapped my confidence because, even as I walked around it, I thought to myself: What can I write about it? A British businessman and his wife confirmed there was nothing to say about Douala except that it was hot and humid and there were no concerts apart from occasional piano recitals at the Goethe Institute. It seemed to me – as the blue sparkle of the swimming pool outside entered the dining room where lunch was brought by a servant of spectacular obsequiousness, all smiling teeth and *Yes-sah*! – an inadequate summary of a city of more than a million inhabitants. I was temporarily tired of my journey, and wished I had taken the *Iberia* flight to Madrid. Equatorial Guinea had struck me as so extraordinary that I feared anticlimax the rest of the way.

There was a debate that night on Cameroonian television as to whether office hours should continue to be split by a long lunchbreak and siesta, as at present, or whether work should continue through till two-thirty in the afternoon. The latter scheme would reduce by two the number of rush hours every day; but it would make it difficult for parents to collect their children from school. It was strange to hear a debate in Africa on so mundane a question, especially coming from a country that had witnessed one of the most vicious massacres of the twentieth, or any other, century. Perhaps it was a symptom of Cameroon's relative success: at last an African country where food production grows faster than the population, and whose exports do not rely on a single commodity.

Such buildings from the colonial era as still stood in Douala were being left for humidity, fungus and neglect to destroy. From now on it was all to be concrete and plate glass, preferably banks and five-star hotels. But while Cameroon was relatively prosperous, it was still not a rich country, and so the number of skyscrapers was as yet fairly small, and open sewers never far away. Along one of the principal streets of the city, the *Avenue de la Liberté*, was an overgrown graveyard, whose luxuriant vegetation two men with machetes were desultorily attacking, though they worked so slowly I think the vegetation must have grown faster than they cut it down. Some of the grass was taller than a man, and was sprung, trap-like, with thistles, thorns and prickles. But I cannot resist a cemetery, and I fought my way through to the headstones. Many of them were of young, pre-First World War *schütztruppen*, the builders of Germany's evanescent colonial empire. Whether the troops died of malaria or in anticolonial revolts the headstones – as granite-fresh as the day they were set – did not record. One of them was a man called Bilharz: any relation, I wondered, of the Theodor Bilharz who discovered the organism of bilharzia? And supposing he were, my Africa-weary self demanded, what then? To what use would I put this recondite information?

The language of the headstones changed to French; and the new concrete graves, in small clearings in the grass, now had little oval photographs of deceased Cameroonians, with vases of dusty plastic flowers placed at their feet. The graveyard therefore served as a reminder that a man might have lived through the arrival of the Germans and the departure of the French. Some have argued from this that colonialism, historically fleeting as it was, will one day be seen as but a ripple on the ocean of African history. I think this is wishful thinking: for the impact of an experience is not necessarily proportionate to its duration. Contact with Europe is overwhelmingly the most decisive fact of modern African history: one sees it from ocean to ocean, in the forests, in the deserts, in the mountains, on the plains, in the cities, in the villages. The impact has yet to be worked through and absorbed; perhaps it never will. That is why one sees in African cities Europe vomited up like an ill-digested meal.

In Douala I bought the English Sunday newspapers – I'm addicted to prophecies of doom, and I hadn't had any since Gabon – and I tried to buy a map of Africa, having long since lost mine. But, as in every other African city in which I tried, there was none. To get a map of Africa you have to go to Europe. Perhaps this is because anybody of any importance in Africa who needs to travel does so by air, and pilots are assumed to know where they are going. There is therefore no market for maps, aimless voyaging not being an African pastime.

It was with a sense of duty rather than with anticipatory pleasure that I took the train to Yaoundé, Cameroon's capital and second largest city. I had been warned sternly by an expatriate that I must approach the station in a taxi, or I should be attacked; but I walked and I was not attacked. I was warned also that, by comparison with Douala, Yaoundé was very dull.

The journey was of no great interest. We chugged neither slowly nor fast for eight hours through uninhabited forest. The carriage was so efficiently air-conditioned that I had to stand on the brake platform to get warm. This at least gave the forest an immediacy and reality impossible through a dirty window. At lunchtime a young man came through the train with a bucket of *baguettes*, to make sandwiches of pâté, with liberal layers of that terrible and ubiquitous African margarine (made by Lever Brothers) that tastes like ointment for eczema.

We arrived after dark. One of my fellow passengers, a man in his early thirties who had not spoken to me during the journey, offered to show me the way to a hotel. As usual in such situations, I was torn between fear of being robbed, or at least being made the object of embarrassing financial requests, and the need for human contact. Perhaps he sensed my dilemma, for he pulled out his identity card to prove he was an off-duty policeman. I wasn't sure how far this was a recommendation, but we took a taxi together and sped off into the ill-lit streets. The first two hotels, ramshackle establishments with a certain charm, the second run by a rotund Greek perspiring olive oil, were full, and we ended up in the *Hotel des Deputés*, modern but going quickly to seed. I do not know why, but contemporary architecture and furnishings seem incapable of going to seed with any grace; they look only stained and sordid. I appeal to architects to take this into account when designing buildings for Africa.

The policeman and I had a drink in the bar. He showed me pictures of his family, his little daughter with ribbons in her hair.

I asked him whether he had ever been abroad.

'Yes,' he said. 'I've been several times to Equatorial Guinea.'

'Recently?'

'No.'

He had, in fact, been during the time of the mad bloodthirsty paranoiac.

'What were you doing there?' I asked.

'I was on official business. I had a diplomatic passport.'

'What kind of official business?'

'Helping.'

I went to the British embassy in Yaoundé. Everywhere else the diplomats had been charming and helpful, only too pleased to share their latest speculations. Here, however, I was shown into the office of a formidable, chain-smoking lady in a dress of fine pink stripes who responded not at all to pleasantries. She was obviously very busy, for she kept looking at her watch.

'What do you know about Cameroon?' she asked.

'Not very much,' I answered modestly and in all truth.

'Well, you shouldn't have come here until you did,' she said. 'You should have researched it thoroughly before coming here.'

Yes, I thought, she's quite right, especially from her point of view; but it wasn't really all that easy to research Cameroon *en route* from Zanzibar.

'I've read a couple of books . . .' I stuttered, multiplying by two.

'That's not enough.' She stubbed out her cigarette in her ashtray as though it were my ego. 'Well, what do you want to know? I can give you five minutes.'

What I asked and what I wanted to know were by now quite distinct. My thirst for knowledge about Cameroon receded before more personal matters: for example, was she always as charming as this, and if so why hadn't there been a war between Britain and Cameroon? What did her staff think of her? Had her struggle to succeed in a man's world embittered her, or was it her natural temperament?

I asked about Cameroon's balance of payments.

I departed her office with the utmost relief. I cravenly thanked her for having seen me.

Her strictures had their effect. I went straight to a bookshop and bought a thick, closely-printed book by a French political scientist about Cameroonian politics and society. If only I had read it before going to see her! What finer evidence could there have been of a conscientious interest in Cameroon than having read this saharan prose, which would have made Judgement Day sound dull but turned trifles into things of transcendental significance?

I walked through the street market reading it. The market was crowded and noisy; every few yards a stereo set played different music at full volume. Otherwise the goods on sale were precisely those I had seen for thousands of miles across Africa: cheap enamel dishes, plastic shoes, hurricane lamps, gaudy printed cloth, imitation jewellery. In the market I lost my way and asked a young man of about twenty. It turned out he wanted to talk. Because of the music, we had to shout.

He had just graduated from the university in biology, and I asked him what work he would do.

'There is no work,' he replied.

'Then how will you live?' I asked.

'I will return to my village.'

'So you will be a farmer again?' My intonation conveyed approval.

'No.' The thought made him shudder. 'I will ask my mother for money so I can live in Yaoundé.'

My flagging enthusiasm for the journey did not revive until I reached the small town of Ngoundéré, where the nocturnal chorus of insects rekindled it. (When you have lived your life with the yellow glare of street lights and with traffic noise, darkness and cicadas have ineffable romance.) I was happy again.

The three-hundred-mile train journey had taken us through forest uninhabited except for little settlements of railway workers. From the way the passengers were dressed, I gathered we were entering the southern reaches of Muslim influence. Some wore splendid Hausa robes, others gallibeyas. The man behind me wore robes of dirty brown that served also as napkin and handkerchief. From time to time he prayed in the gangway, often with an uncertain sense of direction, for he faced Tristan da Cunha more than Mecca. The man next to me was a Christian Bamileke with two wives and twelve children. He ate peanuts the whole journey through, throwing the shells past my face out of the window. As he grew tired, so his aim deteriorated.

There was a colour television in a bar in Ngounderé, and many townspeople had gathered round to watch the news. A report on the air crash in which the Mozambican President, Samora Machel, had died aroused little interest, despite the howls of popular grief which the official newspapers of Africa said greeted the news everywhere. Indifference was the word I should have used. But when there was an item about the former Emperor Bokassa's dramatic return to the Central African Republic it was quite otherwise. People shifted expectantly on their seats, there was a low buzz of excited conversation. When pictures of the ex-emperor-cannibal himself were shown, surrounded by offspring and gilded furniture in his French château, proclaiming his innocence and blaming everyone else for things he said never happened, the audience dissolved into giggles. Eating schoolchildren because they won't buy your uniforms is terribly wrong, of course, as everyone knows; but it is a stern moralist who can suppress altogether a prurient interest in such matters.

A lot of beer was drunk during the news bulletin.

Early in the morning I took a taxi to Garoua, two hundred miles to the north. My bag was seized from me at the taxi stand by a man in a gallibeya and deposited in a taxi in which I was not going to travel. I had some difficulty in reuniting myself with it.

My taxi was a Peugeot estate and there were ten passengers. The driver took 3500 francs from us and gave us receipts for 2275 francs.

'*C'est le vol,*' protested one of the passengers.

'*C'est l'Afrique,*' I muttered.

We departed Ngounderé after everyone's *pièce d'identité* had been inspected by the taxi stand's resident policeman. The roads in this part of Cameroon are good: some of the country's oil revenues have gone to build them. We travelled fast but had to stop several times for *les contrôles* by otherwise idle policemen, who walked round the vehicle staring insolently in, and then took some money from the driver. The country was much drier now, golden-brown grassland stretching in the shimmering air into the limitless distance, broken only by a few rocky outcrops. We scattered troupes of monkeys and baboons as we drove, the big male baboon of the troupe sometimes giving us a valedictory glare of defiance from a prominence overlooking the road; once or twice he seemed almost to shake his fist at us. This was also lion and elephant country, I was told, but I saw only mongooses and little green snakes scurrying busily across the hot surface of the road.

The villages were few and far between, their huts of quite different style from those of the south. They had private enclosures of mud walls, and they were tall, round and delicately waisted. The thatch roofs had pumpkin plants growing over them. The speed with which we flashed past these villages on the new road brought back all my doubts about the value of my journey: its inevitable superficiality and externality. I consoled myself with the not altogether convincing argument that what it lacked in depth it made up for in breadth.

In Garoua, in the middle of the market, some of the passengers announced they wished to continue on to Maroua, a further hundred and twenty miles, in the Cameroonian province of *Extrème Nord*. It was a finer town than Garoua, I was told, and so I decided to join them.

At first the driver was reluctant to take us. Then he drove us several miles out of the town and stopped to haggle the price from a position of strength. The fare laid down by the government was 2000 francs; he wanted 2500 francs. There were many protests all round, of poverty, theft, the need to proceed quickly. The driver said that if he charged only the regulation fare, he would have to pay *le tribut* (his very word) to the soldiers out of his own pocket. A compromise was reached – in which I paid the full fare and others did not – and we started out once more.

While the driver was paying tribute halfway to Maroua, we heard the wail of sirens behind us. Motorcycle outriders with huge white gloves, two black Peugeot 504's with blue flashing lights, and a black Mercedes between them, went by at speed.

'*C'est un grand,*' said one of the passengers, with succinctly disparaging eloquence.

We reached Maroua in just over two hours. The journey that took Gide three weeks to complete sixty years ago had taken me precisely five-and-a-half hours. I was not sure I found this evidence of progress, or comparison with Gide, entirely reassuring.

Maroua is on the edge of the Sahel and has a middle-eastern atmosphere. The houses are of partly whitewashed mud, and the larger streets are lined with stunted trees whose leaves have turned olive-green from the dust that settles on them. In every substantial patch of shade sleep men in long robes, and one wonders whether, in fact, they ever wake. Few women are abroad, and when you look them in the eye they turn furtively away, as though a sin had already been committed. The people have a more semitic cast than in the south, and many are handsome.

Maroua is built on a river, the Kaliao. (A river? wrote Gide. A river-*bed*, rather.) It is a wide expanse of sand with an occasional puddle of brown mud, and in one favoured reach a trickle of greenish slime. Nevertheless, people still go there to wash and do their washing, and some dig pits to the water table which lies only a foot or two below the surface. It is also a convenient place for children and some adults to relieve themselves, the vastness of the space giving them a privacy of sorts.

The water carriers syphon water from large metal tanks supplied for this purpose into buckets strung at the ends of bamboo poles which they balance across their shoulders. They are children, not men, and they have to run so as not to be toppled by their load.

Many of the mud houses of Maroua had *A démolir* painted on their walls in faded red, as though the Angel of Town Planning had passed through one night. However, apart from a wall or two replaced by egregious but modern breezeblock, nothing had come of this visitation other than the incantatory words themselves: and I hoped it never would.

Outside one of the houses scheduled for demolition was a noticeboard:

Prof. NKUEZE, VICTOR Native Healer, Diploma in Occult Sciences, Clairvoyance, Magic and Talismans. What then is this magic whose name some people fear to pronounce? Too much fear for no reason. It is not a question of sacrificing a loved one. No. It acts rather as a spiritual science. For your predicament, domestic matters, business, love affairs and success le Prof. NKUEZE Victor is at your disposal, and cares for all kinds of traditional maladies eg sorcery, poisoning, Venereal Diseases.

I debated whether to consult him about my knee, which ached from time to time, but I doubted I could have done so without revealing an insulting scepticism, so I didn't.

Maroua is a town of considerable physical charm and not just a mess, as many African towns are – for it is built largely of local materials that elsewhere Africans have learnt to despise. But there was one other curious fact I noticed about Maroua: its bird life consisted entirely of vultures.

Le grand who had passed us on the road to Maroua was the Minister of Finance and he was staying in the same hotel as I, a series of thatched cabins in a large wooded garden. His bodyguards sat outside at tables, drinking beer and reading picture novellas. The Minister had a lunch party for ten, including the Minister of Commerce, a Muslim northerner, who was not as important as the Minister of Finance, for his voice did not carry as far and he did not crack jokes constantly at which everyone had to laugh heartily for the sake of their jobs. A latecomer arrived at the table, whom everyone respectfully addressed as *Mon Général*. He was a quiet man and did not stay long; he had an air of calm authority, as though the people at the table, for all their bravado, were but puppets, and he the puppetmaster.

The lunch party proceeded. The waiters gathered round the table. Some of them were terrified into immobility, like rabbits by a stoat. Their eyes bulged, their skins oozed the sweat of fear. How odd, then, that one of Cameroon's élite, Ferdinand Oyono, should have made his name with a famous novel, *Un Vie de Boy*, in which an innocent young Cameroonian houseboy records his observations of the strange and cruelly arbitrary behaviour of his white employers.

'*Poisson, poisson, poisson, j'ai commandé poisson!*' shouted the Minister of Finance.

The waiters had made the regrettable error of serving everyone before the Minister, who alone was left without a plate.

Was it a mistake? Satire? The small rebellion of the powerless? The confused waiters bumped into each other like overheated molecules, seeking the Minister's fish as though it might be under the bar or on the verandah outside. Only one kept his head and made for the kitchen; the fish was produced and the crisis was over. Bonhomie was restored as toasts were drunk.

Suddenly businesslike, the lunch ended abruptly. The manager, a young European, came to shake the hands of the entire party as they left. Outside, the bodyguards had relinquished their novellas and stood to attention. The sirens of the departing cars soon sounded the all clear.

The manager sighed like a deflating balloon and the waiters, who had seemed until then worn down with care, chattered gaily and almost danced as they cleared the table. The Minister of Finance had left a very large tip.

I walked round the town after lunch. It was Sunday and though Maroua was overwhelmingly Muslim, it was a day of rest. I bought a newspaper and while checking its date to make sure it was the latest edition the vendor told me it didn't matter, because in Cameroon the newspaper was always the same. The people found my interest in the vultures, congregated in trees like lawyers waiting for their cases to be called, highly diverting, as we should find a man who stared with fascination at our starlings. Next door to the hotel was a large colonial house, surrounded on all sides by a verandah ten feet wide. The garden which had probably been some colonial wife's refuge from insanity was now as derelict as the house itself; only some upturned and disconnected sanitary ware remained in the echoing house, and an old stuffed toy in what must once have been the nursery. Evidently no-one wanted the house, perhaps because it was haunted or held unhappy associations for local people; in any case, what would anyone want with a large house so cool it did not require air-conditioning?

I walked past a cotton field on the edge of the town. It looked desiccated and near to extinction to me, though I am no judge of cotton. Next to the field were several shacks with walled enclosures from which issued the laughter of a woman and drunk men in boubous; they emerged to relieve themselves, their gait unsteady, their Islamic caps at rakish angles. Goodnaturedly they asked me to join them in their cups but it was fiercely hot and I declined. This struck them as another eccentricity of the everunpredictable white man, and after squatting to urinate in the cotton field – the boubou acting as a kind of moveable water closet – they returned with a shrug and a lurch to their bars.

I took a bus to Mora – there was none direct to the Nigerian border. I thought I was early but most of the buses and taxis had already left from the *gare routière*, leaving a huge, empty, dusty square with a few trees around its perimeter, under which slept the passengers who still hoped to travel at the late hour of eight o'clock. We had to wait until the bus to Mora filled with passengers; the driver, stretched out on the ground, had no idea when that would be, or even whether it would be today. It was all the same to him.

Though I had just eaten breakfast I bought some kebabs to pass the time. They were covered with a salty, peppery grit, and I knew at once I had made a mistake in eating them. It already promised to be a furnace of a day, and I had little water with me. In any case, only time and not water assuaged the heat in my mouth, which felt as though it had been propped open the whole way across the Sahara.

Of time there was plenty. Passengers came one by one, and soon there was a knot of people sufficient to fill the bus in any other continent: but not here, not in Africa. The driver slept on peacefully, in the certainty that time was on the side of his income. Only *I*, whom my culture had taught to hoard time like a commodity, grew impatient; I paced up and down, the words of *Moby Dick* entering my eyes but not my mind, working out how many dams could be built in Africa by the man hours wasted for lack of timetables. My calculations had no validity, but they soothed me.

At last, though, it seemed as if no-one else could be squeezed on board. For myself, I took up – or rather, was moulded into – the foetal position, by no means as comfortable as some notable psychologists have suggested. A notice above my head prohibited certain activities: 'No Smoking, Spitting, Vomiting or Stealing on the Bus'.

We started out. The road was at once rough and dusty, the landscape ever drier. At the first *contrôle*, two large soldiers decided they needed a lift. As they climbed on to the bus I understood at last what Einstein meant when he said space was a relative and not an absolute concept. As for space being curved, it was less of a mystery than how those two soldiers were fitted in. In the process a boy squeezed out of and then back through a window. It would all have been entertaining if it hadn't been so uncomfortable, and even the Africans began to complain. The driver took no notice, however, even if he was no longer able to shift the gears for all the limbs around him.

A mile or two further on a cow had been freshly slaughtered by the side of the road, and a trestle table was piled with its red meat. Most of the passengers wanted to buy and so did the driver. The bus was soon filled with the smell of blood. On the ground by the trestle table was stretched the cow's hide, with several vultures hooking the adherent strips of flesh in their beaks and hopping to tear it away. They were the butcher's unpaid assistants.

There were several more controls and by the time we reached Mora it was so hot that everyone had retired indoors. The *gare routière* was deserted here too, and I was told the last bus to Banki had just left. I briefly considered going to Chad – the lake was only a hundred miles away – but I had no visa and the only way to get one was to return to Yaoundé, which seemed a world away. A young man with a small motorbike offered – for an ample fare – to take me to the border. I accepted, after trying half-heartedly to argue down the price.

We set out not along the main road but along a narrow footpath. The driver said it was because this was the shorter route: actually, it was to avoid the *contrôles*.

It was a fine thing to ride in the open in that vast, dry, fierce, golden landscape, the stream of air in one's face mitigating somewhat the heat that rose in waves from the ground. We passed through villages with huts of a kind new to me: igloos constructed of reeds. These villages were isolated and off the road, and their inhabitants stared at me: I might have been from Mars. Recovering from their shock, they smiled and waved, and naked children ran after us for a few yards. The women of the villages pounded manioc or millet, using a rounded log as a pestle and a hollowed trunk as a mortar. Their naked torsos glistened with sweat. Even the old women engaged in this tiring labour, and I saw some of them, bent and shrivelled with age and work, carrying heavy bundles of kindling on their backs. When liberation came to Africa it was not meant for women.

Round a corner in the track we came to a sudden halt that nearly catapulted me into a tree. In the shade of that tree were two policemen, in short a *contrôle*. They were fat and sluggish and as surprised to see us as we were to see them. They demanded to inspect our papers and it transpired after an argument that the driver had none. While I conversed with one of the policemen the other talked in earnest and threatening tones to the driver.

The tree was by a field of millet. The ground was parched and cracked, as one sees in famine posters, and the stalks of millet so dry they had broken, their heads bowed to the ground like flags lowered in surrender.

'It's very dry here,' I said.

'Yes,' said the policeman matter-of-factly. 'There will be hunger.'

But not, I thought, for you. When we continued on our way, the driver told me the policeman had instructed him to return me at once to the *gare routière* at Mora, and either pay 50,000 francs (£110) or have his motorbike confiscated. Either way, the policemen had done well out of their morning *contrôle*.

But the driver needed my fare more than ever now, so instead of taking me back to Mora he took another narrow track to Banki, once we were out of sight of the policemen. He knew every track in this landscape. And all the while he complained vociferously.

'Why do they treat me like this?' he asked. 'They are Cameroonians just like me.'

I drew the inference that he considered it perfectly acceptable for them to extort from foreigners – like me, for instance.

'Can't you avoid paying them?' I asked.

'Not if I stay in Mora,' he said. 'They know me there.'

He told me he would have to think about moving away: the motorbike was all he possessed.

We came to a large river-bed, completely dry, several hundred yards across. The motorbike could not take us both – it slithered and writhed, and the driver came off several times – and I walked across the deep sand.

Soon afterwards we reached Banki, where once again corrugated metal was king. The town was a mess, even by the standards of border towns, and naturally it was time for the border guards' lunch. The driver and I went to what he called an 'African restaurant', in the tin hut of a woman he knew.

She was fat and friendly, and in no time at all produced several dishes containing crushed millet, a spinach-like vegetable and something upon which I had heard many returned expatriates from West Africa dilate with real horror, namely a glutinous green slime (made, I think, from okra) that leaves a glistening, translucent thread when the spoon or fork is raised from the dish. *At all costs*, they warned me with more warmth of feeling than that of vampire experts warning against nocturnal excursions in Transylvania, *at all costs avoid the green slime*. But that was not the worst of this meal. There was a stew whose chief ingredient was indubitably the intestines of some small animal, a rodent perhaps. The heat of the cooking had congealed them into a vermicular knot which I had no desire to unravel.

Sitting on the ground in the tin-trapped heat, I ate as little as I decently could, citing the heat as the reason for my relative lack of appetite. I drank copiously of the water from the large earthenware jug dug into the sandy soil to keep it cool, but the water seemed to pass directly out of my skin as sweat.

I paid and, in the hut of a tailor who worked at a foot-pedalled sewing machine, we waited for the border to re-open. The driver waited with me: I liked him, and it was as though the injustice I had seen committed against him had established a kind of solidarity between us. He would not leave me until I had crossed safely into Nigeria.

While we waited, men came with boubous that bulged in peculiar ways. They were moneychangers and the bulges were huge wads of money, both Cameroonian and Nigerian, that they carried about with them. I changed my paltry remaining francs into a surprising number of Naira.

The border re-opened. I was not the most urgent case requiring attention. There were two young *Beninois* seeking their fortune further south, but they had no papers, no money and only a thin bundle of rags. They could not have been more than eighteen, and they sat meekly in the corner while officials raved at them. How they had got this far was a mystery and it made the *chef de bureau* (who was dressed in a surprisingly good suit) very angry. He told them to pick up their bundles and go back to Nigeria. They did as they were told, without protest, without comment.

TEN

Nigeria

One hears horror stories about entering Nigeria: of the hours waited and the bribes paid. Here, however, they could not have been more charming.

'You are British,' they said. 'Welcome to Nigeria.'

It was quite the opposite of what I had been led to expect.

'Your National Captain is my hero,' said one of them, 'What do you think of him?'

I was pleased at his pro-British sentiment, of course, but I wasn't quite sure what he meant by our National Captain. Prince Charles, perhaps? Or Mrs Thatcher? But his English was too good to mistake a her for a him. I looked puzzled.

'You mean you have never heard of Bryan Robson, Manchester United and England?'

'I've heard of him, yes. But I'm not very interested in football . . .'

'Can you send me a poster of him? I need a poster of him.'

He also 'needed' subscriptions to magazines with titles like *Goal*, *Shoot* and *Score*. He was not allowed to subscribe to them from Nigeria any more because they had to be paid for in foreign exchange. That was what the fall in the price of oil meant to him. I said I would see what I could do, if he wrote to me. The customs man offered me a lift on his motorbike to where I could find a taxi to Maiduguri. I shook hands with everyone before I left: I felt already well-disposed towards Nigeria.

A green and yellow taxi had just arrived from Maiduguri and was u-turning in the road to go back; there was much high-pitched squealing of tyres and the smell of burning rubber, together with a little acrid smoke.

'Let's go,' said the driver, scarcely stopping to let me in. It was the only phrase of English he knew, or which at any rate was recognizable as such; for the rest of the journey he spoke to me in a language I assumed to be local and he assumed to be English.

Within a very few seconds we were doing a hundred miles an hour. It is, as I discovered, the only speed a self-respecting Nigerian considers worthy of him, whatever the condition or situation of the road. This driver, dressed in Hausa robes and a colourful embroidered hat, peered imperiously, with his head thrown back and his eyelids half-closed, at the road ahead – except when speaking to me, when he turned to face me, disregarding the road altogether. Of course, he did not slow down at such times: he was a man of uncompromising principle, with fine aristocratic features and mien. Before long I had the same disdain of death as he.

The road, fortunately, was straight and without much traffic. The surface was excellent. The oil boom years in Nigeria were a time of personal and corporate plunder, but they did at least leave the country with the finest system of roads in Africa north of the Limpopo. Not that this was an unmixed blessing: there is an annual holocaust on Nigeria's roads that is quite without parallel in the world. I heard a figure of a quarter of a million deaths per year; but like most figures about Nigeria, especially official ones, no-one knows whether it is an under- or an overestimate. As for the army of the maimed this orgy of destructiveness must leave behind, it presumably melts unnoticed into society, to join the limbless and the deformed with whom all African countries, whatever their accident rate, are so richly endowed.

Every so often we would pass like milestones the burnt-out wrecks of Peugeot estate taxis just like our own, as skeletal as the blanched carcass of a cow in an African drought. There would be no difficulty or snag in the road that explained the accident, unless monotonous straightness be such a snag. Perhaps so, for it is generally accepted that whoever sits beside the driver in a Nigerian taxi has the duty of keeping him awake. Another piece of lore I heard – but only later – was that whenever possible one should sit in the seat immediately behind the driver. Long experience of head-on crashes proves that the occupant of *that* seat has the greatest chance of survival.

The country through which we passed was almost flat, brown-green and with vast horizons. One hears a great deal about the size of Nigeria's population: but the truth is, no-one knows how large it is, for a census is not a mere head-count or demographic exercise, but a division of the spoils among the country's diverse and antagonistic regions, which all inflate their figures to obtain a bigger share of whatever is going. Nevertheless, a population of a hundred million, doubling every twenty-five years (in fifty years there will be 400,000,000 Nigerians), seems to be the accepted figure. So the last thing one expects to find in Nigeria is a vast, relatively unpeopled landscape. The statistics and what one sees are – not for the first time – somewhat at variance; and, depending on one's temperament, one can either doubt the statistics, or doubt what one sees.

I saw my first camel on this journey, a creature that always surprises by the ungainliness of its form and the grace of its movements. Just past the camel a group of people hailed us by the roadside. They were short, coppery-black and with sun-wrinkled skins, the womenfolk having their hair done in a fringe of small ringlets tied with aluminium ornaments, and with rings in their noses and ears, and many bracelets and anklets. Their most striking feature, however, was their bright red teeth and mouths, which seemed deliberately stained. Later, I asked several educated people in the town who these people were and why they stained their teeth thus; but all disclaimed any knowledge, insincerely I felt, as though mere knowledge of such things would detract from their status as urban sophisticates.

We squealed to a halt, leaving a trail of smoke behind us. These people wanted to go only two or three miles down the road, and the driver refused to take them. By means of dramatic gestures in the direction of the fuel gauge, the brakes and the tyres, I gathered he told them the wear and tear on his vehicle when stopping such a short distance away would be greater than the 50 *kobo* (half a Naira, or 10 US cents) fare they would pay him. It was, of course, quite out of the question that he should *not* accelerate to maximum speed in that short distance, or that he should come to a gradual rather than a violent stop.

At the hotel in Maiduguri they asked for a deposit in cash of two hundred per cent of my estimated bill, the balance to be returned to me when I left. This, they said, was standard practice in Nigeria, where people were otherwise inclined to depart . . . well, in a manner of speaking, without paying. I asked whether I looked the kind of man to leave, in a manner of speaking, without paying. It was an unfair question, of course, for they could hardly answer in the affirmative, and they were very polite. But they conceded I should deposit only a hundred per cent of my bill, since the regulation had not been intended for such as I, but for . . . well, Nigerians.

I met one of their untrustworthy guests in the lobby. He was sitting, or rather lying, in an armchair, looking bored. His name was Solomon and he was a Yoruba accountant from Lagos. He had spread himself generously over the chair and his pot belly rose like a hummock that stretched his nylon shirt, so that there were big gaps between the buttons. After he had levered himself upright we started talking.

Naturally, we talked of Nigeria; more particularly, of what was wrong with it. This is an inexhaustible subject, one that Nigerians discuss not only with despair, but with tenderness and affection. As Chinua Achebe remarks in his sparkling little book *The Trouble With Nigeria*: 'Whenever two Nigerians meet, their conversation will sooner or later slide into a litany of our national deficiencies. *The trouble with Nigeria* has become the subject of our small talk in much the same way as the weather is for the English.'

Solomon was eloquent on the subject of corruption. He had been brought up in the Methodist tradition, he said, and so was against it, completely against it. What was the point of embezzling hundreds of millions or even billions, he asked? How many meals could a man eat in one day, fuck how many women? Look, supposing one had a hundred thousand pounds sterling in the bank, with the present interest rates in London one would have an income of ten thousand. Wasn't that enough for anyone? Ninety thousand naira! By the way, he continued, he had two thousand in a London account (pounds, that is) and was thinking of using it to import pharmaceuticals into Nigeria. Injectible vitamins, sex hormones, that kind of thing. There was a severe shortage of them in Nigeria at the moment, and he could sell them for ten or twelve times what he paid for them. Did I know of any dealer, someone I could trust? Of course, he would have to go out to the airport the moment the drugs arrived, otherwise they would disappear (as to bringing them by sea, that would be pointless: nothing ever emerged from the docks to its rightful owners). It was terrible. But with a rate of profit of a thousand per cent, who needed to be greedy or dishonest? Why be corrupt? Solomon couldn't understand how people weren't satisfied with what they had.

But would he not have to pay import duty, I asked?

Solomon looked at me hard.

'I can arrange that,' he said.

Then, of course, there was the population problem. The trouble was, people just didn't think of the future. They didn't think, will I be able to feed this child? or what will Nigeria be like if everyone has as many children? No; men just thought, look how strong and potent I am with so many children. It was all primitive, so primitive.

Later in the evening – when Solomon had forgotten all this – he revealed he had two wives and eleven children.

I suggested we have a drink together. There was no drink in the hotel, said Solomon with contempt, because the owner was a Muslim; but he, Solomon, had found a bar not far away. He had, after all, been in this godforsaken town a day and a night.

Solomon's bar was over the road and down a dark alley. There was a small courtyard with a string of coloured lights around it, all but deserted; we went inside. The bar was dark, hot and small, and what little light there was came from a pink lamp. The disco music was so loud we had to shout our orders. Prostitutes entwined themselves round some of the customers and Solomon related how the previous night he had had to fight off a prostitute who had found him irresistibly attractive.

'Go away!' he had shouted. 'I like beautiful women. I don't deal in ugly women.'

Fortunately, according to Solomon, he had been successful in his efforts to fight her off.

I mentioned that, to my surprise, many of the patrons of the bar were Muslim.

'Yes,' said Solomon. 'Tonight they drink, tomorrow they are el Hadj.'

In Africa, beer bottles are big. Solomon grew more loquacious by the minute.

He told me he went to England every year for his holidays: alone, of course, since he'd need a private airline to shift his family. He always stayed in London: Walthamstow to be exact.

I asked him how he found it there and expected a torrent of complaint about British racial prejudice, police harassment, rudeness and so forth.

'There are many types of women in Walthamstow,' he said. 'I can seduce them easily. But Indian women are difficult. They are tough nuts to crack. Indians expect their daughters to be virgins and their wives to be faithful.'

He mentioned these traits with evident distaste, mingled with contempt.

'But,' he said, cheering up, 'I always manage in the end. They love me.'

There was no disguising the fact that Solomon was rather ugly. It was difficult to imagine him a Casanova, even in Walthamstow. And yet his stories of suburban conquest somehow rang true. Perhaps he thrilled bored housewives with stories of wild animals subdued barehanded in the jungles of Africa.

I said I was hungry and we went to the Maiduguri Chinese restaurant which was less than a hundred yards away. It was very large and cavern-like, and decorated as a million other Chinese restaurants through the world. Many of the expatriates in the town ate there every night of their lives, in sad, quiet, bored little groups, or even worse, alone. I met a young employee of a British cotton dealer who had been in Maiduguri some months, supervising shipments from Chad and Cameroon: he had formed the habit of coming to the Chinese restaurant because in the hot season, when the air burnt your lungs and not a leaf stirred, it was the only public place in Maiduguri where there was (sometimes) air-conditioning. And he had discovered the table which received the most cooled air.

Solomon said we should have a drink before our meal, and we joined a man in beautifully-laundered white Hausa robes at the restaurant's bar. Solomon and he set about arranging my itinerary in Nigeria, very noisily. On no account, they said, should I miss Lagos. To do so would be a shame, a tragedy. As tactfully as I could, I mentioned I had heard and read somewhat to the contrary.

'No,' said Solomon. 'Lagos is beautiful.'

'Lagos,' said the slightly drunken Hausa, 'is a city of . . . a city of . . .'

I expected him to extol its vibrant life, its frenetic energy, its markets where anything in the world could be bought, its famous music, said to be the best in Africa, but his eloquence failed him in mid-sentence.

'Of skyscrapers,' suggested Solomon.

'Yes, exactly,' said the Hausa. 'Lagos is a city of skyscrapers.'

'So you see,' said Solomon, proud and delighted at the acknowledged aptness of his description, 'you must go to Lagos.'

After several beers Solomon said he was not hungry: he wanted only soup. Actually, he was starving but, thanks to the two hundred per cent deposit, had money enough only for soup. This money he passed over to me munificently, as if to say *keep the change*, and told me to order what I liked, he didn't mind. When the food arrived, he fell on it and ate so fast he began to sweat and became quite breathless.

Back at the hotel he gave me, by way of repayment, a wad of recent newspapers with which he had finished. Nigeria has the most vigorous press in Africa. It loves scandal and gossip, and even attacks the government, though with circumspection. Only one president, General Buhari, tried seriously to control the press, arguing that a 'developing' country like Nigeria needed a press that drew attention to achievements rather than shortcomings. He soon fell from power. Newspapers in Nigeria are evanescent phenomena, appearing and disappearing even faster than governments. The overall impression is of a many-limbed creature, without co-ordination or serious purpose, and with tremendous, exhilarating but totally undirected energy – like the country itself. After months of government broadsheets, however, it was a pleasure to read the words of men who were trying, at least, to be journalists rather than toadying bureaucrats.

When the prostitutes in a certain town went on strike for higher rates, the headlines of one newspaper read:

PRICE OF FUCK TO RISE

The newspaper announcements alone seemed to epitomize the swarming confusion of Nigerian life: next to a black-edged announcement of the death by armed robbery on his way to work of an accountant in the city of skyscrapers, were an advertisement for an aphrodisiac:

Dear Friend,
    If you have sex problems, potency problems, or even prostate problems, I'd like to send you something that comes in a plain brown wrapper . . .

and an advertisement for a book, *Confession of a Wizard*, about Jeje Karawa, the Wizard of Igbinse:

The book contains exciting revelations about the secrets of coven and what is going on in the meeting places of witches, how witches launch deadly attack on fellow human beings, how coven is organised and governed and how witches and wizards can fly in the night.

The book was on sale at the University of Benin bookshop.

A prominent Nigerian journalist, Dele Giwa, had just been assassin-ated by letter bomb, and this gave rise to much high-flown, if ungrammatical, lamentation:

> What precedence is the older generation setting for the teeming youths of this country . . . These questions and more are imperative because it seems from all indications that the Nigerian society is an idiosyncratic set up . . . Where against what obtains elsewhere, falsehood, triumph and truth and those who uphold it are persecuted wantonly . . . True, Dele Giwa had been physically exterminated from mother earth, but his soul liveth . . . Every of his footstep will be trailed solidly by those of us still alive . . . Dele's spirit must avenge more brutally.

There was much, too, about Lawrence Anini, the most famous bandit in Nigeria, a self-proclaimed Robin Hood figure. He had vowed to rid Bendel State of all its policemen after they had shot his brother, claiming they were corrupt and criminal. So far he had killed eight policemen, and his invulnerability to retaliation was widely credited. Several Nigerians told me stories about him which they believed to be true: the police had once emptied a magazine of bullets into him without ill effect; another time, the police came to arrest him while he was drinking in a bar, but he changed his form into that of a little boy and escaped. Now he had offered to halt his vendetta against the police, providing they were all dismissed and new ones employed.*

A Nigerian journalist had interviewed the President of Togo and was amazed by his informality: 'How on earth can a whole President be riding about town with only one car trailing him? . . . No gun-totting soldiers around him . . . it is meeting any ordinary man, but this is a whole President of a country.'

I turned to a column called *Feminine Touch*. The article was entitled 'What Shall We Do About House Maids?' and it would have been a wonderful parody of colonial womanhood, had it not been in such deadly earnest: the servant problem having been transferred to Africans along with political sovereignty.

---

*Six months later he was captured and executed by firing squad. He took some of the police with him, though, naming those who had collaborated with him. They were executed too. It is well-known that the police often hire out their weapons to bandits for 500 Naira a night.

Not only was it difficult to find a maid at all, but they demanded exorbitant wages: 'The salary level ranges from N40 to N80 (£4.50–£9) per month. This is a cut throat amount, especially as one is expected to clothe, feed and provide shelter . . .' Employers got little for their money, however. Arriving home to discover the work not done, it was because the housemaid ' . . . must have spent the whole day playing or sleeping.' Housemaids ate too much: ' . . . they amongst the household eat at least three times, a luxury the "master" and "madam" cannot afford.' Housemaids are dirty: 'God help (the madam) if she has a maid (who is) scared of water touching her skin. Recently (a madam) nearly died of shock when she discovered her . . . daughter had lice in her hair. No price guessing where she got them from.' Housemaids are dishonest: 'At times they steal things that are not actually useful to them like . . . toys, pants or cloth pegs, books they cannot read, among many others.' In short the life of the madam is intolerable: ' . . . God help the madam if she should do as much as raise her voice two times in a row.' In the centre of the article was a cartoon of a madam caning a housemaid, though whether as recommendation or condemnation I am still not sure. I fell asleep and dreamt of a whole President reviewing a guard of honour, comprising ranks of madams presenting canes.

Outside the hotel was a notice on a small hoarding:

> Dr Nwatadibia Occult
> Home of Wonders
> Why Die in Silence?
> For Your Spiritual Help, Such As, Witchcraft, Good Luck,
> Pool-Secret, To Win Love, Magic Bird Pen, to Collect Debt,
> Love, Talisman, Guard Against Poison, Cast Out Obanje,
> Good Footballer and For Employment,
> We Can Also Make Impossible to Be Possible eg Barren Women,
> We Are the Indian Secret Agents in Talisman of All Kinds

I walked on. Under the shade of a line of trees was a Koranic school, the children writing in Arabic on slates and calling out passages by rote. A little further on, I came across a man walking two full-grown hyaenas and one pup. They were performing animals, but even muzzled they looked mean and dangerous, their eyes glittering with malice and shifting furtively in search of an opportunity to revenge themselves on their master. He beat the unmuzzled pup with a stick, and though still small it snarled at its tormentor ferociously, laying bare its row of foamy, saliva-covered teeth. It looked to me like an animal that would not forget: and somehow I shuddered to think of its master's fate.

Maiduguri that morning was not the busy town I had expected. There were few people about and the traffic was not noisy or impatient. I discovered the reason for this comparative calm that evening by watching television: most of the town had been away at the public executions.

They were of three armed robbers, one a former policeman who had stolen a cow at gunpoint. A huge crowd, said the television announcer, had gathered early to secure a good view, but the executions had taken place four hours later than scheduled because the execution ground was waterlogged. The crowd had worried lest the executions were postponed altogether, but fortunately a piece of dry ground had been found in which to fix the stakes.

A film was shown of the criminals leaving the prison for their execution. Their attitude seemed peculiar, fatuous almost: they made the same gesture as a champion boxer entering the ring. Were they smiling? The picture was too poor to tell; but surely people on their way to their deaths could not have savoured their fleeting moment, à la Warhol, of fame?

Next they were shown being tied to the stakes, their arms wrapped and bound behind them. At this point an interviewer stepped forward to ask them whether they had anything to say to the viewers. The first denied his guilt; the second said it was only for God to judge a man; the third that he wished his parents had been informed of his execution, so that he could have seen them before he died.

A squad of soldiers marched towards the stakes. There was a lot of stamping of feet, British-style, as they took up positions opposite the criminals. The firing itself was not shown, but the announcer said it lasted two minutes, after which a doctor pronounced them dead. Two minutes! It seemed rather a long time for a party of six soldiers to shoot at three stationary men from a few feet away. Later I heard a rumour that men had been executed slowly in Nigeria, shot from the feet up, though whether to increase the deterrent effect of the execution or to make a better spectacle of it for the crowd was not known.

There were several bookshops along the street in which I found myself that morning. This is quite unlike provincial towns anywhere else in Africa, where even the capital may have only one or two poorly stocked bookshops. I was surprised to find Shakespeare widely available: though whether he was studied for pleasure, or for examination purposes, and thus with the ultimate goal of securing a position from which it was possible to enjoy the fruits of corruption, I cannot say. But I met several Nigerians who liked Shakespeare, and this is remarkable when one considers that English is no-one's first language in Nigeria.

I bought a couple of plays by Soyinka – an author whose symbolism I had always found cluttered, inexact, portentous and opaque, and to whom I much preferred Achebe, whose extreme clarity Soyinka once damned as 'unrelieved competence': as though competence in anything in Africa were a quality to be despised, and as though to allow one's ideas into the bright light of criticism were somehow to be superficial.

I bought also two pamphlets of a kind that are ubiquitous in Nigeria, published and printed in the town of Onitsha in eastern Nigeria and sold by the hundred thousand. Soyinka and Achebe are more honoured than read; but Onitsha pamphlets are both. I thought they might, perhaps, offer more insight into Nigerian ways of thinking: just as the *Sun* is more representative of Britain than the *Financial Times*.

As I walked along reading them I was unable to contain my laughter. To passers-by I must have been like a schizophrenic listening to his voices; but Africans are celebrated for their tolerance of madmen, and I was left unmolested. The two pamphlets were entitled *No Condition Is Permanent* and *How to Speak to Girls*. The first was by an author who called himself simply The Master of Life. I think his pamphlet is famous, for later I recognized quotations from it painted on the sides of buses. The pamphlet is difficult to summarize because little consecutive thought is detectable in it, at least to a western mind. The title page has three aphorisms:

MONEY MAKETH A MAN

DRESS MAKETH A WOMAN

A MAN OF STRAW IS WORTH THE WOMAN OF GOLD

The Master of Life proves that no condition is permanent by reference to Onitsha Market, which burnt down for the third time on 11 February 1953.

A large number of rich traders suddenly lost their riches. Some of them became servants, some truck pushers, some load-carriers, some were labourers, some became thieves . . . May God bless those who suffered the incidents. The event enriched many head carriers because boxes of big value were carried . . . The events show us that, No condition is permanent in the world and things are not what they seem and life is nothing but an empty dream.

After this sombre conclusion, the Master advises young men to be industrious: 'Don't be idle. You cannot win raffle when you do not sign it . . . That is, you cannot become rich when you do not work.' Then he warns of 'the Troubles By Our Women': 'Their "showbody" fashion is magnet . . . The contents of their letters are insincere and could scatter one's brain.' Misogyny is a strong theme in the booklet:

When you befriend a woman she will tell you that many handsome young men had applied and promised her a sewing machine, Iron beds, gold and take over all her responsibilities. She can lie to you . . . [He lays charges against wives:]
Many wives today are doing very bad things. I am annoyed with these type of wives and declare windy war against them. Below are my strong charges against them.
Some wives do not cook afternoon food in time.
Some wives receive poison and give to their husbands.
Some women may think I am intentionally criticising them. I have no hatred or malice against anybody. My criticisms and charges against women are justified. [There is advice for men thinking of marrying:]
You should not be seen at randomly in bars and try to secede from the prostitutes because they will jeopardise harmony of your family. Do not beat your wife animalestically, treat her like a human being.

The Master continues by printing letters asking his advice. One is from Tough Girl Pitakwa: 'My choice of marriage is a Minister of Finance. Other important people who are not Ministers of Finance had approached me for marriage but I still abide by my decision and marry one who is a Minister of Finance. Do you support me?' He replies: 'Your high decision is dangerous. Why should you decide to marry a Minister of finance . . .' The Master's booklet ends with a warning against the harmful effects of smoking.

How to Speak to Girls is by J. Abiakam who says in his introduction that he is confidently looking forward to receiving letters of thanks from his readers. By means of a dialogue between Michael and Veronica he shows how boys should approach girls they have never met before:

MICH: Gentle lady, may it please your majesty if I speak to you?
VERO: I have no time, I am in a hurry.
[Michael then declares his love. But Veronica is sceptical.]
VERO: There are so many girls in town, you can go to any of them
      for your so called love.
[Michael replies as though deeply hurt.]
MICH: My dear, why are you proving wicked on me . . .
[Veronica replies that it is difficult to tell the true intentions of boys nowadays. Michael swears his love is true.]
MICH: I strongly promise that I must love you truly but I don't
      know what is your opinion.
VERO: What kind of love is that?
MICH: I believe and trust in love which counts no error.
VERO: Well my dear, if you trust in true love it will be possible.
[Michael is relieved to hear it.]
MICH: You gave me a tough time at the beginning, but now you are
      my very own.

Guidance is then given on the writing of 'Correct Love Letters', an important matter since 'You can easily win a girl's love if you write good love letters'. Not all are successful, however, as Christy Nwanna's reply to Paul Obi demonstrates.

Dear Master Obi,
    Your letter dated 15th September was happily received but I am sorry to disappoint you . . . It is my wish to marry someone who has good educational qualification or a well-to-do trader.
    You know that I am a holder of Higher Elementary Certificate, just imagine the type of worker or trader I should like to marry . . .

Perhaps it was wrong to laugh. But the lack of consecutive thought and the tolerance of blatant contradiction was very striking to a western reader. Here is part of the catechism for boys:

Question: Is it good to think against any girl who rejects your friendship and love?

Answer: God forbid! . . . Friendship and love cannot be forced. It can't be bought with gold and silver.

Question: Is it good to forget your business and think more of your girlfriend?

Answer: Not at all . . . It is business before pleasure. A boy who has money is sure to marry a beautiful girl while a boy who spent all his money carelessly will become hopeless . . .

[The catechism (and booklet) ends with the following exchange:]

Question: If you are a boy or a girl, what reasons will you have in mind when making friends with a boy or a girl?

Answer: There are three reasons only.
1. To write and reply good letters.
2. To encourage for studies and pass examinations or to struggle hard in business.
3. To give and receive good advise when it is necessary.

I am not sure what conclusions can be drawn from these pamphlets. But it seems to me that the intrusion of Europe into Africa, to teach the Africans to consume what they cannot produce, and produce what they cannot consume, has resulted in a hard-nosed materialism by comparison with which Wall Street brokers are other-worldly.

To Kano from Maiduguri is 370 miles, and I went in a taxi with the cryptic words *Sea Never Dry* across the rear window. The road was hypnotically straight, a ribbon of shining, shimmering metal through the brown land. Oncoming vehicles seemed for long to be floating on the waters of illusion. The potholes were few and far between, and as such more dangerous than if they had been every few yards. A falcon rose up from the road, but not fast enough, flapped its wings once and flew into the windscreen, cracking it. Otherwise, the journey was without incident. Near Kano the dwellings changed to mud houses from huts of vegetable matter. The outskirts of the city were the usual confusion of factories, mass housing projects, shantytowns, roads, markets, traffic jams, clouds of dust, unfinished buildings with unsafe scaffolds, herds of goats, open sewers and overfilled buses churning out black smoke and progressing crabwise.

The hotel was of the African failed modern school. There was no water, the telephone was not connected, the windows were sealed to prevent cooled air from escaping (but the air-conditioner did not work), the room was as mouldy as gorgonzola; the light flickered with each surge or reduction in the voltage and the lifts rarely responded to a call. The Nigerian guests took this all in their stride: it was as though they never really expected the appurtenances of modern life to be other than for show. A telephone is a plastic shell whose handpiece one grasps when one wishes to impress someone else with one's importance and sophistication.

I was shown round Kano by an old Muslim who – once he knew I was British – said the old days had been best. The British had been just, severe and uncorrupt: he preferred them to what he called *our own people rule*. But if our own people rule had to continue, he preferred the soldiers to what he called *politician time*, when street meetings had turned into riots, and corruption reached levels that staggered even Nigerians.

Not everyone in Nigeria shared his views, he admitted, particularly in the south. But then he had very little time for southerners. Until the British came, he said, they had nothing in the south: they were savages, they ate leaves and roots, they made nothing, they were idolaters, they were ignorant. Whereas there had been civilization in the north for centuries before the British. In view of the famous bronzes of Benin, I was not sure his outline of Nigerian history was entirely correct, but I said nothing.

We went through the old town together. It was entirely mud-built: not only functional, longlasting and cool, but very pleasing to the eye. No doubt it is hopelessly anachronistic to wish the new city had been built in the same style and with the same materials: for even had it been technically possible, the élite has eyes only for modernity, which it copies without understanding. But I could well understand the old man's pride in the civilization of his forefathers. In Kano the old trades and crafts are carried on still, though by ever-decreasing numbers of craftsmen. The cloth-dyers still use their indigo pits, the leather-workers still stamp leather with intricate patterns, the sophisticated musical instruments are still manufactured. Yes, there had been a high civilization here before cassette recorders and vitamin injections. Why, then, had bastardized culture been so universally triumphant? I suppose the answer is known only to those who have earnt their livelihood or amused themselves by pre-machine methods.

We walked the narrow passages of Kano's market. There were spices in the air – cloves, cinnamon, pepper, cardamom. There were baskets of what the old man called 'native soap' (he used the word *native* unselfconsciously) that looked like toasted cowpats, and 'native medicines' in vast quantities – this herb good for the liver, that leaf good for the kidneys, the other bark good for the digestion. I don't believe that if a certain root or herb has been used by traditional healers for hundreds of years there 'must' be something in it, on the grounds that forty million Frenchmen can't be wrong: for the history of medicine proves otherwise. Still, I wondered whether anyone had ever investigated these remedies scientifically.

There were little shops in the ancient arcades of baked mud that dealt in Tuareg swords, and others that sold only elemental antimony, used for eye makeup. There were shops for the embroidered hats that every Hausa man wore, and others for the pointed leather slippers that were going out of fashion (but cost less than a pound). I was seized by a whim to buy myself a suit of Hausa robes, and as I draped myself in them the traders from all around laughed. I was making a fool of myself, of course; and I asked the old man whether anyone would be offended.

'No,' he said. 'It means you like the people, like the country.'

We went to eat lunch together, in the 'southerner part' of the city. We ate pounded yam and bitterleaf soup. We were back in the urban mess, the realm of dogs, dust and disco. It was dangerous here at night, the old man said: after dark he would never venture out of the safe Muslim quarter. Southerners were hot-tempered and dishonest, and stealing was as natural to them as breathing. In the Muslim quarter one could leave one's belongings in the street and they would be untouched next day. In the Christian and pagan quarters one couldn't even be sure of one's pockets. Was this mere prejudice, or realism? In general it is true that the Muslim cities of Africa are safe to walk in, while many others are not. That very day in Kano market a boy of thirteen had been lynched after he was caught stealing. Whatever the

justice of such proceedings, they kept the incidence of theft low. But that
evening, over the television, the police announced that lynching people
was wrong.

The journey to Zaria, another of the famed ancient cities of northern
Nigeria, was short, only a hundred miles. The road was notorious for its
casualties and its potholes, but none of this, of course, affected the speed
at which the taxi drove. I started out late in the day and arrived as the
evening drew in. The hotel was next to a building called the *Ultra Modern
Conference Hall Complex*. Its plate glass was cracked, the curtains were
grey with dirt, the paint flaked. The hotel had been opened by the state
governor in the days of Nigeria's greatest prosperity, during the oil
boom. The governor himself had been an immensely rich man who once
remarked that he considered India in advance of Nigeria because many
more people there lived on rubbish dumps. By this he presumably meant
that people were able to live on what others threw away, for him a sign of
increasing prosperity. The governor came to an untimely end when he
fell off his polo pony, which kicked him to death.

In the hotel lobby was a bookstall with an idiosyncratic selection of
reading matter: *The Mysteries of Macchu Picchu, Coriolanus* and the 1982
Annual of the Chinese Society of Naval Architects and Marine
Engineers. There was also a paperback volume entitled *Freedom in the
Grave: Nigeria and the Political Economy of Africa*. This I bought, after
discovering it was written by an Englishman living in Zaria. He was a
Marxist, to judge from the preface of his book:

> ... In opposition to literature which only interprets, confirms and
> stabilizes an alienated world of illusions, I write in order to clearly
> explain how extreme inequalities are created and how temporary they
> are once class-consciousness develops ... words are weapons.

I resolved to meet him.

Early next morning I went to Oyinlola Chambers where Patrick, the
author, had an office. The Chambers were a rather grandly-named
Nissen hut belonging to a lawyer, whose picture in robes and wig was on
the wall, together with that of his small daughter, similarly attired.
Patrick wasn't there, and I left a note for him to join me for lunch at the
hotel.

I walked to the old city, down a long street with an avenue of dusty trees. Zaria is a university town, and I passed *en route* one of the campuses. It was not a place of quiet contemplation: rather it seemed to offer an apprenticeship in urban overcrowding. Behind the trees were makeshift workshops and garages, small stores and stalls, wrecked cars and trucks, dogs and crows searching for carrion, and beggars in the dust who seemed to have acted as lightning conductors for the town's misfortunes, insofar as they were burdened with far more than their fair share. Not only blind with milky opacities over their eyes, they had deformed, withered limbs and hunchbacks as well. Some had special rubber pads to fit over their knees as they scraped themselves along; others had formed calluses. Also along the road were academic bookshops.

The old city retained some of its mediaeval walls, but in very poor condition. They were crumbling like stale cake, and now seemed to mean nothing more to the citizens than a convenient place at which to dump garbage, or to *ease* themselves, as the Nigerians put it. As for the old city itself, it seemed to be disappearing before the onslaught of the new. Even the Emir's palace was a curious mixture, and not a very happy blend: its most striking external feature being the no doubt essential silver-painted water tower.

Patrick arrived at my hotel room as I was reading his book. I had speculated on what he would be like. His writing was unsentimental and ruthless. He believed that only an orgy of death could usher in the golden age which was, however, coming.

> The process of ending the human costs of capitalism will in the short run entail massive destruction of life – it could be as great as the present social costs. But in the long run there is no alternative if we wish finally to practicalize the ideals of self-reliance, equality and justice . . .

There was a small, passport photo of him on the back cover: fiercely unsmiling and intense, he looked every bit the uncompromising polytechnic revolutionary, the Nechaev of Nigeria, the Lenin of Zaria.

There was a knock on the door. It was not the confident rap of historical necessity: rather the diffident tap of moral dilemma. I opened the door and there before me was a slight, donnish man with thick spectacles, the frames of which had been repaired with pink sticking plaster.

His movements were precise but timid, almost bird-like and, like his speech, rather pedantic. He was the mildest of men and so terrified of giving offence that even sitting down without having first been asked gave rise to agonizing indecision, as though he were choosing between two terrible alternatives. So much, I thought, for the Lenin of Zaria.

He was a remarkable man. His first degree, from Oxford, was in French; his subsequent career had been in teaching public administration at various universities, first in Europe and then, for nine years, in Zaria. (I admit I had only the very faintest idea of what public administration, as a university subject, could be.) He fell foul of the university authorities for teaching his radical views and they forced his resignation. Instead of returning to Europe he stayed in Nigeria, while his wife, a Nigerian nurse, went to live in England. He, in the meantime, tried to earn a living from writing political tracts. His *Freedom in the Grave* was now in its fourth edition, the previous editions having been 60, 150 and 500 copies respectively. The market for radical tracts was very small, and so he was poor: he lived in a single room with two Nigerians, similarly impecunious. Whatever his views, he held them with complete – one might almost say, frightening – sincerity.

We went to the hotel restaurant for lunch. We were the first customers that day (in fact there were to be no others – the hotel cook was a notorious drunk, Patrick said), and the waiter turned on the little illuminated fountain in our honour. Patrick laughed at this pretension, but not from pure amusement. He said it was terrible that people should think of such trivial things when outside there was so much suffering, so much hunger, so many babies dying. In fact, he disapproved of luxury altogether: he swept his hand round the whole restaurant. It didn't look so very luxurious to me – some of the large fibreglass ceiling tiles, for example, had fallen, leaving gaping black holes – but I had not been living in a single room in a Zaria lodging house with two other tenants. The immorality of the restaurant, however, did not impair Patrick's appetite: or perhaps he was just building himself up for the Revolution.

I ordered a dish called *fura da nono*. I thought it was named for an early Portuguese explorer who penetrated to the interior in the sixteenth century, and whose explorations were the subject of a chronicle: 'And so the Captain Fura da Nono led his men to unknown parts in the land of the caffres, and there saw wondrous great cities whose gold it was impossible to count . . .' *Fura da nono* turned out to be yoghourt with crushed millet, flavoured with lemon, salt and red pepper.

Patrick had to go to Kaduna after lunch on a sales trip, but said he would return next day. On the way out he greeted everyone, including the cook, who by now was swaying in the garden. Everyone on the street seemed to know Patrick too: he was a famous local figure. I remarked on this, and said that everyone liked him.

He tried very hard not to be flattered and fought back a smile. 'Not everyone knows me,' he said. 'And not everyone *likes* me. They think I am dangerous.' And then he added as an afterthought: 'But all the children like me.'

We were passing a child as he said it. He stopped to speak to the child and to embrace it. I thought I detected the same saccharine goodness in his manner that I had seen in missionaries: or perhaps I had seen too many propaganda posters of dictators surrounded by hosts of adoring infants.

'You are a Marxist missionary,' I said.

Not surprisingly, he objected to the analogy. Religion, he said, was just the veil of illusion with which the ruling class, whether they knew it or not, hid reality from the toiling masses. He, on the other hand, was trying in his writing to show them reality directly, without veils or other devices.

A new Mercedes went by. He shook his head: the car cost at least 150,000 Naira, he said, and a beggar was fortunate to get 50 *kobo* a day. It made him very angry; but secretly I wondered whether he wasn't enjoying himself. To be on the side of the angels is not without its compensations, even for an atheist.

That evening I went with the hotel driver (whose car, a golden Peugeot, had tinted electric windows and curtains, arctic air-conditioning, a silvered nymph diving from the bonnet and quotations from the Koran to ensure safe arrival) to a bar on the outskirts of the city. To be found drinking within the old city walls was to risk a lynching, but it was safe elsewhere.

The bar was outside, a group of thatched shelters lit by dim red lamps. We ordered pepper soup, a hot dish of muddy catfish, and beer. From the only other occupied shelter came the sound of an excited political discussion. One of the participants was addressed as *major*, and since the names of two countries I had recently visited – Mozambique and Ethiopia – were mentioned frequently, I asked whether I might join them.

As is often the case in such discussions over beer, the original point at issue had been forgotten, but Africa as a whole – its backwardness and poverty – was the general subject. The major, now retired, was for a military solution, since the people of Africa lacked the necessary self-discipline. He admitted, though, that the soldiers were as corrupt as civilians. A university lecturer in biology thought there was no solution but hard work and gradual improvement, while a man in his late twenties who described himself simply as an intellectual said that Africa must unite to defeat the World Economic System. I disgusted him by remarking that even joined together, Africa hardly amounted economically to Switzerland; therefore its ability to change things on a world scale was small. Besides, if Ibo, Yoruba and Hausa couldn't unite in Nigeria, what chance was there for a united Africa? The lecturer laughed, but the intellectual stood up angrily.

'That is a very bourgeois analysis,' he said. He could think of no worse insult. 'I cannot listen to it.' And he left, which I regretted.

I met Patrick again next evening, after he had returned from his sales trip to Kaduna. I asked him how it had gone; but like an evangelist discussing converts, he declined to talk numbers. With him he had Dennis, a worker from the university hospital, whom I quickly recognized as a disciple. I had seen before the relationship between a Marxist guru and worker-acolyte: a worker who had previously been interested only in beer and skittles until the scales had been removed from his eyes, to discover that the most fundamental laws of the universe themselves were working inexorably for the total liberation of his class – *via* an apocalypse, of course. Dennis, however, had not yet been entirely won over: he still had a sense of humour.

We went to a little restaurant where all of us ate our fill for less than a dollar. Our conversation was completely serious. Patrick felt the ills and misery of Nigeria weigh upon him personally, and what a weight – according to him – they were! He dismissed all statistics about Nigeria as at best unreliable, at worst mendacious; but he unhesitatingly subscribed to the view that practically all Nigerians led lives of unrelieved misery, lives which grew worse every day. I said this had not been my observation in Nigeria, or anywhere else on my journey for that matter. Poor yes, but miserable no.

He replied that my observations were superficial: that people could look happy when in fact they were miserable. And even when they *were* happy, they *ought*, considering their conditions, to have been miserable. He spoke of them as though they were somehow failing in their duty in this regard. Nigerians lived in squalor; their children died in infancy; they lived in terror of unemployment. *Objectively*, in the Leninist sense, they were miserable. My argument that misery was always subjective and depended at least to a degree on one's expectations rather than one's circumstances, cut no ice with him – though Dennis agreed with me, and said that most Nigerians were not miserable.

Patrick's statements, it seemed to me, grew wilder and wilder. The modest, mild little man now decried the whole of heretofore existing civilization, saying it must be swept away *in toto* as it had brought only increasing misery to Africa, Asia and South America. This was a strange assertion, I said, for a man who disbelieved in statistics; besides which, it was simply untrue that the situation grew worse everywhere. He challenged me to name a country where it was not so.

'India,' I said.

He said I should prove it.

'Thirty years ago there were regular famines. Now there are none.'

He let out what I can only describe as a cry of pain. He was far from rejoicing at India's fortune. He *needed* the world to be only a vale of woe, otherwise his sacrifice, his whole life, was pointless.

'India is only one country,' he said.

'With a fifth of the world's population.'

'Statistics again. I don't believe them.'

'And Japan?' I continued. 'A hundred years ago the Japanese were horribly poor. Now they have the highest life expectancy in the world.'

'Japan is tiny, insignificant.'

'With a hundred million people.'

'They're not alive, they're living corpses.'

I felt I was beginning to lose my temper. I wanted to call him an arrogant little shit.

'You don't think that's a little sweeping?'

'No, they're corpses, not alive.'

He turned on doctors. They were corruptly concerned only with keeping decrepit westerners alive, beyond the age of social utility. Only Nigerian babies, it seemed, were worthy of their efforts.

I asked him whether he thought we should let our old people die without relief, or maybe even kill them off?

'Let them die! Let them die!' he exclaimed with fervour bordering on hatred.

It was impossible to break into the paranoid, apocalyptic circle of his thought. We parted in acrimony, our hearts racing, believing each other to be men of bad principle.

I woke next morning with the argument still going round in my head. It was the dialectical equivalent of a hangover. How many witty ripostes and telling examples had my mind conjured up while I was asleep! I considered finding Patrick to tax him with a few, but decided against: instead I took a taxi to Sokoto.

The taxi was, as they say, far from well. Shortly out of Zaria it developed a jerking tic; then there was a puncture and the spare tyre was as bald as a vulture's neck. Then the exhaust fell off, and the noise was equalled only by the smoke. It was with some relief (and surprise) that we juddered and smoked our way into Sokoto: the road had been unrelentingly hot and shadeless, not a landscape in which to linger without preparation.

Sokoto is one of those euphoniously-named northern Nigerian towns that conjure up romantic visions of emirs, mud-walled palaces and gorgeously-bedecked cavalry stampeding across plains in clouds of dust. Actually, Sokoto is not very old, having been founded as an encampment in 1809. Mud looks ancient as soon as it dries; unfortunately, the sultan's palace, painted cream and green, looks very like a railway station. The house of Shehu Shagari, the deposed democratically-elected president of Nigeria (who was said to be personally uncorrupt, though he allowed his son-in-law, the infamous Dikko, to salt away billions while minister of transport) was a plain breezeblock edifice with louvred windows and dirty green curtains. Some of Sokoto's outer streets were pleasantly tree-lined, but on the whole it is a city that disappoints the fervid romantic imagination.

In the morning there was an interesting little report in the newspaper, headed 'Man In Soup'. An unnamed man in Jos had been arrested for attempting to sell his son to another man, described only as *Alhaji*, for

7000 Naira (£780). The Police Public Relations Officer, Mr Smart Irabor, 'advised people not to sell their children in spite of economic hardship' – because it was against the law.

I had the name but not the address of a British lady, the friend of a friend in Tanzania, who had long worked in Sokoto's Department of Antiquities, and who was an expert on the famous *jihad* of the sheikh Uthman dan Fodio in 1804. I had always found precolonial African history difficult to grasp insofar as its political entities were so fluid, with constantly shifting frontiers and capitals, and with tribes and other ethnic groupings moving kaleidoscopically over the continent. I hoped she would be able to clear my mind about one small part of that history.

But first I had to find her. This proved no easy matter, for nobody I asked agreed with any other informant as to the location of the Department of Antiquities. Eventually I was directed to the head of one of the state government's departments.

The capital of each of Nigeria's seventeen states has a double bureaucracy, state and federal. They are housed in vast, warren-like buildings (the federal secretariats being identical in each state): one wonders as soon as one enters what all these people can possibly be doing. Not much, from the look of it, unless endlessly obstructing the flow of files be counted. As I waited outside the door of the department's director, I reflected unfavourably on African bureaucracy, likening it to an eleventh plague of Egypt. I even managed to work myself into a pleasant state of indignation about it. Bureaucrats in Africa were corrupt, lazy, inefficient, obstructive, stupid and cruel, and the thought of them raised my blood pressure. Then I was courteously invited into the director's office.

He was a small man behind an immense desk which quite dwarfed him. His complexion was pale, and he looked more North African than anything else. He, too, had the title of *Shehu* (Sheikh in Hausa). His eyes shone with humorous intelligence; he was a model of natural courtesy. He spoke English perfectly, and said he went to England every year, regarding it as his second home: though he feared Nigerians had now a very bad reputation there (deserved, of course). On his last visit he had taken a taxi in London and when the driver discovered he was a Nigerian he had made him get out of the taxi.

'I don't take Nigerians,' he had said. 'Nigerians are corrupt people.'

I apologized on behalf of England, but the Shehu said he understood the taximan's point of view.

Alas, the lady I sought had left Sokoto some months before, after twenty-five years. But the Shehu said he would find her address in Britain for me and bring it to my hotel: which he did and where, to my surprise, he drank a beer with me.

And so I was left to decipher the meaning of the Sokoto *jihad* for myself, from what I could learn in books. At the time of its outbreak, the region was ruled by a variety of nominally Muslim Hausa sultans who, however, countenanced the continuation of animistic practices. The Hausa were settled farmers; the Fulani were pastoralists whose moving herds of cattle sometimes damaged Hausa crops. There was thus the potential for hostility between the ethnic groups. The immediate pretext for the *jihad* was the outlawing of turbans by one of the Hausa sultans. Among the Fulani was a class of pious and scholarly Muslim preachers, and it was they, with Uthman dan Fodio as spiritual leader, who raised the banner of holy war. Their aim was to create a state of Islamic purity, consciously modelled on the early Arab empire. The *jihad* was soon joined by devout Muslims of many different tribes.

The descendants of Uthman dan Fodio still have more natural authority in the north than the government of Nigeria. But for me the moral of the *jihad* – at least, the one that is congenial to me – is contained in what Uthman dan Fodio's son, Abdullah, wrote soon after his father's death about some of the people who took part in the *jihad*:

> . . . whose purpose is the ruling of countries and their people, in order to obtain delights . . . and the appointing of ignorant persons to the highest offices, and the collecting of concubines, and fine clothes and horses that gallop in the towns . . . and the devouring of gifts of sanctity, and booty and bribery, and lutes, and flutes, and the beating of drums . . . They were many, but the righteous were few; they showed the dissimulation of (the) wicked . . . the sellers of free men in the market.

No puritanical political movement can ever maintain its original purpose: men are just not like that. And for a writer, it is just as well.

One of the enduring effects of the *jihad*, perhaps, is the prohibition of alcohol within the confines of the old city. Ardent drinkers need not despair, however: for outside the old city is an entire shantytown of corrugated tin, consisting entirely of bars – hundreds, maybe even thousands, of them.

My companion there was an Ibo driver who had come to the north to save money, away from the financial demands of his relatives that had kept him poor at home. The religious enthusiasts of Sokoto, he said, wanted to destroy this township of beer: but there was a military camp nearby, and the city fathers knew the soldiers would run riot if deprived of their inalienable right to get drunk off-duty. Even the fanatics were afraid of them.

We chose a bar down one of the uneven narrow roads and sat quietly drinking. For himself, my companion was not unhappy. But he regretted there was so much poverty in Nigeria, in the midst of so much wealth. He was not sanguine about Nigeria's future: he had grown up in Biafra and still believed the only solution to the country's ethnic divisions was to separate it into sovereign states. As for corruption, it was caused by the passion for quick, unearned gain. The squanderomania that had ruined Nigeria was caused by oil money which was essentially unearned. When a man bought a box of matches with his wages, he was careful with each match; when a man was given a thousand boxes for nothing, he lit them just to see the light.

Next evening we went together to the cinema, a great, bare hall seating (I should guess) two thousand. The walls were of latticed brickwork to let in the breeze, if any; the ceiling was an upturned forest of fans, revolving slowly with, as far as I could tell, no effect whatsoever. The audience was almost entirely of young men, each in an embroidered hat and robes: the Ibo driver and I were conspicuous in our western dress. There was a hubbub of conversation, in eager anticipation, I thought, of the film. This was not so, for the conversation continued all through the film at exactly the same volume, obscuring the soundtrack which in any case sounded as though it were relayed through water.

The film was *The Rise and Fall of Idi Amin*. It was not a film in which dialogue was necessary to understanding of the action. The actor who played the part of the dictator caught to perfection his fatuous swagger, his bone-headed incomprehension of his own ignorance. Every time he appeared on the screen in ever more gold-braided and bemedalled uniforms the audience burst into derisive laughter; and when he was shown in a morgue eating the flesh of one of his enemies, they laughed again, but this time uneasily. To the sophisticated Hausa, with centuries

of civilization behind them, the brutal antics of this savage village
potentate were as alien as a game of American football (even if they
sometimes rose against the Ibo in their midst). Idi Amin's Uganda was a
continent away.

I went to Illela, on the Nigeria-Niger border. For once there were only
two passengers in the taxi, the other a young Malian who, surprisingly,
spoke English but no French. He addressed me softly as *Gentleman* and
he had the timidity of someone who has lived long in a society that has no
compassion for the weak and defenceless. He had been working illegally
in Port Harcourt and was returning to Mali. I asked him why.

'Gentleman, my daddy has dead.'

He had $10 (in Naira) to see him to Mali. It was very little, but he said
he would sell his clothes if necessary. Far worse, his only document was
an out-of-date Malian identity card. He was worried about what the
Nigerian authorities would do to him. Rather vaingloriously, I told him
to stick with me.

The sight of a police roadblock halfway to the border threw him into a
panic. He was half-inclined to jump out of the car and run for it. I told
him to tell the police he was going to Illela not to cross the border but to
see a friend. This he did, and the police waved us on.

The harmattan, the wind off the Sahara, was blowing and everywhere
the lines of the landscape were blurred by a yellowish haze of sand. The
harmattan is an impressionist.

I admired the villages with their bell-shaped granaries: the famed
fecklessness of the African being here translated into an anxious care for
the future, the land providing no more than a grudging subsistence and
the desert creeping ever nearer.

At the border my Malian friend gave the health inspector five Naira in
lieu of certificates, and simply ignored the customs. We walked together
into the Republic of Niger.

ELEVEN

Niger

The Niger border official became deeply respectful once he knew I was a doctor.

'*C'est trop fort,*' he said.

Taking advantage of his respect, I said the Malian was my friend. The official made no difficulties, asking only for treatment for malaria, which I gave him.

We waited six hours at the *gare routière* of Birni Nkoni, the town on the Niger side of the border (and the northernmost reach of the Sokoto caliphate). The *gare* was also a market, through which the money changers waddled with bulging robes, seeking customers. Beggars and kebab sellers weaved among the passengers waiting for the bus to Niamey: the driver was stretched out asleep under a tin shelter, which later served as a mosque.

There was a terrible smell of sewage in the *gare*. Next to the tin shelter was a *pissoir*, a small sloping slab of concrete leading to a lake of urine whose outlet was blocked. Sun-drying excrement lay in blobs on the concrete, attracting flies; and across the concrete, heading for the urine, wriggled small white maggots. When the call to prayer came and most of the men in the *gare* bowed and knelt and bowed and knelt again in impressive unison in the direction of Mecca, I remembered once more Chekhov's remark vis-à-vis Tolstoy. But then, being by nature argumentative, if I had met a sanitary engineer I would have said that the Kingdom of God is within you.

We set out for Niamey late in the afternoon, when shadows were lengthening. The road was paved the whole way, 250 miles. It had been built as aid: the old road, narrow and crumbling, ran parallel to it much of the way. The improvement in communications with the capital seemed not to have wrought much change in the countryside through which the road passed. Settlements were few, the land arid and with little vegetation. During the entire journey, which lasted nine hours, we passed not more than a dozen vehicles in either direction. I wondered whether the aid money might not have been employed more usefully.

We were stopped ten times for identity checks. For the most part, the soldiers confined themselves to checking only the passengers in the front few seats, for the bus was crowded and to reach the back would have taken considerable effort. I sat next to two Tuaregs who kept their identity cards in their turbans, which in any case repeatedly unravelled and blew in my face. The womenfolk behind us, in tent-like black garments leaving only a slit for their eyes, decorated with headbands, necklaces, and bracelets of old silver coins, were never asked to identify themselves. A Nigerian who was transporting four six-feet high bales of polythene washbowls had repeatedly to pay an unofficial tax to the soldiers – a tax no doubt incorporated with interest in the final price of the bowls. This explained why the Nigerian accepted the tax with complete equanimity. As for the young Malian, no-one noticed his card was three years out of date: the soldiers were not fluent readers.

We stopped at a village with a roadblock. The beat of drums throbbed through the night air. A hundred yards ahead we could see a large, shadowy crowd in the road. And, by the roadside, illuminated by hurricane lamps, was a big concrete building under construction. The drums were to encourage the workers to hurry. There was a sense of urgency and excitement about the work I had not encountered before on my journey: human chains formed to pass up buckets of water, sand and cement to the workers on the building. The whole village had turned out either to help or to watch and encourage, and I asked two young boys what it was all about.

One of the villagers had made good in Niamey and was having a store built in his birthplace as a kind of thanksgiving. He supplied the materials, the villagers the labour. This they gave willingly, for a store would make everyone's life better, and nothing like it had ever been seen in the village before. Of course, the store would belong to the rich villager, and he would soon be selling goods at a profit to the people who built his store for him: a case of philanthropy and five hundred per cent.

As I had no change, my Malian companion insisted on spending an eighth of his money on a drink for me. I was touched by his generosity; but I suppose when you have so little money it doesn't matter much how you spend it; it is simply insufficient. Nevertheless, I was more confident that he would reach his destination than that I should reach mine.

We parted at Niamey, which we reached at one in the morning. The roadblocks had grown more frequent towards the capital and I had been singled out for special scrutiny which, however, had never been less than polite. But for whom or for what, I wondered, were they searching?

I reached the hotel dizzy with the desire for sleep. The sound of slightly old-fashioned dance music wafted from somewhere within its bowels, and two men in military dress uniform emerged, rather unsteadily, into the lobby, accompanied by women in long chiffon dresses. The American Marines were having a ball.

Niamey is on the River Niger. It is not ancient, but most of its people live in sun-baked mud dwellings of ancient design. It has grown fast since independence, stimulated by two industries: the uranium mines in the north, and international aid. The relatively few modern buildings are, however, still as incongruous as three or four pearly teeth in an otherwise edentulous mouth. Next to the hotel is the one bridge across the river, the *Pont John F. Kennedy*, built fifteen years ago by the Americans. Across it comes a steady, unhurried procession of camels, bringing firewood to the mud quarters of the city. Along the fifty yards of river bank between the bridge and the gardens and tennis courts reserved to the hotel, the women of Niamey come to wash clothes in the far from clear waters of the river, slip-slapping the garments on rocks that substitute for soap. Inside the hotel, from which it is possible to phone Europe direct, it costs $3 to have a shirt washed.

There are two huge construction projects in the city. The first is a new market, built by the European Economic Community on a grand, not to say grandiose, scale. It hardly matters that the country produces practically nothing of its own to sell, and there is no prospect of self-sufficiency in view: for Niger consumes less in a year than a medium-sized European or American town consumes in a week, and this little the aid-donors will always be content to provide – in return for access to the uranium mines, of course.

The other large construction project is the National Stadium, a huge concrete arena that will be able to accommodate a large proportion of the city's population. The government thus seems to be pursuing a policy of circuses, without the bread. It struck me as absurd that so poor a country should spend so large a sum on so useless a luxury. But then I thought, what are the prospects for Niger with even the most rational policies in the world? At least this way they will be able to watch football matches in comfort.

Across from the hotel, curiously enough, was one of the best museums in Africa (not that Africa is famed for its museums). Standing in pleasant and immaculately maintained gardens were a series of small white pavilions, decorated with pretty traditional designs. Each pavilion was devoted to an aspect of Niger's past or present: for example, the uranium industry, tribal costumes and dinosaurs. One came away from the uranium mining exhibit with the impression that it was a rather pleasant social activity, with games of squash and visits to child welfare clinics predominating. One ought not to be too cynical, however: for there is only one thing worse for an African country than being exploited by a multinational consortium, and that is *not* being exploited by a multinational consortium.

There were attendants in each pavilion, whose eyes shone with the light of economic opportunity at the sight of a foreigner. With the fanatic zeal of flunkeys, they cleared out the barefooted, runny-nosed local children who had come to stare at the exhibits and then limped round after me, reading out loud the explanatory placards. For these inestimable services a reward was expected, at least twice as large as whatever was proffered. My nerves, for some reason, were not up to argument: and so I left each pavilion with the attendants bewildered (and I think a little disappointed) at my lack of resistance, and thinking I was an idiot. Yet I denied myself some of the beautiful traditional craftwork – handloom blankets, silver, leatherwork – that was done in the museum's artesenal workshops, for fear of being overcharged. Such are the inconsistencies of the traveller's state of mind.

The museum had exhibits of several kinds of villages from different parts of Niger, uninhabited of course and therefore cleansed of all the domestic sights and smells that might offend. Without the distraction of malnourished children or of chickens shitting on one's shoes, one was able to admire the often beautiful construction of African huts, their variety, their graceful shapes, their adaptation to the environment. I wished I knew more of the ethnology of the lands through which I passed so that I could discourse learnedly on the material and spiritual significance of the several styles of hut: instead I sat on the mud throne in a chief's hut and meted out imaginary justice to all white men – missionaries, agronomists, sanitarians, macroeconomists, arms salesmen, geologists, bankers, irrigation engineers, educationalists, volunteers, experts, and even doctors – consigning them all to the cooking pot.

There was a little zoo in the museum as well, and I went to watch the hippos wallow in their rather small pool. The lion had been thin and rachitic, his skin a threadbare fawn rug stretched over bones: the twitchings of his muscles being too feeble to disturb the flies feeding on a sore. But the hippos were sleek, and I always find them irresistibly comic – providing, of course, they are at a suitable distance. I laughed as they emerged from the water on their absurdly thin and stubby legs. I turned to the young African who leant on the rail next to me, to share my amusement. But he was not smiling: instead, he was sullenly vacant. A dullard, I thought, until I glanced at the side of his neck. It was swollen and pus had dried over the skin, leaving a trail of whitish-yellowish crust. Tuberculosis, in all probability.

I was anxious now to complete my journey. When I look at the map again, it seems full of exciting and mysterious destinations; but at the time I wished only to reach Timbuktu as directly and quickly as possible, to put an end to an undertaking whose utility I doubted once more.

And so I went once more to the *gare routière*, larger than that of Birni Nkoni, but otherwise not dissimilar. The bus that was bound for Gao in eastern Mali was called *Lover Boy*. It was parked between buses called *It's Not Wonderful* and *Oh Don't Worry*. Others nearby – all with Ghanaian registrations, presumably here to earn francs rather than near-useless *cedis* – were called *Good Father*, *To Be a Man Is Hard* and *If There Is Life There Is Hope*. *Lover Boy* also had a couple of slogans emblazoned on its bonnet: *Good God* and *All Shall Pass*, the latter a prediction, it transpired, of some accuracy.

As usual, no-one was able to say to within the nearest twenty-four hours when the bus would go. With a lack of irritation that surprised me – was I at last becoming an African in my attitude to the passage of time? – I settled to reading a Nigerian novel, *One Man, One Matchet*, by T. M. Aluko: a powerful, and surely unfashionable, attack on the hollowness of much African nationalism. But my reading was disturbed by a procession of beggars, blind women mostly, with their arms extended, resting on the shoulder of a child to guide them through the crowds or between the stalls; or the victims of polio, who spent their lives on the ground looking upwards. All sang snatches of song or recited verses from the Koran in exchange for alms, and I was impressed by the generosity of people who were not themselves rich. To give was considered a religious duty; and when I gave a blind woman some money, the young man next to me said: 'You give for the love of God.'

'No,' I replied firmly. 'I give because she is poor.'

I finished the novel, drank iced water sold in polythene bags, and went on to a play by Soyinka. I fell asleep in act one, with still no prospect of departure. When I woke an hour-and-a-half later, there was a distinct stir of activity. Baggage ten feet high was being tied on to *Lover Boy*'s roof; and the crowd round it had grown ominously large for so small a bus. An enormously fat boy – an unusual sight in Africa, where most children are thin – had taken up position in the doorway of the bus, and though the passengers had already paid the full fare he would not let them board without a further payment. A few of the passengers objected and tried to pull him from his position; he shouted at them, struggled, and then defeated them utterly by bursting into tears. I was the only one allowed on the bus without the fifty francs he demanded.

The bus was very small and the windows had no glass. There were six wooden benches, each of which might have seated five passengers, if not with comfort, at least without discomfort. There were, however, ten passengers per bench, so squashed together that for much of the time one's buttocks did not rest on wood but on bone and joints. It was by far the most crowded vehicle I had yet been in, and each time we stopped to alight it took at least a quarter of an hour to fit us all back in again. Movement was impossible; everyone thought everyone else had taken up more than his fair share of room; the driver was angry at the time it took for us to fit ourselves, sardine-like, into the bus; and as for the view, it was little more than occasional glimpses of rocks and tufts of grass at the edge of the road, and a constantly rising cloud of dust.

We left nearly ten hours after my arrival at the *gare*. Fifty yards into our journey we stopped: the driver had forgotten to fill up with fuel.

'Ten hours,' I exclaimed. 'And only now he discovers there is no fuel! How is it possible?'

My outburst was greeted with incomprehension. Did I expect to travel without fuel, then? I was unable to explain the basis of my rage, and it was taken as just another instance of the madness of white men. A man waits patiently for ten hours and then complains about a few minutes!

But filling the tank was by no means straightforward. A barrel of fuel had first to be rolled to the bus and then tipped to fill a bucket. The bucket was then emptied into the tank through a piece of stretched muslin, acting as a filter for the surprisingly large numbers of impurities. All these operations were conducted with a crowd of advisers shouting contradictory advice.

A kilometre out of the *gare* came the first roadblock. Then the sun went down and it was time for prayers by the roadside. In any case, *Lover Boy* needed frequent rests: no longer in the first flush of youth, and terribly overburdened, even an incline of a few degrees produced horrible grindings and judders. The road was dust and rubble, a treacherous surface for bald tyres; the male passengers had frequently to get out and push, while the female passengers stayed modestly where they were.

The plan, insofar as there was one, appeared to be to travel by day and night. But *Lover Boy* had other ideas. On the stroke of ten, a breakdown occurred beyond hope of nocturnal repair. There was only one torch on board, and the batteries were soon dead; *Lover Boy*'s lights, never the strongest, were soon reduced to a barely perceptible glimmer. There was nothing for it but to sleep where we had stopped.

We had stopped at a small village of not more than twenty mud buildings. No-one from the village came to speak to us or investigate what had happened. The moon was not yet up and the sky was magnificently arrayed with stars. On the other side of the road was a camel, hind legs bound with rope to prevent wandering, that swayed gently in the balmy air and from time to time cast a supercilious glance in our direction.

Suddenly the profound silence of the Sahel night was shattered by the sound of shooting, and then of galloping horses and more shooting. The French Foreign Legion, perhaps, coming to *Lover Boy*'s rescue? No; although the village gave no other indication of an electricity supply, one of the mud houses had a video set, and a cowboy film, dubbed in French, was being shown. The silence when the film finished was all the more profound for that sudden irruption of noise.

After more prayers, the passengers lay down by the side of the road. Within five minutes, many were broadcasting snores into the vastness. I went to the camel's side of the road and there found a large pile of hay, fodder no doubt for the camel. Lying down in it, I wondered why the others did not take advantage of its comparative softness. I discovered why at four o'clock in the morning.

I was woken by the sound of an animal, growling and running nearby. A hyaena or a lion? I saw nothing but was instantly alert. I wondered whether danger could be sensed independently of whatever caused it. If so, I sensed danger. I walked towards the bus, towards the sound of gentle snores. On my way there I became aware of a thousand pinpricks all over my body. The straw in which I had lain was full of spiky seeds, mere bagatelles for a camel's stomach, no doubt, but a damnable nuisance, amounting to torture, in human flesh. Why had the other passengers not warned me? Politeness? Indifference? Malice?

It was two hours before they woke, and two hours before I removed the last prickle from my clothes. Once more the passengers prayed; but despite the presence of the rising sun, they were not in accord about the direction of Mecca, and they prayed in all directions at once. Meanwhile, *Lover Boy* underwent swift repair.

The land grew ever drier. Although this southern part of Niger is by far the most populous, any slight eminence in the landscape revealed a vista of uninhabited emptiness. Several times we had again to push. By the roadside grew small, round wild melons with white flesh that I was told was fit only for animals. At times the melons – like small water melons – grew in profusion as far as the eye could see, gathering up and collecting moisture it was difficult to believe existed in all that aridity.

Shortly after starting out in the morning there was another roadblock, where the soldiers demanded a payment of 500 francs each from everyone without an identity card. This paid, we continued on our way (except for minor breakdowns) until within two miles of the Niger border post, which was itself a considerable distance from the border. The driver collected 500 francs from each of us, this being the bribe to the Niger customs and immigration to let us through without any inspection at all. *Lover Boy* forged on at full speed: that is to say, about fifteen miles an hour.

I had become friendly with an off-duty Malian policeman who was returning to his country after a holiday excursion. I asked him whether there were as many roadblocks in Mali as in Niger.

'Oh no,' he said, laughing patriotically. 'Once we reach Mali everything will be all right.'

TWELVE

Mali

We reached Mali at half-past-eleven in the morning, when the world was on fire. The air was so still there seemed none to breathe. To move required great mental concentration: not surprisingly, the officials declared it lunchtime when they saw us, and retired from view. They were not seen again till four o'clock.

The border village was small and wretched. There was nothing to eat, except peanuts in small packets. They were sold under the shade of one of the village's few trees, from a tray set on a makeshift table. The only other item for sale was a packet of *Liberté* cigarettes, sold one by one (but not yet, as in Tanzania at the height of its socialist purity, by the drag). The villagers would not give us water – it was too precious – and so we drank what we had from the previous village. It was hot and brackish, but I was past caring and it tasted good. As for the other passengers, water was simply water to them, the *sine qua non* of life, never the harbinger of disease.

I went to sleep on the concrete step of the border post. It seemed to me the acme of luxury. When I woke, the temperature had fallen from furnace to oven heat. Next to me was sitting an elderly man in a white gallibeya. He soon let me know he was a man of the world, that he had not spent the whole of his life in this diabolical village of Labbezanga. On the contrary, he had served with the French army, rising to the rank of sergeant. He had been in Vietnam, at the battle of Dien Bien Phu.

I wondered what the battle had meant to him; whether one of the most important defeats of European colonialism had changed his attitudes, or been a clarion call to action. I asked him about Dien Bien Phu.

'It was very good,' he said. 'Now I have a French army pension.'

This made him by far the richest man in the village: he was able to go to France every year. Thus, fortuitously, I had discovered a footnote to the history of one of the most important wars of the twentieth century: it made the fortune of the richest man in Labbezanga.

An argument had broken out between the *chef* of the *douaniers* and the driver, about the amount of the bribe to be paid to let us pass without inspection. No agreement was reached, and so the *chef* ordered the bus unloaded. This was no slight undertaking, especially in the heat, but it had to be done. By pure coincidence, the duties levied on individual travellers added up to what the *chef* had asked for in the first place. It was no end of a lesson.

We left Labbezanga between five and six. We bumped and shook along the dirt road, leaving a trail of smoke and dust and noise, until we reached the small town of Fafa. It had taken much longer than the distance on the map seemed to merit, and the moon was up, casting black shadows on a silvered world.

Fafa was beautiful beyond description at night. There was no artificial light anywhere, the streets between the flat-roofed mud houses were of deep sand, muffling the sound of dogs barking and murmured evening conversations. The moonlight was clear and bright enough to read by, and the leaves of the date palms rustled gently in the faint breeze. It was cool now, and many of the townspeople slept in the sand outside their houses. Beyond the town, which was on a slight elevation, one could see a vast plain, bathed in the cool light of the moon.

But we had not stopped to admire the beauty of the Sahelian landscape on a balmy evening. We had stopped because there was another customs post at Fafa. (As I soon learnt, customs posts are present in Mali not only at borders but throughout the country, not to raise revenue for the government, but simply to pay the wages of the customs men whom the government has employed but cannot pay. It is a solution of a kind to the problem of what to do with potentially disaffected secondary school graduates.)

First, the *chef* had to be found. Though Fafa was by no means large, this proved not easy. I settled to rest on a bed of fine sand. When found, the *chef* simply sent a message stating how much we should pay, and this was remitted without demur: it was midnight and we had suffered enough delay.

Once more we were on the road. But the driver had not reckoned on the police post at the edge of the town. We were stopped for an identity check. I was dealt with first and in complete separation from the others.

The police were polite and asked for no payment. When they had finished they told me to return to the bus while they dealt with the other passengers. An hour later, not all of them had returned to the bus: the ten without *pièces* were under arrest and locked up in a mud cell, pending the payment of a sum whose size was still a matter of negotiation between the police and the driver. By half past two the difference between offer and demand had narrowed to 2000 francs, but it was unbridgeable. I decided to pay it, and the men were released. But the driver was understandably too tired to continue, and so we slept where we were. The pleasant cool turned to chill, the sand having lost all the warmth of the day.

I woke early, before the others. It was not yet five, and though no light yet streaked the sky, the town cockerels crew and distant dogs barked. The passengers snored on oblivious; until suddenly, in unison, they woke. After clearing out their noses and bronchial tubes, they prayed; and this time there was unanimity of opinion as to the direction of Mecca.

We started out at six. Our progress was slow and, together with the tiredness, the overcrowding made this one of the most uncomfortable journeys of my life. My buttocks ached, my hips were sore, the struggle for an extra millimetre of room had taken its toll. I almost wished for a breakdown, that I might escape the interior of the bus. I saw little of the country on the way to Ansongo, but I imagine there was not much to see.

We reached Ansongo, the biggest town between Niamey and Gao, six hours after setting out. The distance was not much more than thirty miles.

The driver celebrated our arrival by accelerating straight into a sand dune from which it seemed impossible that we should ever be extricated. The passengers got out to dig and push but four of us, petulantly rebellious, said we had paid our fares and were damned if we were going to propel the bus as well; besides, we had hardly eaten for two days and were desperately hungry. We marched off in search of food, but the scorching heat and the energy-sapping sand soon cooled our ardour. Our quick march became a slouching stagger.

We found a restaurant – or rather, *the* restaurant – near the market. The sun had driven practically everyone indoors, or at least into the shade. Nearby was the River Niger, sparkling in the sun and looking invitingly cool. Along its banks grew palms. The map showed the road from Niamey following the river, and every settlement on its banks; but this was the first time since leaving Niamey I had seen it. We ate on the floor of the mud-walled restaurant: rice and meat. Ordinary as it was, rarely have I enjoyed anything more. The others did not want meat until they realized that I would pay; then they devoured it with enthusiasm bordering on savagery. We drank copiously of the River Niger, as earthy-tasting as *retsina*. Even the coffee (Nescafé, incidentally, is a product quietly ubiquitous, to be found where even Coca-Cola has not reached) tasted of mud.

After lunch a boy came to us and asked us whether we should like to see something special. Always intrigued by small mysteries, I said I should; and the boy led us to a large, crumbling colonial era building of Roman-style red bricks. A long dark passage ended in an archway; and there in the room beyond, standing on a pedestal and looking like an idol in a pagan shrine, was an old paraffin refrigerator – or rather, *the* refrigerator, for I was told there was not another one in Ansongo. We approached it reverently. The high priest was not present, and we waited for him to return (there was a padlock on the door). And what did it contain, this one refrigerator of Ansongo? Polio and other vaccines, as Aid Workers and Relief Agencies would have wished? I knew from experience that it did not. Instead, there were rows and rows of Heineken beer, smuggled into Mali from Niger. We each had a beer, a can of which cost six times more than lunch. As a reward for bringing us here, I gave the boy a refrigerated bottle of sickly orange drink: the one refrigerator of Ansongo had already made him discontented with the tepid water of the Niger.

We rejoined the bus, which had been dug out of the dune and now was outside the Ansongo customs house. We had to wait for the officers to return from lunch, but matters were soon settled (in their favour) thereafter. We drove a hundred yards into the main square of the town, to be halted by the police. They insisted on an inspection of our baggage as well as *pièces*. This was to be avoided only by payment of a sum, the amount of which was the subject of acrimonious debate. By now, I had come to believe the debate was almost as much desired by the authorities as the bribe, just as a fisherman values the fight put up by the fish as much as the fish itself.

I sat out the debate on the edge of the square, taking tea by a foetid alleyway leading to the river bank, up which toiled a procession of hunched old women with bundles of firewood on their heads. They had come from across the river where there were still some trees.

The tea was boiled in a tiny pot over some charcoal, and then so saturated with sugar that it looked like green syrup when poured into the small, thumbprinted glasses. Though normally averse to sweet drinks, I found it good. While I was drinking the young town idiot came to dribble over me, and a bright, smiling child with polio-withered legs dragged himself to sit at my feet. The townsfolk tried to shoo them away, thinking it was what I wanted; but when I gave them 100 francs each they were allowed to stay, and the town idiot's flow of saliva increased in appreciation.

We climbed into the bus once more, the customs men having been at last paid off. The idiot and the polio victim came to wave me goodbye. But we had only gone another ten yards when some soldiers stopped us: another identity check. I was shown into the commander's cockroach-infested office while the other passengers were herded together in the square outside. My passport inspected, I was told to wait in the bus while the other *pièces* were checked. I did as I was told.

After more than half an hour, however, when none of the passengers had rejoined the bus, I went to find out what was happening to them. A group was standing disconsolately outside the commander's office. They told me their identity cards had been taken by the soldiers, who refused to return them without a payment of 1000 francs each. As for those without *pièces*, they had to pay 2000 francs each to be released from the lockup. I recalled Ibn Batuta's remark about the ancient empire of Mali, after which the modern state was named, that one could travel its length and breadth in perfect safety and without molestation, so respected were the Emperor's laws.

My friend the policeman was particularly outraged that no special consideration was given to him: he had to pay like the others to get his police identity card back. 'Of course, you never do this,' I said to him. He did not reply.

At first the passengers were resolved to resist the soldiers' demands, but as time went by, one by one they paid, until all resistance crumbled. However, several of the passengers without *pièces* simply did not have the 2000 francs to pay. We were in for another long wait as negotiations went on. They were temporarily suspended at sunset, when the soldiers emerged to salute the lowering of the Malian flag in the square.

Everyone stood patriotically to attention during the brief ceremony; then the soldiers returned to their deliberations over how much they should extort from their fellow-citizens. I was deeply impressed by the instinctive solidarity of the passengers. No-one ever suggested leaving those without *pièces* (who were, after all, travelling illegally and causing us untold delay) to languish in their cell. It was accepted without argument that we could not move without them.

At seven in the evening the driver told us to climb on to the bus. Our hopes rose. The negotiations had been successfully brought to a conclusion, we thought. But no: we drove only to the edge of Ansongo, near a dune, where we should sleep the night. Three were still locked up. I discovered only another 3000 francs stood between them and release. I said I would pay 2000, and I told the driver to offer it to the soldiers, but to tell them we should not pay a single franc more. Absurdly enough, in the light of all that had gone before, it seemed to me of the utmost importance that the soldiers should not get *all* they asked for. The 2000 francs were accepted and the men released. They came to thank me, and I received their thanks with a guilty conscience: for I had paid not for their sake, but for my own. We set off once more, our complement complete. It had taken us more than seven hours to go a hundred yards.

It was dark and we made what was, for *Lover Boy*, good progress. The moon came up and the desert landscape glowed in the pewter light. Weariness was replaced by a strange elation, a feeling that life, despite officialdom, was good. We should soon be in Gao, and I would be on the last stage of my journey.

Perhaps, after all that had happened, it was odd I could have imagined we should complete the journey to Gao without further interruption; but hope generally triumphs over experience. Fifteen miles from Gao, at a small village, there was a roadblock manned by a single soldier. Next to the red and white barrier he had set up his mosquito net round his camp bed, sagging with constant use and covered in crumbs. At the head of the bed was a radio, relaying music loudly enough for a dance hall, but through a wall of white noise caused by the poor reception.

The soldier was specific in how much he demanded to let us pass: 15,000 francs. He said it was a fine for all those without *pièces*.

There was no question of this sum being paid, and so the passengers settled by the side of the road to sleep. The soldier, confident that we should pay in the end, retired under his mosquito net and prepared himself to sleep with the radio at his right ear.

I had had enough.

'*Pots de vin! Pots de vin!*' (Bribes! Bribes!) I went shouting up and down the village.

When I was a short distance from the soldier's bed he asked me why I was angry. His bewilderment was genuine.

Choking with fury, I related how we had been stopped and fleeced innumerable times that day; how it had taken sixty hours to go less than four hundred kilometres, not because the road was bad (I omitted to mention *Lover Boy*'s deficiencies), but because of Malian soldiers, police and *douaniers*, all demanding money from poor people.

The soldier, not without dignity, explained he had not received his wages for three months. What was he supposed to do? I said nothing. It was wiser not to remark he was collecting far more than merely his salary; or that I doubted he would cease his exactions if ever his salary *were* paid. All the same, I was somewhat deflated by the nagging question of how honest *I* should be in his circumstances. He asked me my profession, and I told him. There was a lull in our conversation. Then, a few minutes later, he addressed me plaintively.

'Monsieur, monsieur,' he said weakly. 'I am ill, monsieur.'

This was really too much. My anger came flooding back. First he held us up with his demand for an illicit payment; now he wanted a free consultation. I was about to say I hoped his illness might prove rapidly fatal, when I saw in it the opportunity for a *quid pro quo*. I asked him what was wrong.

'Malaria, monsieur,' he said. 'Chronic malaria. I need chloroquine.'

'I have chloroquine,' I said.

We struck a tacit bargain that in return for tablets we should be allowed to continue. After expressions of deep mutual regard we were soon on our way, once the snorers had been roused from their roadside slumbers.

Again my spirits soared. Surely now we should reach Gao within the hour?

The *douaniers* stopped us three miles from the town, which gave off a faint orange glow in the distance. The *douaniers* did not detain us long (about half an hour), being relatively modest in their demands. The night air was cold for them too.

At last we entered Gao. I felt battered and bruised, but triumphant and almost virtuous. The glow of the town had been caused by very few lights, and most of it lay in darkness, buildings being merely a denser shade of black. We drove to a yard which turned out to be a lair of sleeping *douaniers*, whose permission we needed before unloading the luggage. This they would not give until after sunrise, when they had received their bribe.

Alone of the passengers I sought out the *Hotel Atlantide* (a name with strange connotations for such a town, except that Sahel means shore and Sahara ocean). The night watchman showed me by lantern to my room, not luxurious but more so than the stony ground. The other passengers were in for an uncomfortable few hours, and I fell asleep wondering why they never turned on their tormentors, or simply ignored them and their demands altogether. Exaggerated respect for authority? Fear of guns? Or reading too much later Tolstoy?

Gao was once the capital of the vast Songhai empire, the successors to the Malian empire and greater in extent. It disposed of large resources and during its time Timbuktu reached the apogee of its reputation as a centre of Islamic learning. Nothing remains of Gao's former glory. Perhaps there never was very much: after the Battle of Tondibi in 1591, when a force of 3000 Moroccans defeated 15,000 Songhai cavalry and 60,000 infantry who turned and fled for reasons which will never be known, the Moroccan commander Judar entered Gao and found it very disappointing: 'The house of the shaykh of the donkey-drivers in the Maghrib (he wrote) is superior to the *askiya*'s (king's) palace.'

The Malian policeman whom I had befriended on the bus woke me early with my luggage. As a reward he requested a pair of shorts and shoes. I summoned up the energy at first to refuse his request as excessive: but in the end he prevailed. I was a European, he said, using the same argument as Michel in Zaire, which meant I could easily buy more shoes and shorts. But for a Malian it was the chance of a lifetime. His absolute belief in my infinite wealth reminded me of my childhood, when I thought all adults could buy and do anything they wished.

Delighted with his new possessions, he said he would return in a few hours to show me the town.

The *Hotel Atlantide* was a watering hole for young European adventurers who had just crossed the Sahara through Algeria in their air-conditioned, tinted-windowed four wheel drive vehicles. I wondered what the local people thought of these casually but expensively dressed Swedes and Italians to whom the Sahara was but a pleasure ground? Or of the groups of unshaven German hippies and their girlfriends who dressed with no concession to local custom or feeling, and who changed unimagineable sums of money in the bank (after nine different forms had been filled)? And what of the policeman I saw who paid a thick bundle of notes – the night's takings, perhaps – into his account?

Later, *my* policeman returned, proudly wearing his new shoes and shorts. He invited me to lunch at the police lines, where his sister (an ambiguous term in Africa) had cooked a meal for me. We walked together through the market, where the stalls were rigged with torn sacking, cripples mingled in the dust, and tiny heaps of millet and powdered milk – a Gift of the People of the United States – were sold.

We walked towards the police camp across a piece of open land, dry as desert. First we passed a school, a collection of long, low buildings with holes in the walls for windows. On the blackboard of one empty classroom were written the words:

LA REVOLUTION DANS LA VIE ECONOMIQUE

In another classroom, a few twelve year olds attended a lesson on the Enlightenment. The teacher scratched some words across the blackboard:

DIDEROT, VOLTAIRE, GOETHE

I looked around: unfed dogs, rusting water towers, little eddies of dust, a woman carrying a baby tied to her back and a load on her head. Mali had once been one of the most politically radical states in Africa, but it had long since fitted into the IMF mould. Even so, the Sahara was continuing its southward advance.

The police lines were like all labour lines in Africa: rows of small, soot-blackened, tin-roofed rooms, dark and unlit, with no running water, the land around a dump for litter, a haven for flies and mosquitoes, freezing in the cold and baking in the heat, ugly beyond the wildest dreams of a modern British architect. In the policeman's room was a veritable Tutankhamun's tomb of broken hand-me-down goods: a baby walker without wheels, a gas ring without gas, a shower curtain without water, a doll without a head, a bicycle without tyres, a record without a record player. The policeman saw me notice it all, and was embarrassed.

'We are very poor, monsieur,' he said.

Suddenly the meaning of never possessing anything new, of wearing other people's cast off clothes, of living one's life entirely among rubbish, was clear to me: the humiliation of it. And so far, at any rate, he had not extorted his way to wealth and comfort.

His 'sister', a nurse, brought us rice and meat in aluminium bowls. There was no room here for concern over the possible dangers of the metal. She was shy and modest, and after I had praised her cooking she left us. The policeman then took the opportunity to touch me for 3000 francs. Was this the sole purpose of his hospitality? I might have been angry; instead I was resigned. I gave him half of what he asked, and left him wondering whether a fool and his money were not soon parted.

By one of those coincidences which seemed to have happened regularly throughout my journey, a river boat was leaving Gao that afternoon. It was uncertain when, or whether, there would be another that season, for the Niger at Gao is navigable only five months of the year, and the water was falling fast after the cessation of the rains. I bought a ticket to Kabora, the river port of Timbuktu, and boarded.

The river ferry of the *Compagnie Malienne de Navigation* was far less crowded and life on it far less exuberant than on the Zairean equivalent. There was no music and even the lower decks were quiet. There women sat among piles of water melons and seemed not to care whether anyone bought or not. Conversation was a murmur, not an excited babble.

On board I befriended two French nurses, one of whom came every year to Africa for her holidays. The previous year she had gone walking in the Dogon country of Mali, and after six days without food had almost died of exhaustion. Undeterred, she had returned to Mali. Also on board was a young Peace Corps volunteer *en route* home from his tour of duty in Cameroon, which he had spent in a small, isolated village. The experience seemed to have had the same effect as smoking too much marijuana: a vacancy which was as much neurological as meditational. From time to time he bestirred himself to ponder the philosophical questions (What is life for? Why am I here?) that his sojourn in Africa had raised; but he was not an educated man – he had been a rebel a school, he said, and had not gone to college, preferring to become a carpenter – and his command of his own language was inadequate for coherent philosophizing. Nevertheless, he had come to doubt the materialistic values of his native California, and he was apprehensive about his capacity to adopt them once more when he returned. His horizons had broadened, to the detriment of his peace of mind.

The Niger was broad but shallow, to be navigated with care. Much of it was converted to rice paddy, and the boat steamed in passages between brilliant green fields. The river banks were desert, rising at times in the graceful golden arcs of sand dunes, but for the most part flat and hostile-looking, with only scrubby vegetation, and the horizon always blurred by a yellowy-pink haze of sand. The few villages were of flat-topped mud houses, with only the conical mud tower of the mosque and the fronds of a few palms rising above them.

Early in the afternoon we stopped at a small town situated at one end of a long, sweeping bank of sand fifty feet high. Along the crest of this gilded dune, silhouetted against the azure sky, ran in single file a score of townspeople in red and white and dark blue robes, rushing to greet the boat. Many others had put out in pirogues, which clung to the side of the boat as iron filings to a magnet. We pulled up beside the quay: the town was untouched, to all appearance, by the last century or two. Aesthetically, and possible in other ways too, it was in perfect harmony with its surroundings: the twentieth century had little to teach it.

At midnight, with a full moon up, we stopped at another town, Gourma-Rharous, built on the crest of a large dune. As soon as the gangplank was lowered, excited crowds streamed across in both directions. Despite the lateness of the hour, the entire town had turned out to greet us. Everyone gathered by the water's edge. The two nurses, the Peace Corps volunteer, a young Malian who had sought my advice about his peptic ulcer (at every meal he opened a vial of B vitamins for intramuscular injection and drank it) and I walked through the deserted town, looking back on the boat and the crowd from the top of the dune. The town was deathly quiet, a monochrome world where everything was a shade of silvery-grey. At the end of the broad, cool central street stood the Governor's house. One half-expected a *tricoleur* to unfurl from its flagpole, and legionnaires to salute it to the sound of trumpets. We returned to the boat, to a chorus of the one word of French all the children knew:

'*Cadeau! Cadeau!*'

The Malian was less fastidious than we: he cuffed the nearest child smartly round the ear, the only *cadeau* he received that evening.

We went to the bar in second class for a last drink: unnaturally pink and sweet grenadine. I described the exactions of the officials from the border of Mali to Gao. A soldier in the bar, a member no doubt of the extorting classes, overheard, and when I finished asked why I did not continue. There was something mildly insidious and threatening in his manner. At first I pretended not to understand; then I looked him in the eye and said:

'Because that is all there is to say.'

He slid off his stool and left.

Timbuktu is not on the River Niger and neither any longer is its little port, the village of Kabora, which is now reached by a short canal. After all the difficulties Mungo Park faced in getting this far down the river (he and all his party were soon to die in 1806), he sailed straight past Kabora and missed the city which had been the object of his explorations.

A pirogue took us from the river to the village: the water in the canal was already too shallow for the boat. Kabora was once a centre of Islamic learning in its own right, but is now little more than a scruffy landing-stage for the larger town inland. We watched sinewy young men carry hundred-kilo sacks on their heads from pirogues the last few yards to the quayside, and return at once for a further load. They waded waist-deep in water and then ran up a ramp. They did not pause a moment for breath. Waiting in the shade for a pick-up taxi to take us the five miles to Timbuktu exhausted us.

Sitting on sacks of dried milk – another Gift of the People of the United States to the merchants of Africa – in the back of the taxi, I congratulated myself on the completion of my journey, at the same time acknowledging that a journey to Timbuktu is not what it once was. The short road from Kabora to Timbuktu, for example, used to be infested with aggressive Tuareg who attacked, robbed and murdered travellers. The first European known for certain to have reached the fabled city, Major Alexander Gordon Laing of the 2nd West India Regiment, was carried there in 1826 after being left for dead by the Tuareg who attacked him; and when, eight days later, he left the city, the Tuareg strangled him with a turban.

But why had *I* come, I asked myself as we bounced about (I had no idea milk powder could be so hard)? Why end my journey in Timbuktu? The African Association who sent Mungo Park had no doubts: in

Timbuktu, even the slaves wore gold. 'If we could get our manufactures into that country' – wrote one member – 'we should soon have gold enough.' The legend of Timbuktu's wealth was born in the fourteenth century, when the Malian emperor, Mansa Musa, left Timbuktu with 8000 followers to go on the pilgrimage to Mecca. He took so much gold with him that when he reached Cairo, the price of gold there fell by a tenth. The legend has long been exploded, of course, but the name alone continues to exert a fascination. As a child I heard the name of Timbuktu as a byword for distance, obscurity, mystery and isolation. When something was irretrievably lost, it had gone to Timbuktu; and I wondered whether, like Heaven, it was a real place or an invention of adults. Another reason for going there was to give a title to my book: for everyone has heard of Timbuktu, and most have wondered what it was like.

First I glimpsed a water tower, and then some long, low buildings faced with rough-hewn stone: government offices. Soon we reached the heart of the old city, however; and walking through the narrow, sandy streets, mere winding passageways between mud houses, with free-standing clay ovens at many corners, I felt a pale intimation of the joy of Réné Caillé, the French explorer who in 1828 was the first European to return alive from Timbuktu: 'On entering the mysterious city, which is the object of curiosity and research to the civilised nations of Europe, I experienced an indescribable satisfaction . . .'

The house – now only a façade – in which Caillé stayed while he was in Timbuktu was decked out with little French and Malian flags. We had contrived to arrive on the same day as a flying visit by President Mitterand, accompanied by President Traoré of Mali. We missed the camel races in his honour, but we saw the presidential motorcade, consisting of every serviceable vehicle in the town, including some (I was told) that had been stolen in France, driven across the desert and sold lucratively in Mali as part of a regular trade. M. Mitterand was on his way to lunch, looking pale and distinctly unseduced by the charms of Timbuktu. His aides in the cars behind waved regally to the non-existent crowds while the Malian presidential guards slouched hungrily, waiting for the afternoon departure of the two presidents. The guards had a bizarre costume: they looked as if they had strayed from an amateur production of a Lehár operetta. They wore bright green trousers with a crimson stripe, yellow shirts, maroon cloaks, orange epaulettes and black boots. Mitterand must have needed all his *savoir faire* not to laugh. It was funny, but also inexpressably sad. For all around were men of great physical dignity in traditional costume, a costume rejected by the Malians in favour of a sub-comic opera get-up, because it was 'modern' and European.

Foreigners must register with the police and have their passports stamped at every place they stay in Mali. (There is a club in New York whose membership requirement is a Timbuktu stamp in one's pass-port.) We went to the police station, a dark cavern in the *Place de l'Indépendence*. We later discovered that the children of Timbuktu always ran past it, as I ran in childhood past a house where an old lady lived whom I believed a witch; though I understand there is a more rational basis for the children's fear of the Malian police. There was a lengthy and detailed form to fill, and labouring over it we found a young Japanese who had spent nine months travelling alone in Africa, without a word of French and not much more English. The last time he had filled the form it had taken him three hours (I think that is what he was trying to say): hardly surprising, for it is difficult to convey the meaning of questions like *In the event of an accident who should be informed?* by means other than language. We filled it for him, making up his wife's name, his address and occupation, and he bowed to us in gratitude.

While waiting for the presidents to leave and for Timbuktu to return to its normal somnolent state, we went to one of the town's few bars, a mere afterthought of a building, hidden away from view, with *I hate the hand that destroys*, *Make love not war* and *Alcohol = Dialogue* scrawled on the walls. Other than the owner, there were two Americans there, a husband and wife. He was an irrigation engineer, working for a charitable organization a hundred miles from Timbuktu, the metropolis of the region; she was a housewife, swayingly drunk and high (or low) on some kind of drug. He was quiet, the kind of man who did not waste words or speak of what he was ignorant; she made up for his taciturnity, but her loquaciousness was not equalled by her coherence. Her speech was slurred, her mind a blur of impressions fighting for simultaneous expression. As for her French, it was murderous, even to my ears.

She stood up and swayed with a bottle of beer in her hand. She was dressed in khaki shorts and a pink vest.

'Timbuktu,' she said, 'say le finn de le monde.'

The bar owner was offended.

'Timbuktu,' he said, 'had a university in the thirteenth century.'

'No, really?' she said, lurching back into her seat and raising the bottle to her lips. 'You don't say.'

Not realizing that her lack of interest was terminal, he mentioned that Timbuktu was also the city of three hundred and thirty-three Islamic saints. She turned to me.

'I'm kinda bored,' she said.

She hadn't been in Mali long: a couple of months. I asked where she was from.

'Springfield, Illinois.'

'And what did you do there?'

'I guess I was bored there too.'

Boredom was for her a sign of superior sensibility, or at least of sophistication. If I had admitted to an interest in anything, I think she would have laughed.

Her company was dispiriting. As we left the bar and walked in the harsh sunlight, I thought: go on, *prove* that life is worthwhile, that your so-called interests are not illusory and fleeting, that – contrary to the slogan I saw painted on a Nigerian truck – all life is not vanity.

We stayed in the *campement* on the very edge of the desert. If the Sahara began anywhere, it began here. Nearby was a large man-made crater a hundred feet across, dug down to the water table thirty feet below the surface. The sides of the crater were terraced and divided into tiny plots by mud barriers a few inches high that retained the water that was brought up by hand from below to irrigate the soil. Brilliant green but fragile shoots grew vulnerably from the cracked mud, to shrivel in the fierce sun if neglected for half a day. It is scarcely surprising that the colour of the desert religion, Islam, is green, or that the Islamic conception of paradise is so horticultural.

Across a few hundred yards of the desert was a new luxury hotel, built in the midst of a small oasis and in the expectation of a large increase in the tourist trade. But, far from increasing, the trade had severely diminished, for Air Mali had crashed just outside Timbuktu with the loss of all passengers, and could not afford to replace the aircraft. Though it was French owned and managed, the hotel had the unmistakable atmosphere of defeat, of another failed project in Africa.

The *campement* was simpler. My room was the one in which, before the luxury hotel was built, Giscard d'Estaing had stayed. I found it not easy to associate its torn mosquito net, its map-like fungus on the wall, musty smell, and prehistoric shower which alternately dried up or shot bullets of cold water to the sound of battles within the shaking lead pipe, with the patrician, high-domed Giscard, and my respect for him increased. Did he also eat the camel stew, rice and bread, all liberally admixed with sand? Did he take breakfast on the fly-infested verandah?

All day we were followed round by young children, as persistent as the flies but rather more pleasant. Françoise, one of the nurses, asked them whether Timbuktu was *the mysterious city*. They replied that no, for them Bamako (the capital of Mali) was the mysterious city: from which came wonders like headsets, torches, radios and batteries. Their ambition to leave for the capital had hardened into resolve by the age of eight.

We went to the most famous of Timbuktu's mosques, the Djingare-ber, founded in the thirteenth century. It was built of mud – mud being a permanent material in this climate. A young man offered to show us round: his tour was peremptory and rushed, and when we asked to climb the stairs of the mud minaret he said they were unsafe. The reason for his dispatch became clear when the white-robed muezzin appeared on the scene. The muezzin ran after us shouting abuse, and when he caught up with us began to beat our erstwhile guide about the head. He ejected him forcibly from the mosque (he made no attempt to defend himself, though he was larger than the muezzin and more muscular); and then the muezzin turned on us. He pushed us towards the exit, while we protested our innocence: we had not known our guide was unauthor-ized. He relented and said he would show us round the mosque himself, though the physiological concomitants of his anger – a quavering of his voice and a tremor of his hands – had not yet subsided. We walked together through the cool, dark building with its colonnades of crude columns to support the heavy mud roof. There was no decoration and nothing that spoke of high artistic endeavour, though the whole was harmonious with its surroundings. The muezzin showed us the tombs of twin brothers, both of them saints.

Françoise asked what one had to do to be an Islamic saint.

'Believe much in God,' said the muezzin.

We climbed the 'unsafe' stairs, on to the mosque's uneven roof. Before us was a scene not much different from Caillé's day:

Nothing was to be seen in any direction but immense plains of quicksand of a yellowish white colour. The sky was a pale red as far as the horizon: all nature wore a dreary aspect, and the most profound silence prevailed; not even the warbling of a bird was to be heard. [Nevertheless, he was glad to be there] . . . Though I cannot account for the impression, there was something imposing in the aspect of a great city, raised in the midst of sands, and the difficulties surmounted by its founders cannot fail to excite admiration.

A *great city* is now an exaggeration. But that there should be anything there at all is indeed amazing.

It was on the roof that the muezzin first brought up the subject of his remuneration. He had no salary, he said, and depended entirely on voluntary contributions. Our first offering was refused as derisory (one soon learns to offer half of what one is prepared to give, since first offerings are refused however large they may be, as a matter of principle). Soon we were haggling as though in a market, and understood at last the muezzin's extreme anger at our former guide. It was not outraged piety, as we had thought at first; it was that a tip rightfully his was going to another.

We went to a restaurant that evening, an establishment that boasted a table, three chairs and a bench. The owner and cook was an elderly man who showed us with pride his visitor's book: a passing Swiss or Dutchman would eat in his restaurant every two months or so. It was not a thriving business, then; he half-expected us to recognize the names in his book. Eventually he produced some macaroni and fried meat; unhappily, his only crockery was soup-plates and his only cutlery spoons. We took turns with the carving knife. Throughout the preparation and the meal, the owner fanned us at the table with a Heath Robinson contraption, a rug suspended from the ceiling connected by pulleys to near his single-ringed gas stove.

Before we finished, a group of six tough-looking Frenchmen arrived, bronzed by the desert sun. They worked in a camp in the harsh north of the country and came into Timbuktu from time to time for a rest: to them it was a resort of comfort and luxury. They sent for beer and whatever food, in addition to what the owner cooked, could be found. Their appetites were huge, for food and drink. As they tore at the meat and drank straight from the bottle, I felt ashamed of the puniness of my journey: what was it compared with living in the north of Mali?

Officially the Frenchmen were performing a cartological survey for the Malian government. But – as they told us in a kind of stage whisper that meant 'This must not go a step beyond the Northern Hemisphere' – their *real* work was tracking satellites and missiles for President Reagan's *Star Wars* project. They were uncertain whether the Malian government knew this or not; a group of Frenchmen was less conspicuous in Mali than a group of Americans.

In the narrow sandy streets, where people lay down to sleep, where the langorous murmur of conversation came from open doorways that flickered with the pinkish light of oil lamps, it seemed a thousand years and a very long way from the conflicts of great powers. No corner of the earth, however, is too insignificant to attract the attention of the players of the Great Game.

I watched the sun go down, sitting on a dune a mile from the edge of the town. I had passed a group of men who were digging down to the water table, constructing another of the traditional vegetable gardens. They passed buckets of sand upwards from hand to hand, until they had reached the rim of the hole they dug. A large labour for an inevitably small result: but the desert left them no choice.

A young Tuareg in a stained, sky-blue robe struggled up the dune towards me, and sat down beside me. He was on his way back to his camp, another mile into the desert, after work.

After work? I had thought the Tuareg were nomadic pastoralists.

My Tuareg companion told me he had once been a nomad, but the disastrous drought had killed his tribe's herds and driven the Tuareg towards towns to seek relief. He had lost his camel and now had nothing. Some American missionaries were offering the Tuareg a dollar a day if they worked on an agricultural project the other side of Timbuktu. It meant he had to leave camp at five in the morning, not returning till after six in the evening; but it allowed the hope, however faint, that one day he would be able to save enough for another camel and resume the traditional life.

He invited me to tea at his camp. We walked together: the going in sand was easy for a camel but laborious for a man. The camp was a group of widely-spaced shelters, sticks of wood supporting blankets and sacking. His black-clad wife fetched charcoal and he brewed the sweet green tea. He talked of his fear that the Tuareg would never be able to return to the old ways. It grew dark and the stars in the sky were such as we in the civilized world will never see again. There wasn't mere silence: there was *peace*.

He accompanied me back to the town but was afraid to enter it. He said he'd be arrested as a thief. In this respect, things had changed greatly since Caillé's day: 'They (the Tuareg) roam about . . . and behave in the most arbitrary way, making the inhabitants give them provisions and other property – in fact, seizing whatever they can get their hands on . . .' The town that once the Tuareg terrorized now terrorizes them: and thus the whirligig of time brings in its revenges.

Out of curiosity, I went to see the American missionary project. It was nearer Kabora than Timbuktu, some hundreds of yards off the road. The government, desperate for aid from wherever it came, had suppressed any religious qualms it might have had, and granted the mission an area of land to develop.

The project was only just beginning. Land had been cleared and wells were being sunk. Pumps would irrigate the land via a system of pipes and channels. Each Tuareg who joined the scheme was to be granted a parcel of the irrigated land on condition he worked it. Whatever profits he made were to be his to keep. Thus the Tuareg were to be introduced for the first time to the rigours of regular work and market forces. The change in their way of life was to lead to a change in religion.

'How many have converted so far?' I asked.

'Our congregation stands at fifteen,' said one of the missionaries. 'It's not growing because converts face persecution.'

He thought the Tuareg belief in Islam was superficial, though at the same time deeply ingrained: a question more of convention than belief. He doubted they had any theological, as against superstitious, opinions. He hoped one day they would realize the difference a personal relationship with Jesus made. The best chance was for a whole tribe to convert *en masse*, to avoid persecution.

The missionaries were fluent in the local languages. Their parents had been missionaries in Mali too, and they had grown up there. They had lived in America only to attend Bible College and acquire necssary technical skills. I watched them at work, fixing some irrigation pipes. A few Tuareg looked on with the amused and superior air of people observing the antics of the insane. And the missionaries were full of doubt.

'We don't know if this is going to work,' one of them said. 'The natives have known for centuries that nothing will grow here.'

But if they could make the desert bloom, what a harvest there would be for Jesus! *That* was the hope that kept them going.

Unfortunately, they were short of cash. Tomorrow was a day of prayer for funds.

I went indoors. The house was spartan, but unmistakably middle American. Two wives, surrounded by children and chaos, looked pale and miserable, blanched by a thousand cares. What if the children got sick, what if the government changed, what if the natives rose? They were weighed down.

'Do you like it here?' I asked.

'I'm happy here,' replied one, 'because I know this is where the Lord wants us to be.' Her eyes darted about, avoiding mine. 'But otherwise – Timbuktu's the pits, the absolute pits.'

So that was it. I had come all this way to find the absolute pits.

Life, though, is often like that.

EPILOGUE

From Kabora I took a pirogue to Diré, sixty miles up the Niger. After the owners of the pirogue and the port officials had taken their cut, the boatmen received 1000 francs ($3). The journey took twenty-four hours, with four hours to sleep in an abandoned village on a small island in the river. Otherwise, the two boatmen punted the pirogue against the current the entire time. They never complained; they chatted and laughed the whole way. When Diré came into view, they broke into song. They took their leave with a carefree wave.

I rejoined the river boat at Diré – the last of the season. It was very crowded. Several young Europeans, travelling cheaply, slept on the sundeck. Some Africans joined them. Soon afterwards the Africans, but not the Europeans, were rounded up by soldiers and made to strip. Those who could not or would not pay the soldiers 1000 francs were locked in the leaking and revolting showers. There were murmurings against this outrage, but no one protested.

I saw much during my journey of the petty tyranny that, now more than ever, oppresses Africans. As a white man I was spared the worst of it. Yet despite the oppression, the corruption, the ever-worsening economies, the ignorance and disease, the poverty, the dirt and the disorientating change, Africa is not a continent of misery. There is more general gloom in Europe. For Africans, I discovered, have a unique talent for finding happiness where others would find only misery.